WARREN SPAHN

A BIOGRAPHY OF THE LEGENDARY LEFTY

LEW FREEDMAN

SPORTS
PUBLISHING

Copyright © 2018 by Lew Freedman

All rights reserved. No part of this book may be reproduced in any manner without the express written consent of the publisher, except in the case of brief excerpts in critical reviews or articles. All inquiries should be addressed to Sports Publishing, 307 West 36th Street, 11th Floor, New York, NY 10018.

Sports Publishing books may be purchased in bulk at special discounts for sales promotion, corporate gifts, fund-raising, or educational purposes. Special editions can also be created to specifications. For details, contact the Special Sales Department, Sports Publishing, 307 West 36th Street, 11th Floor, New York, NY 10018 or sportspubbooks@ skyhorsepublishing.com.

Sports Publishing® is a registered trademark of Skyhorse Publishing, Inc.®, a Delaware corporation.

Visit our website at www.sportspubbooks.com.

10 9 8 7 6 5 4 3

Library of Congress Cataloging-in-Publication Data is available on file.

Jacket design by Tom Lau
Jacket photos credit: AP Images

Print ISBN: 978-1-68358-199-4
Ebook ISBN: 978-1-68358-200-7

Printed in the United States of America

CONTENTS

INTRODUCTION

WARREN SPAHN WAS good enough that baseball could have named its top pitching award after him, but the honor had already gone to Cy Young. Instead, Spahn won a Cy Young Award (1957) and had the trophy for best left-hander named for him.

With 363 wins, Spahn is the winningest southpaw in Major League Baseball history. More than a half-century after retiring, he remains the winningest overall pitcher among those who played their careers since the live ball era began in 1920.

His was the most extraordinary of careers. Not only did Spahn win at least 20 games in a single season thirteen times—a feat every pitcher today strives to achieve just once—but the manner in which he accomplished the deed was greatly against the odds. His mastery of the pitched ball made Spahn a seventeen-time All-Star. He ranks sixth on the all-time wins list and tops among left-handers.

Spahn was twenty-five years old before he won his first big-league game. He thus began his lengthy career and pursuit of so many victories with a deficit of sorts. It would have been inconceivable for anyone to imagine in 1946 that this late bloomer would capture so many wins and that he would still be pitching at the major-league level until the middle of the 1960s.

While Spahn was not anywhere near the fastest of throwers, he may have been the craftiest. He was not the largest of men at 6 feet tall and weighing about 175 pounds, but he was extremely durable.

* * *

Warren Edward Spahn was born in Buffalo, New York, on April 23, 1921. By the time he turned twenty-one, he had shown enough talent and promise to be promoted to the Boston Braves of the National League. His stay was brief—then.

Soon enough, Spahn would be wearing a different uniform, representing his country in World War II as a member of the United States Army. Spahn spent three years at war and was discharged as a decorated veteran, winner of medals—including the Purple Heart—and famously serving at the Battle of the Bulge.

The left-hander returned to the sport he loved for the 1946 season, again with the Braves organization. Spahn's baseball career began anew and in earnest at age twenty-five. A year later he was a star.

The southpaw was a leading pitcher for the Boston Braves when they won a National League pennant in 1948, and he was one of the luminaries of the team when the club shifted to Milwaukee. Representing that city, the Braves won pennants in 1957 and 1958 and the World Series in 1957.

In Boston, Spahn was teamed with right-hander Johnny Sain as a formidable pitching duo. Down the stretch in 1948, however, the rotation was shorthanded and a sportswriter wrote an enduring poem about that, which is remembered as "Spahn and Sain and Pray for Rain."

These were not the same old Braves in Milwaukee, even if it was the same old Spahn, continuing to win 20 games in a season year after year. Milwaukee may once have been a thriving minor-league baseball town, but the community viewed the big-league Braves coming as a Christmas present. Fans were delighted for the majors to come calling, and they were also blessed with a team that, by the early-to-late 1950s, was as exciting as any in the game.

Sixty years later, Milwaukee baseball fans still remember and revere the Braves of 1957 and 1958, despite the passage of time and the presence of the well-established Brewers franchise.

Stylistically, Spahn's pitching motion was propelled by a big right-leg kick, his foot rising above his head and his leg obscuring his delivery from the hitters. There were not many like him.

For all his long-term greatness as the new decade of the 1960s dawned, Spahn had never thrown a big-league no-hitter. In September of 1960 he rectified that situation by hurling one against the Philadelphia Phillies. He was thirty-nine at the time. A year later, at age forty, Spahn recorded a second no-hitter, against the Giants.

In July of 1963, when he was forty-two, Spahn became engaged in one of the most riveting pitching duels in baseball history with twenty-five-year-old Juan Marichal of the San Francisco Giants. The enthralling game lasted 16 innings, and the men threw more than 400 pitches combined.

Spahn won a Cy Young Award and led the National League in various pitching categories several times. He was part of pennant-winners and a World Series championship. Spahn stands out in baseball history as a southpaw with a better record than anyone else but also as a mid-twentieth-century figure who was a throwback in accomplishment and durability to the early-century pitching stars. He showed that with his longevity, shut-outs, and complete games.

Spahn had left Buffalo behind long before and settled in Oklahoma, where he owned a ranch. After his playing career ended, he stayed in the game, even coaching in Mexico City and Japan. Spahn also managed the Tulsa Oilers for five years, a minor-league club which played its home games a stone's throw from Spahn's ranch.

Elected to the Baseball Hall of Fame in 1973, Spahn's selection defied the joking comment made by contemporary St. Louis Cardinals star Stan Musial that Spahn would never get into the hallowed museum because Spahn would never retire and accumulate the five years of waiting time necessary.

After retiring from both pitching and working as a pitching coach, Spahn spent much of his time in Broken Arrow, Oklahoma. He was an adopted son of the state and is enshrined in their sports Hall of Fame. The Atlanta Braves built a statue in his honor as well.

Spahn was eighty-two when he died in 2003 and is buried in Elmwood Cemetery in Hartshorne, Oklahoma, not far from the ranch that gave him so much pleasure.

1

A NO-HITTER AT LAST

THE DRIZZLE COULD have ruined everything. Instead, it was just an annoyance. The humidity and dampness did discourage the faint-hearted from attending that night at County Stadium. Most of Milwaukee stayed home drinking beer on September 16, 1960, instead of traveling downtown to witness history.

That choice made for bad luck and bad timing for most Milwaukee Braves fans. The venerable southpaw Warren Spahn was going for his 20th win of the 1960 season, and only 6,117 ticket-holders showed up. Spahn was thirty-nine years old and by that age most baseball players had put away their youthful toys and hung up their uniforms as they pondered a new career selling insurance or cars.

By then, anyone who had followed his career knew Warren Spahn was not just the average guy, nor the average baseball player. He routinely defied odds, others' expectations, and the norm.

Spahn was not going to shy away from circumstances. If it was his turn in the rotation, every fourth day, he wanted his manager to hand him the ball. If the game was on, so was he. Inclement weather was irrelevant. One of Spahn's traits during his long major-league career was dependability. He never looked for a way out. If it was his turn to pitch, he was ready to fulfill his obligation.

Probably the foremost thing on Spahn's mind before the game was getting that 20th victory. The Braves were 81–61, a far superior team to their opponent, the Philadelphia Phillies, whose record was 52–90. The teams were at opposite ends of the National League standings in what was then an eight-team league.

Yes, a suitably armed Braves team with a future Hall of Fame pitcher on the mound was going to be favored against a club that for a decade had to buy tickets to watch the postseason. Yet how many times does the better team fail to sweep a three-game series from the inferior team?

So many variables figure in. Warren Spahn might have had a hangnail or a blister that day. He could have been trying to get by on short sleep. He could have awakened with a stiff neck. As it happened, the bad news for the Phillies was that Spahn did not suffer from any of those minor afflictions and shrugged off the irritating weather too. At this stage of his career, Spahn had terrific concentration on the mound.

During that era, the Phillies were regularly one of the weakest teams in the National League or the majors. That year, out of the sixteen teams in both leagues (before expansion), the Phillies finished with the second-to-worst record, just one win better than the American League's Kansas City Athletics.

Including Spahn, the Braves had three Hall of Famers in the lineup for the game: Henry Aaron was in right field and Eddie Mathews was at third base. Plus, Joe Adcock, Del Crandall, and Johnny Logan had all been All-Stars. There was no mystery about which was the better team. But still, on any given day the Phillies might win. In fact, just a day later, Philadelphia beat Milwaukee, 5–2.

But on September 16, Warren Spahn was on the mound, and after two hours and two minutes of extremely efficient pitching, Spahn had recorded the first no-hitter of his long and storied career.

This was one achievement Spahn had always coveted but was starting to wonder if he might ever accomplish. That was a reasonable worry for an athlete of his age. Although he was not entertaining the idea of retirement, being thirty-nine put him at the far end of his pitching career. It was the wondrous Satchel Paige who coined the phrase "Maybe I'll pitch forever," but it was Spahn who had the thought in the back of his mind.

The opposing pitcher was right-hander John Buzhardt. Buzhardt was 4–15 on the season at game's start. Buzhardt spent eleven years in the majors, mostly with the Phillies and Chicago White Sox. His best season lay five years in the future with the 1965 White Sox, when his record was 13–8. Overall, he finished 71–96 in his career. Although his place of birth was Prosperity, South Carolina, Buzhardt enjoyed limited prosperity in the big leagues, though he did throw a one-hitter in 1959 while playing for the Chicago Cubs. At the time of this game versus Spahn, Buzhardt was twenty-four.

The biggest threats in the lineup for the Phillies were left fielder Johnny Callison, who was batting leadoff, first baseman Pancho Herrera, and center fielder Tony González. Second baseman Tony Taylor was not in the starting lineup that day but was later inserted as a pinch-hitter.

Spahn definitely was thinking more about obtaining a 20th win for the eleventh time in his career than the prospect of pitching a no-hitter for the first time.

"The difference between winning 19 games and winning 20 for a pitcher is bigger than anyone out of baseball realizes," he said. "It's the same for hitters. Someone who hits .300 looks back on the guy who batted .295 and says, 'Tough luck, buddy.'"[1]

Long before managers and front-office types employed sabermetrics, video replays, or any highfalutin technology to analyze every pitch and at-bat, Spahn carried such information in his head. The famed baseball writer Roger Kahn viewed Spahn as a computer genius before anyone besides UNIVAC mentioned computers. Spahn, who threw far more pitches during his time than modern-day pitchers do, knew what he threw to everyone in a game.

In an issue of *Sports Illustrated* that appeared on newsstands shortly after Spahn died, Kahn recalled introducing his wife to the pitcher and saying, "After a game, Mr. Spahn remembered each one of the 125 pitches he had thrown, where it was, what it was, and the sequence."[2]

If Spahn committed a mistake he would certainly recall that pitch well—only there were to be no mistakes against the Phillies.

With the Braves the home team, Callison led off the game by flying out to right. Phillies second baseman Bobby Malkmus then grounded out to short and right fielder Ken Walters struck out.

When he was a young man, Spahn's fastball was fast enough, though he was never considered as much of a flamethrower as Walter Johnson, Bob Feller, or Sandy Koufax. As he aged, Spahn relied more on mixing his pitches and fooling batters than blowing them away.

The most notable aspect of the first inning was Walters's strikeout. Walters was victim number one. At the end of the game, Spahn had 15 Ks.

Buzhardt was in trouble almost immediately in the bottom of the first. Outfielder Billy Bruton walked but was caught stealing. Del Crandall singled, Eddie Mathews singled, and Henry Aaron walked, loading the bases with only one out. Only Al Dark hit into a double play, so Buzhardt escaped.

Spahn's turn again. The second inning was an impressive one for Spahn and a baffling one for the Phillies. He set down Herrera, González, and catcher Cal Neeman, one-two-three, all by strikeout. This was an early indication Spahn might have something special going.

Although Spahn led the National League in strikeouts four times in his career, he hadn't done so since 1952 and had never reached 200 strikeouts in a season. Spahn struck out 2,583 men lifetime, but that was spread across 5,243 2/3 innings. He was no Nolan Ryan when it came to super-speed or blinding batters. For him to strike out four of the first six hitters for outs was enough to put Braves fans on alert he had his good stuff going in this game.

Although Spahn's arm was not the most powerful around (most people gave the nod to the Dodgers' Sandy Koufax during this era) and he stood just 6 feet tall, he was an intimidating pitcher. Besides his well-ingrained reputation as a great pitcher, Spahn could give you that scowl as he stared in at the plate, a look that could shiver your timbers. Spahn's windup seemed more energetic and stronger than most, a windmill revving up.

Yet beyond all that was the big foot. Spahn's delivery style featured a high kick that made it seem as if the sole of the spike on his right foot was much closer than 60 feet, 6 inches away. Indeed, it could appear as if the big foot from the big kick might come down on your head. Although it is unlikely the thought ever crossed his mind, Spahn's big leg kick might have qualified him for a tryout for the chorus line in a Broadway show. Sometimes it almost seemed as if Spahn might tip over backward from his lean with the leg high over his head.

Jim Woods, Ruben Amaro, and Buzhardt were the three hitters up in the third and Spahn struck out Woods and Buzhardt. Amaro fouled out.

Walters became the Phillies' first baserunner in the fourth when he walked. Callison, Malkmus, and Herrera made routine outs, although none of them struck out.

Until the bottom of the fourth inning, Buzhardt matched Spahn with zeroes on the scoreboard. Henry Aaron, already a well-established superstar, singled to start the inning. Dark, who would become better known as a manager than a shortstop, smacked a triple to center field and Aaron scored easily. Joe Adcock followed with a sacrifice fly, and Dark scored for a 2–0 Braves lead.

The Phillies were looking for any spark to start a rally in the fifth, but Spahn started the round by fanning González, caught looking. Cal Neeman worked Spahn for a walk, but he was stranded.

Milwaukee added a run in the home half of the fifth with Spahn stroking a single as the first batter up. Spahn, who batted lefty, was no Murderers' Row contributor at the plate. He batted .194 lifetime in 2,056 plate appearances. Billy Bruton followed in the order with another single. Spahn stopped at second base. Del Crandall made an out, but the pitcher scored on the Braves' third single of the inning by Eddie Mathews. So the lead was a little cozier 3–0.

Buzhardt led off the sixth, but neither he nor the next two batters could do anything with Spahn's repertoire, and there were no Phillie baserunners. Ken Walters, Herrera, and González never got anything good to swing at, and Spahn collected two more strikeouts in the seventh.

After the seventh-inning stretch, the Braves scratched out a fourth run. Bruton singled to right after Spahn led off with an out. Bruton then stole second, and Del Crandall drove him in with a single to center.

It was getting late in the game, and the Phillies were not getting anywhere. They showed not a hint of solving Spahn's stuff. So manager Gene Mauch believed it was time for some tricks. Philadelphia's season had begun with Eddie Sawyer at the helm, the same manager who was in charge when the Phillies Whiz Kids won the 1950 pennant. Sawyer presided over the decline of the Phils, too, and one game into this season decided he had made an error in returning. Mauch stepped in at age thirty-four and began a much-admired managerial career. He later managed the Expos, Twins, and Angels, but never won a pennant.

Cal Neeman made the first out, grounding out to first with Spahn covering. Then Tony Taylor, who played 19 seasons in the big leagues, stepped in as a pinch-hitter for Jim Woods, who had a very short career. The third strike on Taylor was called. Then Mauch called on Lee Walls to swing for Amaro. Walls was an outfielder, making one All-Star team in 1958, but was renowned as a pinch-hitter during a ten-year major-league career, plus additional time in Japan.

Spahn rung up Walls with a strikeout. That was evidence of his control of Philadelphia's bench, as well as its starting lineup.

Buzhardt was still on the mound for the bottom of the eighth inning and the Braves went down in order to set up a suspenseful ninth with Spahn seeking to preserve the no-hitter.

The Phillies pitcher was the scheduled first hitter in the ninth and Mauch sent up another pinch-hitter in Bobby Smith. Smith, primarily an outfielder, hit .286 in 1960 and was an upgrade at the plate over Buzhardt. Spahn struck him out. Bobby Del Greco was next up, still another pinch-hitter, although it was a mild surprise he stepped in for Johnny Callison. That move didn't do the Phillies any good, either. Del Greco struck out, the 15th K casualty for the Phillies that night.

Spahn was cruising. The no-hitter looked like a sure thing. But there are no such things in baseball, especially when fate, luck, and a peculiar bounce can conspire to kill dreams.

Bobby Malkmus, the Philadelphia second baseman, stepped to the plate. Malkmus spent six seasons in the majors, basically as a part-time player. His lifetime average was .215. Malkmus had seen all he needed to of Spahn throughout the evening, so he swung at the first pitch. The ball shot back at Spahn. Spahn threw up his glove but only deflected the ball toward shortstop Johnny Logan. Cutting to his left, Logan sprinted behind Spahn, scooped up the ball on the bounce and whipped a hard but off-line throw to Adcock at first as Malkmus steamed down the first-base line.

Spahn's no-hitter rested in others' hands. Adcock bent, stretched, and reached. The ball was low and outside, yet he grasped it in his glove while keeping his foot on the bag. Bob Hayes was the world's fastest human at the time, and it helped that Malkmus wasn't in his heat. Malkmus was out, and Spahn was in—in the pitchers' no-hitter club after throwing 105 very accurate pitches.

Later, Spahn said he was not nervous about throwing the no-hitter until that last out when Malkmus was the threat.

"Funny thing, but I had always had a much more dramatic view of a no-hitter, but last night's game was just another ball game for eight innings," Spahn said. "All I can say is I'm glad Malkmus isn't a fast runner."[3]

It was decades in the works, but Warren Spahn finally had a big-league, no-hit game after previously throwing two one-hitters, in 1951 against the St. Louis Browns and 1953 against the Phillies.

There is always bedlam and celebration when a pitcher hurls a no-hitter. This was no different; by then, Spahn had been in the majors since 1946 and many thought that one milestone had passed him by.

In the locker room, after the 4–0 victory was in the books and Spahn had coasted to his 51st career shutout, he posed for a commemorative photo. In the picture, a grinning Spahn, his uniform jersey removed, his dark hair disheveled, holds up a long, white placard. "No. 20" in large letters (for his expected win) had been stenciled across the width of the piece tacked on the clubhouse wall. Spahn took over and added a second inscription. "Plus No-Hitter" was written in.

Spahn's young son Greg made his way to his dad in the locker room and gave him a hug and a kiss.

"Just don't wake me up," Spahn said of his satisfying triumph.[4]

It was notable the no-hitter came at the same time as Spahn's 20th win, and catcher Del Crandall, who shared years and memories as a battery with Spahn, teased him about that very thing.

"You couldn't pitch a no-hitter when you won 19," Crandall said. "You had to save it for 20."[5]

Spahn had nothing to say to that. He would have taken a no-hitter any time over the last fifteen years, in any game, against any team, whether it was his fourth win of a season or the thirteenth. What he marveled about was the sudden extra juice in his fastball. Abruptly, out of nowhere, it seemed, the fastball began behaving like a sports car again, like the fastball of his youth. There was no way to explain that, but there was no other way to explain 15 strikeouts, either.

"I should be in the twilight of my career and tonight I had a fastball I haven't had in 10 years," Spahn said.[6]

There was all this dissection and reflection in the locker room, but overall joy for the veteran whose latest feat was up on a big board for everyone to read, all of those zeroes strung out in a row, one-through-nine for runs and that other singular zero, the one signifying the number of hits the Philadelphia Phillies cranked out on September 16, as in none.

First baseman Adcock, who made the last putout—and not an easy one at that—drifted past Spahn's locker stall and let him know what he thought about what he saw that night. Adcock was going on thirty-three years of age right after that season, so he understood some of the physical demands baseball made on the body once it turned the corner toward retirement age.

"I don't know what there's left for you to do in baseball, but I know you'll do it," said Adcock in a marvelous teammate compliment.[7]

Spahn knew. This was his 288th major-league victory, and he wanted to get to 300. Anyone who records 300 wins is an automatic Hall of Famer. The 300 level is the absolute elite level, the way 3,000 hits are for a hitter. That's where Spahn wanted to go—300 wins. Since it was mid-September, there wasn't enough time left to reach that goal during the 1960 season.

"What do I want to do?" Spahn asked, repeating a sportswriter's question. "I want to win 300 games before I'm through. And it's killing me I can't do it this year."[8]

At the time there were just twelve pitchers with 300 wins in baseball history. Now there are twenty-four. During his fortieth year on the planet, Warren Spahn still had something to look forward to when taking the mound in 1961.

2

BUFFALO AND BEYOND

ALL THE BASEBALL instruction and coaching for Warren Spahn began with his father Ed in Buffalo.

Baseball was the team sport of most import to fans across the United States in the 1920s and 1930s. Pro basketball did not even gain a serious foothold in the American sports fan's consciousness until after World War II. The National Hockey League was confined to six cold-weather cities, four of them in Canada. The National Football League was first organized in 1920.

Baseball was the national pastime, and even if you lived in Buffalo, New York, where there was no major-league team, baseball was still the game to follow when you weren't paying attention to Triple Crown horse racing in the spring or the heavyweight title fight of the moment.

Present-day Buffalo's population is more than 256,000. The city's population in 1920 was far larger, more than 500,000. The principal city of Upstate New York, located 380 miles northwest of New York City, Buffalo is the gateway to Niagara Falls on the Canadian border, long one of the United States's main tourist attractions.

Buffalo's lower east side was the home of multitudes of immigrant groups. Thousands of African Americans settled in the community beginning in 1920, many seeking work at automobile factories or in the growing chemical manufacturing industry.

Warren Edward Spahn was born on April 23, 1921. His first name was inspired by President Warren Harding. His middle name came from his father. The future pitcher's mother was named Mabel, and he was the fifth born of six siblings. The family lived in the blue collar east part of the city where dad was a wallpaper salesman who made $27 a week.

That income kept the family under shelter and put food on the table but in no way funded a fancy lifestyle. The Spahns did not own an automobile when Warren was a youngster and the menu rarely included a deluxe cut of meat and definitely not more than once a week. One report on the family's early existence indicated new shoes were not always purchased when a foot outgrew a size. Rather they were passed down to the next in line in the family who might have to shove newspapers into them to shape them into a better fit.

Warren Spahn's first coach was his father Ed, a huge baseball fan who dreamed of playing in the big leagues. However, he did not rate his chances very highly when he stopped growing at 5-foot-7 and stopped adding pounds when he hit a range around 130 (apparently never topping 150). He kept playing ball on the semi-pro level locally and he was an avid, solid bowler. Warren was one of only two sons—he had four sisters—and Warren was the chosen one in his father's eyes when it came to baseball. His dad fanned Warren's interest by taking him to Buffalo Bisons minor-league games. This was not a hard sell because young Warren liked baseball and wanted to play. Big Bill Kelly was a longtime star of the Bisons, and Ed Spahn was an old local teammate. That was before Kelly set team records for the club and got a couple of sips of coffee in the majors in 1920 and 1928, accumulating 84 big-league at-bats for both Philadelphia teams. Kelly's lifetime average was just .179 in limited play, but he did experience the big time.

Kelly was a first baseman and Warren's first goal in baseball revolved around that position. Although his father pushed him to pitch, Warren initially was more interested in playing the field than making the mound his life's work.

Ed Spahn was friendly enough with Kelly that Warren could chase balls in the outfield during Bison batting practice. The little boy did not remember all of the home players' names, so he called them all "Kelly." As a joke in return the players called him "Kelly Spahn."⁹

As an illustration of the limits on the family finances, Spahn said when the Bison games ended, his father often gave him the choice of taking the trolley car home or of buying an ice cream cone and walking home together. Usually, the kid took the ice cream. But the walk was still enjoyable time spent together. "Many times we took the ice cream and rehashed the game walking home," Spahn said.¹⁰

Although Ed Spahn attempted to influence his son toward pitching rather than first base, Warren's first inclination was to work at the full-time position. Ed's theory was there were many fewer left-handed pitchers to compete with if one wanted to make the majors and there were plenty of power-hitting first basemen.

Warren was born into Prohibition and the Roaring Twenties and soon enough at elementary school age was feeling the effects of the Great Depression. Ed Spahn kept on playing on local teams and passed on knowledge to Warren about baseball.

"He loved the game, and of course his son played baseball," Warren said. "I didn't even have a left-handed glove. I had a right-handed glove, one of his. I didn't know the thumb was supposed to be on this side, so I played with a glove that had the thumb over here. And, I guess, I learned how to catch maybe better than kids do today because they've got the big, long gloves and all that sort of thing. And it was a love affair. I enjoyed playing baseball. I played in a great municipal league that they had in Buffalo, along with my high school, American Legion. I think I was playing almost every day."[11]

Spahn could play every day because he was playing first base, his choice, for those teams, including the semi-pro club his father was still on playing third base. Decades later he recalled the team name as being something like the South Bethel Businessman's Club. Other reports spread over the years suggest the official name of the team was the Lake City Athletic Club. It was a treat for father and son to compete on the same team, even if they good-naturedly ragged on one another about their respective infield play.

"And I used to give him heck for throwing me bad throws and he'd give me heck for not catching the ones that he threw badly," Spahn said. "I was a first-baseman. I was supposed to catch those. And we had a good relationship and baseball was the catalyst that made it closer together as father and son."[12]

There was a slight disparity in the development of their talents at the time. Warren was thirteen, and Ed was thirty-seven. Warren was literally the boy among men, lucky to be able to take the field at first base or anywhere. Dad was a perfectionist and did want Warren to do things right, from taking ground balls to throwing and catching even when it was a simple backyard catch, never mind in a game where score was kept.

"You'd think he was going to throw it right through me," Spahn said of those days in the games with his father. "I weighed only about 110 pounds in those days. But he was teaching me to play hard and it did a lot of good."[13] Spahn also once said of his dad's throws, "I thought some of them would knock me into the third-base bleachers."[14] (That sounded a little strange because Warren mostly played first.)

It is always helpful to learn how to do something the proper way, and Ed Spahn definitely wanted Warren to absorb this tutoring in that manner. Warren's desire to advance in the game at first base ran into a roadblock when he reached his sophomore year in high school. The team already had an all-state player at that position. As Spahn observed many years later, he promptly realized he was not going to beat that player out for a starting job.

Coincidentally, the team (as most are) was in need of pitching. When the coach pondered where else Spahn might be able to play given that he was a left-hander, it was either pitching or the outfield. Spahn was a pitcher second and an outfielder basically never. So the choice was easy enough and the opportunity on the mound was plain.

This was what Ed Spahn was waiting for and had slyly trained his son for all the way, even while giving him the leeway to experiment at first base. The elder Spahn had long pressured Warren to use proper form when throwing. He was not content to have simple games of catch with no rules attached. Warren knew when he was playing catch with his father he was going to get pointers and adhere to the form demanded.

Because his father was not a big guy, Warren said, he had to compensate for lack of power by taking advantage of the gifts he did have and using proper form.

"And he realized the value of giving all of what God gave you," Spahn said. "Momentum, etcetera and he insisted that I throw correctly and use my whole body to pitch. And, you know, he was responsible for that. I used to hate to come home from school because he wanted to play catch when I came home and he would make me hit the target and that sort of thing. Not that I hated it, but just the fact that he was a taskmaster. And thank God for it."[15]

So Warren Spahn evolved into one of the greatest pitchers of all time, the initial push coming from his father.

The most distinctive aspect of his pitching style, that high kick, was also encouraged by Ed Spahn. Every pitcher finds his own rhythm and own form on the way to success. Spahn's emphasis on the leg kick definitely came from his father, but he would not have stuck with it if it didn't work. "That was part of my father's influence," Spahn said of the high right leg kick and the reason behind it. "Use all the momentum that I could create."[16]

Repetition was also critical to the backyard lessons between father and son. No one counted the pitches thrown, but the number would have been impressive. The core of what Ed Spahn preached was control. That was the art of pitching to him, not just mowing a batter down with speed.

"There's no substitute for practice," Ed Spahn told his son, "especially to learn control. You've got to pitch and pitch and pitch, until you can put your foot up on the mound, set yourself, close your eyes, and throw a strike right down the middle. If you can throw the ball where you want to son, you can last for years, even when your fastball's gone."[17]

Decades later that's exactly how Warren Spahn transformed his style. If he ever did so it was not prominently recorded, but one must wonder if Spahn ever did close his eyes while throwing a pitch.

It was only later, when Spahn gained experience and realized athletes never really stop learning their trade, that he initiated talks with hitters to discover what they thought his strengths and weaknesses might be. The leg kick was distracting to hitters, he learned, and it helped mask how he held the ball when making his delivery. They could not see the position of his fingers. They found it more difficult to pick up spin on the ball when it was released.

"And then talking to hitters, I realized that I hid the ball pretty well so that it looked like it was coming out of my uniform," Spahn said. "So I tried to encourage that. I didn't want to talk to pitchers (about what they did). I wanted to talk to hitters. And I think hitters are the same way. So over the years, I realized where the assets were and embellished on it."[18]

Also over the years, Spahn developed his own philosophy of pitching. He repeated it many times to different sportswriters and interviewers. It defined the way he brought the ball in on hitters and the way he dealt mentally with umpires. Since after his earliest years in the big leagues his fastball wasn't going to overpower many hitters, Spahn needed smarts to outwit them when they stepped into the batter's box.

Roger Kahn, the esteemed baseball writer, once declared that Spahn might have been the most intelligent of ballplayers, although Kahn did deliver a version of the compliment in a back-handed way, saying that Spahn was the smartest person ever named for President Warren Harding, the chief executive in Kahn's estimation who was "our most limited president."[19] Well, Harding couldn't throw a curveball like Spahn, or he might have chosen a profession other than politics.

During a discussion with Spahn long ago, Kahn took note of that oft-repeated philosophy of how the southpaw viewed his right to home plate.

"Home plate is 17 inches wide," Spahn said. "All I asked for were the two inches on each corner. The hitters could have the

13 inches in-between. I didn't throw there. Batting is timing and pitching is upsetting timing."[20]

Spahn is not credited with originating that phrase. It has been used by more than one pitcher. But he did subscribe to its gospel and used it as a guiding precept.

During that era in American history just about every youth wanted to grow up to become a major-league baseball player. It was the rare boy whose attention shifted to another sport. And every dad wanted to father a major-leaguer. Whatever Warren Spahn's skill level as he grew beyond backyard and local ball, he was off to a fundamentally solid start.

It all begins with a dream, but there are many pitfalls along the path of a starry-eyed thirteen-year-old to the diamond in a major-league ballpark. Sometimes there is just too much competition. Other times injury intervenes. Good timing and good luck always help.

But young Warren Spahn certainly possessed baseball talent.

3

HIGH SCHOOL
AND AMERICAN LEGION

SOPHOMORE WARREN SPAHN may have had a lot of youth baseball experience when he entered South Park High School in Buffalo, but even he recognized immediately the first baseman holdover from the previous season was a lock. The position was not up for grabs, and Spahn recognized the other guy was better.

So excited to be moving up to high school ball initially, Spahn's mood was dampened. When coach Joe Schumaker gave him the word, Spahn was disappointed. But he quickly piped up and said he could pitch. Although he had almost nil game-pitching experience, Spahn had those years of private workouts with his father to call upon.

The boy had spent hour upon hour learning technique and control. Also, he had inherited a strong arm from his dad. While Warren Spahn is not recalled as one of the great fastball pitchers of all time, the high school level batters he was then facing found his heater pretty darned swift.

The coach asked Spahn to show him what he had. When he pumped his fastball in over the plate, Schumaker asked the catcher if the pitch was as fast as it looked. "All I know is, my hand hurts," the player responded.[21]

Once the coach also established Spahn had a curve that could break six inches and totally freeze bats, he figured Spahn had the goods. Given that show of good stuff the coach wondered why on earth Spahn would want to be a first baseman.

The throwing session lasted only a matter of minutes with the coach proclaiming on the spot Spahn had made the team. Schumaker was surprised, however, when he told Spahn to pick a number for his uniform jersey and he chose No. 13. Not many athletes wish to tempt fate and display No. 13 because they fear it will bring bad luck. More of them were superstitious than not, but Spahn didn't care. Indeed, he said No. 13 usually brought him good luck.

Future Hall of Famers in other sports, from basketball star Wilt Chamberlain to football star Dan Marino had success wearing No. 13.

Not everyone he encountered during his baseball career was so careless about flaunting superstition, and in the majors with the Boston and Milwaukee Braves Spahn wore No. 21, which remains on the retired list for the Atlanta Braves.

During Spahn's junior and senior years in high school in 1939 and 1940, South Park went undefeated and captured the Cornell Cup, emblematic of the city championship. Schumaker raved about his young pitcher's abilities and the likelihood he would go far in the game.

"His biggest asset as a youngster?" Schumaker was asked nearly twenty years after Spahn graduated but before Buffalo named a street after Spahn in the neighborhood of his high school. "He had perfect control. That's rare in any young pitcher and even more so in a left-hander. Look back in the old newspapers. I said then Warren would be another Lefty Grove. They thought I was nuts, but I'm enjoying it now."[22]

When Spahn was in high school, Robert "Lefty" Grove, the ace of the Philadelphia Athletics and Boston Red Sox, was just coming to the end of his 17-year, Hall of Fame career. Grove retired in 1941 with a record of 300–144. At the time Schumaker was speaking, Spahn was closing in on 300 victories himself.

Even as late as the 2017 baseball season there have only been six left-handers to win at least 300 games: Spahn, Steve Carlton, Eddie Plank, Tom Glavine, Randy Johnson, and Grove. Plank was the first lefty to 300 wins. He retired in 1917 with 326 wins, including the 21 accumulated in his one season in the Federal League in 1915.

As for southpaw wildness, there are some well-documented cases of eventual superstar hurlers suffering from such early-career afflictions. Perhaps most notable among those fitting the category was the Dodgers' Sandy Koufax. Under the bonus-baby payout rules of the time, Koufax had to remain with the parent club as a nineteen-year-old rookie in 1955 when he would have been better served by a stay in the minors. So Koufax rode out the season with the Brooklyn Dodgers, appearing in just 12 games.

It took three seasons for Koufax to obtain much more action and considerable time for him to regularly locate the strike zone without a map. Of course, then he had one of the greatest five-year periods in baseball history before an arthritic elbow forced him into retirement at age thirty.

Certainly, Randy Johnson was finding his way his first few seasons in the majors in the late 1980s. Even after that stretch,

Johnson did not truly have his scary-fast fastball harnessed. For three straight seasons in the early 1990s with the Seattle Mariners, he led the American League in walks. And then suddenly, he became Randy Johnson. The 6-foot-10 flamethrower led his league in strikeouts for the first of nine seasons (on his way to the second-highest K total ever of 4,875) and won his first of five Cy Young awards in 1995. If anything, Johnson had been wilder than Koufax during his early major-league seasons.

Spahn may have been fast for a high school pitcher, but he was not in Koufax's and Johnson's class as a fastball hurler. Spahn admitted that his father's emphasis on control was a factor, but real life also played a part.

"Well, that might be part of it," he said, "but I think the hitters made me have good control. You don't throw through the middle of the plate. And when you stop to think about it, a hitter goes up to home plate and he stakes a stance to protect most of the strike zone, or what he is comfortable with, so you pitch against that grain."[23]

Spahn did not deny the perception of left-handers throwing wilder than right-handers, or even acting that way, although sometimes the polite euphemism "unorthodox behavior" has been used as a synonym for southpaw behavior. Rube Waddell, the early-twentieth-century Hall of Famer for the Philadelphia Athletics, was considered flaky in his time, dashing off the mound and out of the ballpark in mid-game to pursue fire engines, although some later concluded he was actually mentally ill.

The 1980s reliever Tug McGraw was viewed as an off-beat comic. At times, supposedly sage baseball elders summed up a player with the description of "Oh, he's left-handed" without even meaning which side the guy threw from, but applying it to the fellow's head.

In past eras, leftys following their own drummers were sometimes labeled "screwballs." McGraw actually threw one.

Mickey Lolich won 217 games mostly for the Detroit Tigers in the 1960s and 1970s and made three All-Star teams. Because he was portly, people laughed when he opened a doughnut shop after retiring. "If you're left-handed and a pitcher, then people automatically think you're flaky," he said.[24]

Lolich did not seem to be a left-hander to deny flakiness. He imbibed twenty-five Pepsis in a day and said he became a southpaw after crashing a tricycle into the girl next door at age two and breaking his collarbone.

Spahn was a pretty even-handed guy and he counted on that ingrained accuracy more than the fastball to set down opposing players.

"I think I might be the exception," Spahn said. "I don't really know why left-handers are more wild than right-handers. And then there were also theories that pitchers were unorthodox as left-handers, and then the heart is closer to the left side. I don't know any of those things. I know that there's a great demand in baseball today for left-handed pitchers."[25]

Spahn said his father was his best coach during his youth and teen years. American Legion was a bonus added to high school games. "It was an opportunity to play," he said.[26]

Spahn's American Legion experience helped him mature as much as did his high school play. In a northern climate like Buffalo, the season is shorter than in warm-weather locales such as California, Texas, and Florida. It might snow into April in Buffalo and that was not conducive to an early baseball start, so the extra games played in American Legion ball were extremely valuable for aspiring players.

Spahn did not look back and credit his high school or Legion coaches for his development. It always came back to his dad's instruction, passion, and forceful personality in insisting on doing things properly.

"I guess most of the things that I learned throughout my baseball career were just picking up a piece here and a piece there to develop what I had to work with," Spahn said.[27]

Even when pressed by an interviewer when he was well into retirement, Spahn said he was never really influenced by other notable southpaws. He was aware of the achievements of Lefty Grove, Carl Hubbell, and Herb Pennock, but he never saw them pitch and didn't know them so he never quizzed them for information. Unlike later generations growing up after World War II, there was no baseball on television in Buffalo during Spahn's youth, no Game of the Week, only radio baseball. Grove, with his 300 wins, Hubbell, a nine-time All-Star with 253 victories and a 2.98 lifetime earned run average, and Pennock, who won 241 games and was part of six World Series champions, all ended up in the Hall of Fame. They would have been worthwhile role models who could have offered Spahn tips.

Instead, for the most part, Spahn went it alone after he moved on from his father's tutelage. Actually, Spahn barely overlapped with the final lap of Hubbell's career and said he recalled batting against the screwball artist who was known as "Meal Ticket" because he could always be counted on to produce.

"I remember hitting against him," Spahn said. "First of all, you're looking for him to break the ball away from you and he threw me a screwball that was bigger than any right-hander's curveball. It looked goofy coming from a left-hander and then (broke) in on me like that. That influenced me a great deal."[28]

Only in a general way, perhaps, because Spahn was not a screwball pitcher early on, and as even he said few left-handers toyed with the pitch.

Although Buffalo was hardly close enough to be classified as a New York City borough, Spahn did follow the Yankees. His favorite player was Lou Gehrig, who was active for New York into the 1939 season and died young from amyotrophic lateral sclerosis, later known as Lou Gehrig's Disease.

"I never saw Lou play," Spahn said. "I never got to meet him. But I idolized him."[29]

Spahn cited Gehrig being an Ivy Leaguer and more handsome than Babe Ruth as reasons why he also favored the slugger, who of course also played Spahn's first-love position, first base. He also said Gehrig scored points with him because he reminded him of Tarzan.

Spahn was probably unaware Gehrig once tried out to play Tarzan in the movies. In 1936, after Olympic-medal-winning swimmer Johnny Weissmuller gave up the role, Hollywood was looking for a new Tarzan. Gehrig took a screen test, but for whatever reason he did not pass muster with the studio.

Once Spahn settled in on the mound for South Park High he became a star. He was excellent as a sophomore and undefeated as a junior and senior. In one of his last high school games Spahn pitched a no-hitter against Buffalo High. So at least he had one on his resume long before that 1960 big-league no-hitter against the Phillies, albeit against slightly less-experienced competition.

Throughout high school, Ed Spahn repeatedly fanned the notion that Warren could become a major-league pitcher if he kept improving, kept working hard, and kept learning. Sometimes he tossed out the idea scouts were probably coming to his games, even though he did not know that to be the case.

Much later, Warren said while in high school "I never dreamed I was going to be a professional."[30]

Scouting was far less sophisticated then than it is in the 2000s. Nowadays players and their parents and coaches put together personal highlight tapes. They appear on websites while social media drives attention. In the late 1930s, there was no cooperative scouting between teams, no draft, and it was up to individual teams to search for the hidden gem.

Word-of-mouth and personal connections played a much larger role. Sometimes it was who you knew or who your coach knew. Spahn had the advantage of living in a fairly large city rather than in a rural part of the country. But still, a bird-dog scout had to find you, assess you, and pass the word along to the big club with an endorsement so you might get signed to suit up for some Class D team in a small town far away.

There were only sixteen big-league teams, eight in the American League and eight in the National League. But each team might be affiliated with a dozen minor-league franchises. With the need to fill out rosters, teams were more willing to take chances on signing boys with that gleam in their eye. They might last a single season with the organization, but it was worth checking them out.

For a time, the St. Louis Cardinals under vice president and general manager Branch Rickey nearly cornered the market on prospects. It seemed Rickey was willing to give just about anyone a chance as long as he could tie his spikes, reach the plate with a pitch, or catch a fly ball. His was a revolving-door operation until complaints led Commissioner Kenesaw Mountain Landis to intervene.

In 1938, as Spahn was working his way through high school, Landis freed seventy-four St. Louis farm players from contracts with the big-league team and ruled six clubs broke rules tying up players. Rickey's big-tent approach of signing guys who at the least would not be able to harm his Cardinals if they were stuck in his minors rather than elsewhere was deemed unfair to the players. Careers could be ruined as they were buried on depth charts. Coming off this spanking, if Spahn was being scouted, there was less chance it was the Cardinals doing the investigating than anyone else.

One day at South Park practice, it happened. A scout named Bill Myers asked Coach Schumaker to introduce him to Spahn. Myers worked for the Boston Braves, and he informed Spahn he liked the way Spahn threw a baseball.

Warren went home and told the family about this meeting. This contact particularly excited father Ed. Although the Spahns were basically Yankee rooters, the pragmatic Ed recognized it might be tougher for his son to work his way through the minors into the rotation of a perennial world champion. While the Braves had not lit a fire in the National League for quite some time, that might mean Warren would have a better chance of working his way onto a big-league roster.

Ed Spahn knew of Myers and believed he had a sound reputation as a fair man based on his previous scouting for the Boston Red Sox. It was said Myers left the Red Sox and switched to the Braves because he did not believe the American League club gave another Buffalo player, Sibbi Sisti, whom Myers scouted, a fair deal. Several years later, Sisti and Spahn would be teammates with the Braves.

Warren wanted to sign with the Braves immediately, but his father insisted he wait until after high school graduation. He was confident the opportunity would still be there. Today the same debate occurs in many households, only the focus is on whether or not a player should take big bucks or go to college. Those weren't the issues on the table in the Spahn household. Warren worried nobody would make him an offer if he waited until after graduation. Dad counseled patience.

The Yankees did come knocking but lost interest because they did not think Spahn was heavy enough or strong enough. They looked but turned away.

Spahn graduated in the spring of 1940 and did sign with Bill Myers and the Boston Braves. It was the kind of contract that loomed fairly large to an innocent teenager whose family life experience had just carried through the Great Depression but one that would be laughed at now.

The deal called for a $150 signing bonus and two suits of clothes. That sounded pretty good to Warren Spahn in those very different times.

He was nineteen years old when he departed Buffalo to play for a Bradford, Pennsylvania team in the Pony League. It was his first out-of-town adventure, and it was the first step toward launching a big-league baseball career and perhaps one day gaining access to another suit of clothes, one belonging to the Boston Braves with a number on the back. His first salary in professional baseball paid Spahn twenty dollars a week.

"I grabbed it," Spahn of getting the chance with a pro team. "And I remember that the guys that were graduating out of high school with me were making like $15, $17 a week working in the steel mills. I was making $20 playing Class D baseball, so I was delighted to play baseball, number one, and make more than those guys did."[31]

The richness was less in the dollar amount and more in the opportunity.

4

LEARNING THE TRADE IN THE MINORS

WARREN SPAHN'S FIRST professional manager, Jack Onslow, was an old-timer even in 1940. Onslow was a baseball lifer who never got to play much major-league baseball but had a long career as a coach and manager.

A catcher from Pennsylvania, Onslow had two brief stints in the majors, totaling 77 at-bats, zero home runs, and a .169 average. He could instruct a better game than he could play. Onslow played 36 games for the Detroit Tigers in 1912 and nine games for the New York Giants in 1917.

Adroitly making the most of his limited skills, Onslow toured the country between 1909 and 1924, suiting up for minor-league clubs in Dallas; Fort Wayne, Indiana; Buffalo; Richmond; Kansas City; and Portland, Oregon. He rarely played in 100 or more games in a season and just about as rarely hit higher than .250.

In 1948, Onslow, who had toiled long and loyally with minor-league teams in the dugout, was rewarded at age sixty when named the manager of the Chicago White Sox, his only big-league skipper role.

The Onslow young Spahn ran into in Bradford, Pennsylvania was the crusty sort, a traditionalist. When deployed to the club Spahn was asked what number he might want to wear. Thinking back to the good fortune he had decked out in No. 13 in high school, that's the digit he requested. He was immediately scoffed at by Onslow and the Bees' equipment manager.

"Just what we needed," Onslow said, "a screwball lefty.[32]

"Fella, we don't carry any number thirteens," Onslow, who may or may not even have known Spahn's name at the time, continued. "A guy's liable to run into enough tough luck around here without wearing any number thirteen on his back."[33]

Spahn may have been indifferent to superstition, but his boss wasn't. Spahn got off to a solid but not brilliant start, statistics-wise, but statistics are not always what officials in big-league organizations study first. They are more apt to look at a young pitcher's makeup and his stuff. All players fresh out of high school are rookies, usually away from home for the first time, as Spahn was, and teams want to know what kind of pure talent they bring in their inaugural professional exposure. However, since many of those young players were the kings in their neighborhoods in high school or American Legion ball, as Spahn was, they think they should be just as dominant in their new environment.

During his season in Bradford, Spahn compiled a 5–4 record with a 2.73 earned run average while throwing 66 innings. He was not wild, that bugaboo of concern about young southpaws. However, for a player who had not lost a game during his last two years at South Park High, Spahn was disturbed by his seemingly so-so record.

After all of those years with father Ed around to coach him and to drum the usual lessons into his head about control and form, for the first time Spahn tampered with his delivery. He sought to provide more oomph to his curve and went about throwing it from a fresh angle. Bad mistake.

Spahn flung a fateful curve and grabbed for his left shoulder. The pain was unlike anything he had experienced on the diamond. He knew he was hurt, knew he should not throw another pitch. Onslow promptly recognized the distress and asked Spahn what was wrong.

"It's like as if my arm's coming off, Skip," Spahn said. "My shoulder's on fire."[34] Those are the worst words a manager wants to hear coming out of his pitcher's mouth. There is never any way to know when the last good pitch may be the last pitch of a pitcher's career. Especially in 1940, when the sophistication of treatment in no way approached the medical cures available more than seventy-five years later, there was every reason to worry. Surgery could well mean the end, not a rebirth. Tommy John, who had the career-saving operation for pitchers named after him when many such injuries seemed hopeless, was not even born until 1943.

The team doctor poked Spahn's shoulder with his fingers and concluded he was hurt and needed more treatment than could be offered in a ballpark clubhouse. Spahn was sent to a hospital for X-rays, and the verdict was torn tendons in his throwing shoulder.

Spahn was sidelined, ordered not to throw a baseball for quite some time, and to adopt the power of positive thinking, wishing and hoping his meal ticket arm would heal and allow him to resume his fledgling pro pitching career.

The uncertainty was bound to eat at Spahn, as it would any young player, until he could again prove himself on the mound. Spahn was sent home to Buffalo to rest and recuperate. He wore a sling on his left arm when he departed, a symbol of the wound.

Spahn had to demonstrate an upbeat outlook back home because his dad was depressed enough for both of them. Ed fretted about the entire matter, wondering if all the doctoring Spahn had received in Pennsylvania was good enough. Spahn told his father the injury wasn't all that bad and he would be as good as new, ready to throw again in a few weeks. Ed Spahn worried his son's chance at big-league ball had been lost. Back in Buffalo, Warren and Ed took in Bisons games together, just as they had when Warren was younger.

After two weeks, Warren could not stand sitting at home while his team was playing and took a train back to Bradford where he informed Onslow he was ready to pitch again. Onslow was suspicious of the quick improvement and asked if Spahn was so healthy how come he was still wearing the sling. Well, there was that.

Thinking quickly, Spahn said he wore the sling on the trip as a precaution against re-injuring it. Onslow gave him the okay to do some light throwing and test the arm. However, right away, as Spahn peeled off the sling, pain shot through his shoulder. Still, Spahn did engage in some light tosses, fooling himself he was ready to go.

Onslow didn't trust Spahn's enthusiasm, knowing that young players tended to think they were invulnerable. He consulted with the team doctor, right in front of Spahn. The medical man agreed the shoulder had improved but warned if Spahn cut loose and the tendons tore once more his pitching career might be dead on the spot. This was a risky moment for the nineteen-year-old who if proven wrong might have disappeared into the baseball mists as a never-was.

Spahn wore down the older men, who gave him permission to throw batting practice. Even though he was instructed to take it easy, Spahn ignored that advice, and his first pitch to the cage was a hard one. Spahn threw fast, and it cost him. In instant pain, he staggered forward from the mound, dropped to one knee, and involuntarily flashed his hand to his shoulder protectively, as if it might fall off without support. There was no masking this agony.

The next move for Spahn was a visit to another X-ray machine, which only confirmed what everyone knew. The shoulder had been re-injured. Spahn bravely predicted he should probably take a month off this time before returning. He was told by the older men to take the year off. That was an optimistic assessment. They hoped some day Warren Spahn would throw off a professional mound again, but they knew there was no guarantee.

Onslow told Spahn he would always have a uniform for him. No telling how that resonated with a young player who was undoubtedly not looking for a repeat performance in Class D, but at least it sounded as if someone in pro ball cared about him, even with a bum wing.

Spahn headed off into the unknown, but he did make a smooth recovery, earning him another shot for the 1941 season. The fears dissipated and Spahn was assigned to Class B Evansville in the Illinois-Indiana-Iowa League, better known later for short as the Three-I League. Class B was a big jump up from an incomplete, injury-interrupted season in Class D. Spahn's 5–4 record hadn't been a major influence in the Braves' front office. People watching believed he could pitch and deserved a shot at tougher competition. Given his limited time at Bradford, this was an unexpected and welcome reward for Spahn.

Fresh off his shoulder recuperation, Spahn reported to spring training in Bradenton, Florida. However, soon after, on a road trip to San Antonio, Texas, Spahn suffered a fresh injury. Anyone who has ever viewed a photograph of Warren Spahn from his years in the big leagues can't help but notice the hook in his nose. It was not a feature he was proud of or had much tolerance for listening to jokes about, but it was pronounced.

During spring training Spahn took a teammate's throw flush in the face, and his nose was emphatically broken. For the rest of his life, Spahn looked like a boxer who had taken one wicked shot to the puss. It was not the flattened nose from repeated ring punishment but a crooked one from the impact of the one blow.

Many years later, Greg Spahn, Warren's son, told a story he heard from his dad when the incident occurred. The Braves talked Spahn out of obtaining reconstructive surgery with the argument, "Warren, we will send you to a specialist to have your nose fixed, but most people that have that done end up with sinus problems and you're not a very good-looking guy."[35]

What a soothing bedside manner. What this also indicated, in an era when management ruled all and was usually on the cheap side, was the Braves didn't think it was worth the investment for a cosmetic procedure, whereas when Spahn's arm was afflicted the year before, they were gung-ho to help.

This was the period when Spahn first encountered Casey Stengel. To some, Stengel is the greatest manager of all time. However, his reputation was made near the tail end of his career when he led the New York Yankees to ten pennants in twelve years between 1948 and 1960.

A former outfielder for the New York Giants with a lifetime batting average of .284, Stengel broke in on the bench for the Brooklyn Dodgers in 1934. The Dodgers of that era were mostly a losing team before Stengel took over and during his tenure, which ended with a third losing season in 1936. The Dodgers were first called "Bums" by their own fans.

Stengel became the Braves (or Bees for a couple of seasons) manager in 1938 and remained in that job through 1942. Although the two Hall of Famers had their differences a little bit later, Stengel's first impression of Spahn as a pitcher was very favorable, and he predicted good things for the left-hander.

"He's only twenty years old and needs work," Stengel said, "But mark my word, if nothing happens to the kid, he can be a great one. Someday he's gonna be one of the best left-handers in the league."[36]

That kind of praise from the field boss was not issued lightly. Then Stengel shipped Spahn out to Evansville. Spahn pitched a full and impressive season, going 19–6 with a 1.83 earned run average in 212 innings.

Evansville was the right place at the right time for Spahn's accelerated progress and people he worked with there in Western Indiana were just the type of tutors he needed at that stage of his career. Spahn took the next step forward in his career with the help of some seasoned and knowledgeable tutors.

Manager Bob Coleman was born in 1890 and was already fifty going into the 1941 season. He was the type of unsung, loyal minor-league leader every franchise needs. He was another of those baseball lifers who lucked into a short stay in the majors but stayed in the game pretty much the rest of his adult life. Coleman's lifetime average was .241 in 116 games as a catcher, spread over three seasons with the Pittsburgh Pirates and Cleveland Indians between 1913 and 1916.

Between 1910 and 1927, when he wasn't making those appearances in the bigs, Coleman bounced around the minors.

He had his finest hitting season of .320 for Terre Haute in 129 games in 1920 and even at age thirty-three in 1924 he batted .312 for San Antonio in the Texas League.

Spahn credited Coleman as the man who helped smooth out the delivery he had tampered with the year before while playing with his curve, an effort that preserved Spahn's arm for the next two-decades-plus.

"That sort of teacher was perfect for me," Spahn said years later. "I never wanted to make the same mistake more than once. And Bob was like a second father. He knew when to be easy, when to be firm, when to criticize, and when to praise."[37]

Spahn acquired an unofficial helpmate that season, too. His roommate, Willard "Bill" Donovan, who was from the Chicago suburb of Maywood, also strove to make the big leagues. Donovan was not blessed with the same amount of talent as Spahn, but he was a smart pitcher, and he possessed one skill superior to Spahn's. He had a gift for holding runners on first base that might be a threat to steal.

At this point in his career, this was not a Spahn strength. Donovan was also a left-hander. Southpaws in general have an advantage over right-handers in keeping runners close to the bag because they are facing them as they start their throw to home plate, while right-handers go into their windups facing the other way. Spahn marveled at how Donovan was able to fool baserunners and sought to adopt a similar motion to keep them closer to the base.

"Donovan had the most deceptive move I've ever seen," Spahn said. "Really the greatest." Recognizing differences in their pitching approaches, Spahn realized he could not copy Donovan precisely, but he could borrow some aspects of it. "But I tried to incorporate the best points of his move into my own style."[38]

Donovan did reach the majors for Boston, briefly, but did not have nearly as much success as Spahn. His career mark was 4–6 combined in 1942 and 1943.

In 1942 at the Braves' new spring training home in Sanford, Florida, Spahn learned his superb season at Evansville and apparent maturity at age twenty-one had given him his shot at the big leagues—he would be moving up to Boston. Stengel was going to see if his prophecy was correct. Spahn, who had endured so much so recently in Bradford, was making his— and his father's—dream come true. He could not have anticipated how swiftly his ascension to the big club would turn into a nightmare.

Another future Braves star pitcher, Johnny Sain, who became Spahn's best early friend in baseball, was also promoted from the minors that season. Sain noticed the smooth delivery Spahn's father had taught him. "I'd give anything to have your form," Sain told Spahn. Spahn retorted, "I'll swap it for your curve."[39]

Whether it was Stengel being cantankerous, just in a bad mood that day, or sick of losing, which he had done regularly with the Dodgers and Braves, he picked on Spahn late in a game on April 20 against the Dodgers in Brooklyn. The Braves lost 9–2 that day at Ebbets Field, but not primarily because of Spahn.

Spahn came into the game in relief in the fourth inning after Tom Earley allowed five earned runs in three innings. This was Spahn's fourth game in his rookie season, and he had been used in limited fashion. He was hit pretty hard during his three innings, also surrendering five runs, four of them earned.

But what inspired Stengel's ire and the temper tantrum that followed was Spahn's failure to headhunt Dodger shortstop Pee Wee Reese to his satisfaction. Spahn remembered the incident quite well since it was life-changing at the time.

"We were playing the Dodgers, and the Dodgers always beat the devil out of us," Spahn said. "Of course, Pee Wee was pretty agile. Of all the guys with the Dodgers, why do you knock Pee Wee down? The Dodgers also got our signs (stole them) from second base and relayed them to the hitter. I remember Casey was going to have a switch, and one was going to be the curveball and two the fastball. Casey gave me the knockdown pitch, and I threw inside. I think I threw back here (inside again), and Pee Wee just moved his head out of the way. Casey jumped up, and when he did, he hit his head on the top of the dugout, which was concrete. Now, he's real mad. And he gave me the knock-down again, and I threw and missed him. So Casey came out to the mound."[40]

Although Spahn threw inside to Reese three times, his inability to plunk him infuriated Stengel, who believed the southpaw was disobeying his order. Spahn was replaced for the last two innings by Lou Tost, but being replaced was the least of Spahn's punishment.

"Young man, you've got no guts," Stengel accused Spahn. "Go pick up your railroad ticket to Hartford."[41]

Stengel cut Spahn on the spot, the pitcher he seemingly so believed in, exiling him back to the minors for the rest of the 1942 season. That was a strangely emphatic move by Stengel, but he stuck to it. The brief foray into the majors left Spahn with a 0–0 mark and an unsightly 5.74 earned run average in 15 2/3 innings.

Spahn pitched the rest of the season in Connecticut in Class A ball with similar results to his 1941 season in Evansville. His won-loss record was 17–12 and his earned run average of 1.96 in 248 innings once again showed he was overpowering batters.

In an era when there was no such thing as free agency, Spahn was bound to the Braves and all he could do was hope that the Braves and Stengel would give him another chance at spring training in 1943.

Only there would be no spring training for Spahn that year. He would not throw another pitch for the Braves organization until 1946, when he was a not-quite-so-young twenty-five-year-old prospect.

5

WAR AND RETURN

WORLD WAR II was alive with bitterness, hatred, and rage by 1939 as Adolf Hitler's troops growled across the European continent.

Poland fell first, and France followed. Great Britain was teetering. Isolationist policy still ruled in the United States. Citizens did not want to go to war and did not want to become involved in someone else's war. President Franklin D. Roosevelt recognized war was inevitable to halt the voracious land appetites of Germany across the Atlantic Ocean and Japan across the Pacific Ocean.

He did not feel he yet had the will of the people behind him, nor did he believe in the readiness of the American military. It took the bombing of Pearl Harbor in Hawaii on December 7, 1941, for Americans to erupt in outrage. The United States was drawn into the conflagration, and once in patriotism coursed through men's veins. They were ready to serve and protect.

Baseball was hardly an essential service such as cultivating wheat and other foodstuffs, working to produce munitions in factories, or raising cattle to feed the troops. There was hesitation by Commissioner Kenesaw Mountain Landis to unequivocally support the continuation of the sport at its highest level when other young men were being shipped around the world to fight.

Landis wrote to FDR to ask what to do. In his famous so-called "green light" letter, Roosevelt endorsed the idea of baseball continuing. Players would be treated like any other young men eligible for the draft, but he thought it wise to continue play so as to provide entertainment for the masses on the home front.

So baseball played on throughout the seasons of 1942, 1943, 1944, and 1945 while the war raged elsewhere and millions died from bullets, bombs, and famine. It was watered-down baseball, as many of the game's greatest stars enlisted or were called up to defend their country in the Army, Navy, Marines, Coast Guard, or the fledgling US Army Air Corps, which later became the US Air Force.

Some of the greatest players of all time traded baseball woolens for newer uniforms. Cleveland Indians fireballer Bob Feller, Detroit Tigers slugger Hank Greenberg, New York Yankees star Joe DiMaggio, St. Louis Cardinals great Stan Musial, and Boston Red Sox leader Ted Williams all joined the military. So did Yankee catcher Yogi Berra and barrier-breaking Jackie Robinson, who in 1947 became the first African American to play in the majors in the twentieth century. It was later revealed journeyman catcher Moe Berg, who attended Princeton and learned several languages, was an American spy.

These well-known players, all Hall of Famers besides Berg, were far from alone. More than 500 major-league players served during World War II. This was clearly something bigger than all of them. World War II was the fight to preserve freedom and the American way of life.

At the time Warren Spahn was little-known outside of the Boston Braves' organization, or more accurately unknown. He had just those four appearances with the Braves on his resume from 1942. Later, his name would be mentioned alongside Williams, Musial, and others as one of the best players of his generation. When Spahn went off to war in 1943, he was essentially invisible at the top level of the game.

Before the Stengel incident, Spahn had advance warning his days might be numbered with the Braves in 1942. He was thrilled to come out of training camp on the big-league roster, but coach Johnny Cooney, one of his favorites, said his ascent did not mean he was permanently chosen. Cooney issued a foreshadowing comment, noting circumstances could change the picture.

"One of them will be how many pitchers we lose to the Army by June," Cooney said.[42]

A year later, Spahn was one of those guys, Boston and Hartford both in his rearview mirror.

Spahn was drafted into the Army as a private as soon as his 1942 minor-league season ended, although he had delayed enlistment a few months to finish the campaign. Then he was sent to Camp Gruber in Muskogee, Oklahoma, now used as a National Guard training facility, but in 1943 used to train men on their way overseas.

"I remember when war was declared," Spahn said. "I certainly was eligible and I certainly felt I was going to be drafted. I was scared to death. I didn't want to go. I didn't want to be a soldier. But I was drafted. Again, if I'm a soldier, I wanted to be the best soldier I could possibly be. If I'm a pitcher, I want to be the best pitcher I could be."[43]

Spahn said the Army didn't appear prepared to deploy him in a useful way that had anything to do with his background. There were no special battalions for pitchers. It wasn't as if he was going to be trained to adapt his motion into a more effective way to toss hand grenades. Asked what he did in civilian life, Spahn seemed to baffle the first Army rep he spoke to when he answered professional ballplayer.

"What the heck are we going to do with you?" the man said. "If you were a truck driver, they made a baker out of you, and if you were a baker, they made you a truck driver. They wanted to teach you their way."[44]

Spahn started with the 14th Armored Division, moved to Company D, and then moved again when the division was streamlined, ending up with an engineering outfit. Digging holes and working on bridges, he said, was "the dirty work nobody else wants to do."[45]

Although Spahn grew up in Buffalo, he found Camp Gruber's weather to be surprisingly chilly when he was stationed there. At one point he said to a friend from Buffalo named Roy Reimann that he pined for spring training days in the sunshine. "I could be living like a king in Florida now, in the warm sun," Spahn said.[46]

By the time Spahn went into the Army, his baseball career had not been secured, but his girlfriend LoRene Southard was a permanent fixture and marriage was on their minds. Spahn did ultimately marry her. Reimann's wife introduced them, and LoRene worked nearby at an oil company office in Tulsa. This was Spahn's first flirtation with Oklahoma, the bad and the good. He wasn't fond of the weather, but it was his future wife's home. Later, Spahn settled in Oklahoma and spent about fifty years residing there.

Spahn was not an enthusiastic entry into the Army, but he recognized the import of what he was doing, both for the role he must play and for his country during a terrible time.

"I was drafted, but my country was in trouble," he said. "And I think we all felt—I think that generation felt—that we had an obligation and that we'd rather fight Hitler over in Europe than have him invade this country. So everybody dropped what they were doing to preserve what we felt America was all about and our style of living."[47]

At times he did wonder about the value of his contribution.

"I dug ditches and I cleaned up minefields and all those sort of things like everybody else did," Spahn said. "I thought, 'I don't want to do this.' I remember when I got to be a private first class and a corporal, I thought I did want to do that because I didn't have to do KP, which is kitchen police, you know, peeling potatoes. Each of the times that I got a promotion I got away from the lower level of the Army. So I became a corporal, a sergeant, a staff sergeant, and I got a battlefield commission."[48]

Spahn remained stationed in the United States until 1944. He played for the post baseball team with Reimann as his catcher. Spahn was always conscious about the number of casualties American servicemen suffered, either killed or wounded, even wounded badly enough to be maimed through the loss of a limb. That was the daily reality at the front and everyone knew it. Why wouldn't a man worry?

Eventually, Spahn's stateside assignment ended, at the base and on the diamond. He was a member of the Gruber Engineers, the 276th Engineer Combat Battalion. By then, no longer a private but a sergeant, he shipped out for Europe aboard the *Queen Mary* in the summer of 1944, landing in Scotland. It was believed the Allies had gained the upper hand in the war and had German troops on the run.

Instead, the Germans regrouped, mustered a last charge of men and tanks, and engaged the Americans in one of the most famous conflicts of World War II, the Battle of the Bulge, which began on December 16, 1944, and did not end until January 25, 1945. The fierce fighting occurred in the Ardennes region, which spanned parts of Belgium, Luxembourg, and extended into a section of France. This was the last Nazi surge on the western front, the last-gasp hope of repelling the enemy and preventing a rush into Berlin.

Spahn's engineers latched onto the 9th Armored Division, their job to keep roads and bridges open for advancing soldiers and blocking them from the enemy. Even in uncomfortable and dangerous situations at the front, baseball came into the conversation. In movie after movie about the World War II experience, characters separated friend from foe by quizzing them about Babe Ruth. Spahn said he and his fellow soldiers did that very kind of thing, although he said they asked a different question. "Anybody we didn't know, we'd ask, 'Who played second base for the Bums?' [meaning the Dodgers and Lord help anyone who didn't recognize they were synonymous]," he said. "If he didn't say 'Eddie Stanky,' he was dead."[49]

Though Spahn was an unknown when he went to war, several other stars who served were well into their careers. One what-if game baseball historians play is trying to guess what the lifetime stats really might have been for players like Williams, Feller, and Greenberg in particular. Williams came up short of 3,000 hits because he lost about five and a half years total in World War II and the Korean War. Feller, who was at the peak of his game, won 266 games, but it was conceded he certainly would have won 300.

Feller, a right-hander from Van Meter, Iowa, was a teen-aged fastball phenomenon, most definitely starting his major-league career younger than Spahn. Feller won five games for the Cleveland Indians when he was seventeen and won 24, 27, and 25 games three years in a row in 1939, 1940, and 1941 before joining the military for more than three seasons. He had just turned twenty-three, not much older than Spahn, who had zero wins on his record at the time.

On his way to negotiate his next contract with the Indians brass, Feller heard the announcement on the radio of the bombing of Pearl Harbor. Within days he enlisted in the Navy. Years later, Feller recalled his thinking upon learning the shocking news.

"The last thing on my mind right then was playing baseball," Feller said. "I immediately decided to enlist in the United States Navy. I didn't have to—I was twenty-three and strong-bodied, you bet, but with my father terminally ill back in Van Meter, Iowa, I was exempt from military service.

"It didn't matter to me—I wanted to join the fight against Hitler and the Japanese. We were losing that war and most young men of my generation wanted to help push them back. People today don't understand, but that's the way we felt in those days. We wanted to join the fighting. So on December 9, I gave up the chance to earn $100,000 with the Indians and became the first professional athlete to join the Navy after Pearl Harbor."[50]

In a comment made after retirement, Feller once said if he had played baseball uninterrupted by war service, "I'd have won more games than Warren Spahn."[51] Maybe, maybe not. If he won 80 games, a not unreasonable total, over the three years he missed, Feller would have ended up with 346 victories.

Spahn was thrust into action at the Battle of the Bulge at the Siege of Bastogne, the Belgium community that was the gateway to the harbor at Antwerp. That was the prize the Germans sought when they caught the Allies off-guard. This was a major turning point of the war, from the American side involving the 101st Airborne, the

82nd Airborne, and eventually General George Patton's Third Army. The Battle of the Bulge was going to provide renewed faith for the Germans or the Americans were going to crash through German lines and march on Berlin.

Much fighting occurred in the dimly lit forest and some German troops stole uniforms off American dead and impersonated them. Spahn and the Americans allowed safe passage to those who could answer the key question: Who played second base for the Dodgers?

"They had our dog tags," Spahn said. "They had our equipment. And Hitler would have been successful, I think, had he not stretched himself on his supply line. They were well-prepared, but you know, they didn't have the American pride and the gung-ho thing that the Americans had."[52]

In Belgium, Spahn was in the midst of one of the most important and telling conflicts of World War II. The Battle of the Bulge was no one-sided rout. Thousands upon thousands of men of determination fought to the death, knowing much was at stake.

Spahn and his engineers were at the front. The Germans sought Antwerp. The Americans sought to push them into retreat. US troops wanted to cross the Rhine River in droves. The engineers erected pontoon bridges. But there were also solid, stand-alone, wider bridges generals wanted to take and hold so the Americans could cross and the Germans would no longer have access. Initially, Spahn was at Bastogne when the Germans were on the offensive.

"I remember one time we were surrounded by the Germans," Spahn said.[53]

That's when they used the Eddie Stanky code to make sure all of the foes were German.

After the Battle of the Bulge, the Americans recouped and regrouped and the 9th Armored Division, its tanks rumbling through the fields and over debris, picked up speed toward the Rhine as February turned to March in 1945. Fleeing German demolition squads rigged those established bridges with explosives, with the aim of halting the Americans at the water. Some 6,200 pounds of explosives were lashed onto the Ludendorff Bridge in Remagen, Germany, about an hour from Cologne, France, but when the Germans set off their detonators, some did not work. The bridge was damaged, but it held and the Americans faced little resistance.

This was a major blunder by the Germans, giving the Americans a major access route to dash across. A small group of Germans was left behind as the body of troops headed out, and they were killed on the scene by the Americans.

Spahn's engineers were sent to the bridge to repair it, to shore it up, and to transform the damage so men and tanks could cross. But the Germans recognized their mistake. Rather than run for it, they fought back, daily throwing manpower and equipment at the bridge to blow it up.

Frogmen swam underwater but were spotted and killed by Americans, for the first time using special glasses that enabled them to see beneath the surface. The Germans came at the men by plane and Spahn retained vivid images of that attack.

"The minute we started working, it was like the Fourth of July. It looked like the whole sky was lit up with those tracers," Spahn said as the Americans moved in artillery and machine guns to shoot back.[54]

Once the bridge was completely secured, the Americans sent some men to the other side to set up a defensive spot near a mountain to hopefully contain the fighting there, farther away from the bridge.

"It was such a maze, and I remember crawling away from that bridge through cow dung and everything else and didn't even realize that you're so full of this stuff," Spahn said. "We were taught to cradle your rifle between your elbows to make sure it didn't get dirty. When I got to a farmhouse, or a barn, I remember I looked at my rifle and I couldn't have fired that thing, you know, if the Germans had captured me. But we were scared."[55]

Those who have seen the movies *The Battle of the Bulge* or *The Bridge at Remagen* or read extensively about this battle are aware much fighting took place in snowy conditions. Soldiers were bundled up as if on a mission to the North Pole. Buffalo is a cold and snowy place, but Spahn indicated there was no comparison with the kind of cold he felt in combat. Yes, he was scared, but no, the shivering was not from fear, but the elements.

"Our feet were frozen when we went to sleep and they were frozen when we woke up," Spahn said. "We didn't have a bath or change of clothes for weeks."[56]

The bitter cold lingered in Spahn's memory for a long time.

"I remember we had half-tracks and we had rations in cans and put them against the motor of the half-track to warm it up so that, you know, you could eat it," he said. "And we couldn't light a fire. There were days, weeks, maybe months, that we couldn't even take our shoes off. And, you know, your shoes and feet would get cold and your socks were wet all the time."[57]

The US troops gained control of the bridge on March 7. When Hitler was alerted to the faux pas, he was furious and ordered a follow-up attack to destroy it at all costs. That fighting lasted ten days and the bridge withstood numerous and varied assaults. Spahn recalled the sight of one German plane being hit and spiraling into the ground, its pilot a charred corpse when found. Historians say the Germans sent seventeen planes at the bridge, all of them missing with their bombs, and thirteen of them being shot down. Hitler raised the ante and ordered V-2 rockets fired at the bridge. Still, it stood. Howitzers were unleashed and damaged the Ludendorff Bridge but did not wreck it.

While this assault was ongoing, the Americans sent about 25,000 troops across the Rhine. On March 17, after the United States built other temporary bridges, the Ludendorff Bridge collapsed. Some twenty-five soldiers perished in the incident and sixty-three more were injured.

Spahn and some others provided security at times and then went to work repeatedly fixing any holes Germans blew in the bridge. Spahn was nearby and witnessed the crash into the water, men and pieces of debris being quickly swept away in the current. A piece of the bridge struck him in the foot and he nearly went down with the bridge.

The fighting on the approach to the bridge, the fighting to hold onto the bridge, and this accident produced many casualties. By then a sergeant, Spahn received a battlefield commission as a lieutenant. He had worked his way up from private.

"We lost a lot of people, including officers," Spahn said, "so they needed replacement people for these officers we lost. And my company commander recommended me as a potential officer."[58]

The strange part was being entrusted to order around the same men he had been with, and he found that challenging, especially since his old friend Roy Reimann was in the group. They had known one another for years, played baseball together, been in boot camp together. Spahn said tradition dictated that a best friend pin the bars on his uniform and he actually woke up Reimann to do it. Reimann laughed at the sight of his old friend as an officer.

"And I had a heck of a time getting him to salute me," Spahn said. "I said, 'Remember, you're saluting the uniform.'"[59]

Spahn went on into Germany as the war approached its end. But he was not allowed to leave Europe right away with his company when peace broke out. There was a rule he had to serve at his new rank for a year. Spahn said he had considered that possibility when the Americans had the Germans on the run, and he accepted the commission. But at the time he was sure he would just be transferred to the Pacific front to fight the Japanese. He did not foresee the coming of the atomic bomb and the power unleashed on Hiroshima and Nagasaki in early August of 1945.

As American troops began administering a ravaged Germany, Spahn was sent to Nuremberg to supervise the building of a hospital by German workers. All this meant Spahn was not back in the States to participate in the 1945 baseball season.

While fighting, Spahn received minor wounds in his foot and back from shrapnel. He was awarded a Purple Heart and the Bronze Star, a battlefield commission, and a presidential citation, officially making him a war hero. It was not something he ever boasted about, but he would discuss his wartime service when asked. Once, in later years, Spahn was asked if he ever worried about the threat of damage to his left arm or shoulder, incapacitating those body parts in such a manner he would not be able to pitch again. He said he did not. He saw many servicemen dying or being maimed and for that reason wondered if he deserved a Purple Heart for what he considered scratches, but baseball seemed like a faraway world when he was at war.

"That was a part of my life that I hoped would happen," he said. "But it was a long way away. I think you live for the present rather than the future. I think you would go stir crazy if you thought about the duration of the war and how long it would take."[60]

Many months passed before Warren Spahn was given his discharge in April 1946. Another baseball season was starting and Spahn wanted to pitch for the Boston Braves. He had no idea whether or not he had retained his skill, but he wanted the chance. After missing three full seasons and spring training, Spahn was twenty-five.

There was no reason to believe the Braves were counting on him. He would prove how badly they needed him.

6

ROOKIE WARREN SPAHN

WORLD WAR II left Lieutenant Warren Spahn behind in Germany for months, even as another baseball season threatened to tick away on him.

Baseball was his career, but he did not know if he still had that career. Spring training came and went and the 1946 season began. He had to worry about what was next. He hoped the Boston Braves would still be his employer, but he had spent only a few weeks with the major-league club before entering the service.

Casey Stengel, with whom he had feuded, if only briefly, was no longer the manager. He was ousted by owner Lou Perini during the 1943 season and replaced by Spahn's minor-league patron, Bob Coleman. Wartime baseball was uneven, especially with so many men fighting for the country instead of the pennant. A manager was dealt what he got, and able replacements were not always at the ready. Coleman finished up the 68–85 season at the helm. He also ran the Braves in 1944. Only thing was, even with the new leadership in the dugout, the results were almost identical, 65–89.

Coleman got one more chance in 1945, but didn't last the season. The Braves' finish was remarkably similar again, 67–85, but Coleman was watching from afar by the time it ended. Del Bissonette took charge August 1, but his share of the wins and losses amounted to 25–34.

Spahn would have loved to have played in the majors for Bob Coleman. After Bissonette could not rouse the Braves, Perini and general manager John Quinn pulled off a coup. Billy Southworth was a dugout star, the flavor-of-the-month, just the way college basketball coaches who produce surprising NCAA tournament runs become hot properties.

"We decided we wanted the best manager in baseball for the Braves," said Perini, who bought the team with his family's construction company money in 1945. "Then we asked ourselves who the best manager was, and of course we had to answer 'Southworth.' We determined to get him if it was at all possible."[61]

Over a three-year period during the war, Southworth led the St. Louis Cardinals to three pennants, two World Series crowns, and three seasons in a row of at least 105 wins. That was the beginning of establishing his Hall of Fame managerial credentials. Naturally, St. Louis owner Sam Breadon did not want to part with Southworth. But in the context of the times Boston was talking big money for multiple years, $35,000 a season, plus bonuses for winning. Breadon acted honorably on behalf of the manager he admired. Once he determined he could not match the dollars, Breadon let Southworth go.

While surely Spahn would have preferred to be part of those three dismal seasons instead of wearing a military uniform, taking wounds to his body and fighting Germans, it might be said he did not miss much. What he did miss was time. Although because of wartime service baseball scouts looked at veterans differently, Spahn had no real track record. He was still all potential on the mound. Some must have remembered Stengel's analysis of Spahn's potential future before their falling out.

Spahn may have been a rookie on the books, but he was no longer an impressionistic refugee from Buffalo. Rather than send him to the minors for more seasoning, the Braves brass decided to keep him around and put all their chips in right away on his left arm. The team's dire need (as if there wasn't more than one) was pitching. Boston blew through twenty-two pitchers during the 1945 season. Only the most serious baseball aficionado would recognize more than a few names. None of those hurlers won 10 games. Jim Tobin was the staff leader with a 9–14 record in his final season in the majors.

Bill Lee (not to be confused with Bill "Spaceman" Lee of the Boston Red Sox a generation later) was a formerly solid thrower for the Chicago Cubs who retired with 167 big-league wins, and he went 6–3. Ed Wright, who won just 25 games in his career, finished 8–3. Mort Cooper, excellent during his prime years with the St. Louis Cardinals, came over during the season and was 7–4 for Boston. He was a keeper. But really, all mound slots were open for 1946. No wonder the Braves chose not to waste any more time on Spahn fiddling in the minors.

The hitting was not much better with only outfielder Tommy Holmes a star performer with 28 home runs and 117 runs batted in. But Spahn wasn't going to remedy that issue.

When Spahn returned to the United States, he immediately went to LoRene's house. She surprised him by informing him Braves officials had been calling regularly asking where he was and when he would be back. Apparently, he had not been forgotten, and apparently he was also wanted. That was reassuring.

Spahn joined the Braves roster on June 10, 1946, and offered a pithy comment. "This is the first time in years I've reported to anybody without saluting."[62]

Today Spahn would have been sent out to a minor-league club to throw some innings, but in 1946 Boston instead gave Spahn a week to work out to regain his form. He stayed with the Braves and on June 17, on the way to a 9–6 loss to the Cardinals, Southworth waved Spahn into the game in relief. He was Boston's fourth pitcher of the day, and he threw four innings, giving up four hits and one run, an unearned one, while striking out two.

Spahn said much later Southworth had remembered him throwing before the war and that's why he wanted him around. But Spahn had to be patient. He wanted no part of the bullpen, but that's where he resided for a month. There was little glory in being a relief pitcher in the 1940s. It was almost like being a fringe player on the roster and Spahn thought that way. If you were a starter, you were a real member of the team. If you were a reliever, who knew when you might get into a game? When Halley's Comet came around?

Southworth had to like what he saw from Spahn's relief stint against St. Louis, but he had just spent years in Missouri, the Show-Me-State, and wanted to see more. It was July 14 before he gave Spahn a start. Spahn held the Pittsburgh Pirates down and won 4–1. Spahn's short pre-war appearances had left him with an 0–0 record, but now Spahn was finally a winner in a big-league game. Fritz Ostermueller was out there for the Pirates and stuck through eight innings, giving up 12 hits and all four runs.

Spahn's numbers in the box score were solid. He went the distance, as most pitchers did in those days unless they were truly clobbered, and gave up eight hits and one run. Spahn did not manhandle the Pirates' lineup with his fastball, striking out just two, but beat Pittsburgh with his control.

If the pre-war Spahn was nervous, young, and trying to prove himself, the war-hardened Spahn was more mature, more of a man, and with those wartime experiences, that combat, Bronze Star, and Purple Heart behind him, it wasn't going to be easy to rattle him. He viewed pitching as a lark compared to war, a proper perspective, and he knew the difference between life-and-death pressure and a game's pressure. Sure, the guys wielding the bats in the batter's box were a new kind of enemy, but they were nothing compared to the real deal. Spahn had served on the front lines, had been shot, seen men killed, had not always been able to eat three square meals a day, and had endured freezing, uncomfortable weather conditions. He said when he got back to the United States he was appreciative of everything available in daily life, hungry for this opportunity, but also grateful he was alive to obtain it.

"When I came back after the Army," Spahn said, "I thought, 'Wow, if I don't do well, nobody's going to shoot me.' I think my service helped me with my baseball career. What a wonderful world this is. What a wonderful country we live in. What an opportunity to play baseball for a living."[63]

When he returned stateside, Spahn wanted to get moving on another aspect of his life, as well. LoRene was still his girl, and he wanted to get married. Southworth tried to talk him into waiting until after the season, but Spahn said no way. He was married on August 10, a team day off. Perhaps Southworth was so old-school he was like the trainer in *Rocky* proclaiming, "Women weaken legs." Or maybe he just didn't want Spahn to be distracted by such a major life-altering decision. This was one time Spahn disobeyed an order from a superior officer.

Spahn was conscious of his good fortune of going to war and returning alive and healthy enough to resume his career as a professional athlete. Approximately 500 professional players served the United States during World War II, and remarkably, just two died.

Elmer Gedeon, who had been a football, baseball, and track star at the University of Michigan, played five games with the Washington Senators in 1939. On a bombing mission to France in 1944, Gedeon's plane was shot down.

Harry O'Neill, a multi-sport star at Gettysburg College, played one game for the Philadelphia Athletics in 1939. He was killed during the attempt to take Iwo Jima.

When Spahn discussed his war years, he said he only lived in the moment, never thinking about baseball or wondering if baseball still lay ahead of him. He believed that outlook enabled him to easily morph into Spahn the pitcher once more as soon as he got the chance. When asked if he thought he had lost speed off his fastball, Spahn noted that there were no radar guns around at the time, so he didn't know how fast he threw before he joined the service and didn't really know how fast he threw when he came back.

"The hitters will tell you a story," Spahn said. "I know that if I threw a fastball by a hitter I was throwing pretty good. And if I threw my curveball and they swung over the top that was pretty good, too."[64]

That viewpoint all seemed to stem from the Keep-It-Simple-Stupid philosophy of life.

"The guy that pitched before I went in the service was a different guy than the guy that came back," Spahn said. "My confidence level was so much better. Again, which comes first, the chicken or the egg? I felt that I could do my job."[65]

However, he still had to win a job. To Spahn that meant taking over one of the regular starting turns, not merely being summoned from the bullpen every now and then. In the 1940s, there was no such role as a "closer." There was not even a statistic called a "save" to quantify the work of a reliever and take note of his value. For Spahn, pitching was all about starting. And that was true throughout the game. Relief specialists virtually did not exist, although the first ones would be making their mark before the end of the decade. This was the ultimate put-me-in-coach scenario.

For seven years in a row before Spahn joined the team full-time, the Braves were awful. Each year they won between 59 and 67 games, never coming closer than 15 games to .500. Maybe Spahn couldn't even tell the difference between the minors he left behind and the majors he joined in 1946. But Billy South-worth was not a losing manager. He was brought in to win, and even though he was not blessed with intimidating talent, that's what he planned to do.

Southworth was willing to try anything. What did he have to lose? Boston sent forty-eight players to the plate that season, though of course pitchers batted in those days. By far the most dependable hitter among the everyday starters was Tommy Holmes. Holmes was a left-handed hitting and throwing outfielder who was coming off the best season of his career in 1945. Not only did he hit all of those home runs (the 28 led the National League) and drive in so many runs, but he batted .352 and was runner-up for the Most Valuable Player Award after smacking a league-leading 224 hits. Holmes played 11 major-league seasons, all with the Braves, and hit .302 lifetime.

But outside of Holmes, the Braves lacked pop. Johnny Hopp hit .333 in 129 games. An aging Billy Herman appeared in 75 games and batted .309 with a .409 on-base percentage.

The starting pitching was much better than it was in 1945. Right-hander Johnny Sain, soon to become Spahn's best friend on the team and a star himself, also missed three years of play in the service. He was back and blooming. Mort Cooper was solid with 13 wins and Ed Wright (12) had the best year of his career. It was basically a last hurrah for Bill Lee with 10 victories.

Sixteen other pitchers who were sent to the mound for the Braves at one time or another did not do much for the cause. Standing between the four key starters and all of the rest was Spahn. He was neither instant sensation nor bust. Mostly, when Southworth deployed him, he did a good job.

Juggling players, bringing in some tried-and-true fill-ins, Southworth pieced together a winning team. Southworth liked Hopp, whom he counted on while both were in St. Louis, and who batted .296 in a 14-year career. Herman, who had also missed two seasons because of the war, help Boston finish 81–72, the Braves' first winning season since 1938 when the team went 77–75.

A mere .500 record was like playing for pennies to Southworth. After earning two World Series rings, he knew what the big prize was in this game. For him, a winning record was nice, especially after all of those losses Boston fans absorbed. But he came to town to win it all, even if he knew it was going to take more than a year or two. Few of the players he inherited were ones he could lean on as he aspired to win 90 or 100 games. He knew he needed more talent.

Warren Spahn had talent, and even better he already belonged to the Braves. They didn't have to scout him in the boondocks or trade for him.

Spahn's beginnings in 1946 were promising. His delivery remained smooth. He retained the lessons dad Ed imparted. Only suddenly, as happens to many rookies after their first time around the league, hitters began teeing off on him. Spahn lost four games in a row, twice to the Brooklyn Dodgers. After the second time, Dodger manager Charlie Dressen belittled him.

Dressen was a good enough athlete to play some pro football in the 1920s and to shift to major-league baseball. But he was always regarded as a better manager than player and generally a smart one. However, he also possessed a smart mouth that could alienate others in the game. After Brooklyn topped Spahn twice, Dressen began bragging. He claimed Spahn had a flaw in his delivery so he couldn't fool Dodger hitters.

"We can beat Spahn every time he pitches," Dressen boasted. "We know every pitch he throws."[66]

That was an alarming bit of news and likely one opinion Dressen should have sat on. Rather than blow off such a warning, Spahn took it seriously. He and coach Johnny Cooney worked on polishing his delivery, masking any hint of giving away pitches and also developed a new pitch, a slow curveball. Spahn was not going to let anyone make a chump out of him. If there had been a leaky faucet, it was repaired.

In 1946, despite his late arrival, Warren Spahn appeared in 24 games for the Braves. Of those, 16 were starts. He had achieved his ambition and became a regular starting pitcher. Spahn finished 8–5, acceptable if not startlingly successful. His earned run average of 2.94, however, was excellent, a tease of what he might bring with his sharp control.

The highly imperfect Boston Braves of 1945 had attracted just 374,178 fans to their home games at Braves Field off of Commonwealth Avenue. Fans were distracted by war and sick of the inferior product on the field. After peace broke out and baseball was back to full strength, America was a different place.

The predominant American mood in 1946 was relief. The secondary one was excitement. The country was starting over again. Soon, after many war wounds healed (though some never would with the deaths of so many fathers, sons, husbands, and brothers), the television age dawned, more people than ever were buying and driving their own automobiles, and the national pastime regained its hold on sports fans.

Johnny Sain, more than any other Brave player, seemed to herald the start of a new age for Boston in National League baseball. He was 20–14 with a 2.21 earned run average in 1946, the front man for stirring fans' souls. The team's attendance jumped to 969,673 fans for home games that year. That was heartening. Maybe if the Braves became a pennant contender even more would embrace them.

While Spahn did take Dressen's comments as an ominous warning, he was also right about listening to the hitters. He still did not have much in the way of numbers to back up his confidence, but some players recognized that barring injury he could become the next big thing. Some praised his curve, and some were thrown off by his delivery.

Future Hall of Fame slugger Johnny Mize had a different outlook. "The curve and change of pace are all right," Mize said. "But it's that fastball. It does tricks as it reaches the plate."[67]

Now, it seemed, everyone was aware of Warren Spahn's talent and was just waiting for him to bust out. Of course, Ed Spahn knew all along in his heart that his boy was going to become a baseball star. Even the one-time, too-angry Casey Stengel recognized the pitching gene in the player he had demoted to the minors with an ugly insult.

Although Spahn was now in the majors and Stengel was not, Ed Spahn still fumed about Stengel's insult. He could point to Warren's World War II service at the front and snarl, "No guts, huh?"

7

A STAR IS BORN

WARREN SPAHN BECAME Warren Spahn in 1947. That season, one which changed Major League Baseball for all time, Spahn became a first-rate star. When the 1946 season began, Spahn was still in the Army. When the 1947 season began, he was in the Boston Braves' starting rotation.

When the 1947 season ended Spahn was the talk of baseball—at least the talk that wasn't focused on the first black man to play in the big leagues in the twentieth century. Jackie Robinson of the Brooklyn Dodgers integrated baseball decades too late for many African American players, but his was as much a societal as sporting development as post–World War II America began awakening to new stirrings from people whose rights were supposed to be legally protected and who now demanded those rights be respected.

Spahn was an unknown when he went off to war. He was known only to the Braves when he returned from war. Even after his partial 1946 season, his 8–5 record was not the type of mark that left opponents fainting.

Everything was different in 1947. Spahn stood 6 feet tall and weighed in at 172 pounds officially. Even if his true weight was a little heavier, he was no giant. Yes, he had a reliable fastball, but his real stuff, the pitches foes couldn't hit, were the curveball and the slow curve with the fastball mixed in, not as the overpowering out pitch.

In 1947, Spahn finished 21–10 and led the National League in earned run average at 2.33 and in innings pitched with 289 2/3. His seven shutouts also led the league. Now that the Braves used Spahn regularly he never wanted to leave the mound, and he posted 22 complete games. He started 40 games, and he loved the workload. And at twenty-six years old, he made his first All-Star team.

Although the Braves were significantly improved in 1946, manager Billy Southworth wanted more. He had an owner-ship group behind him willing to make changes, willing to chase new ballplayers to uplift the team. The recent losing history was annoying to all, and owner Lou Perini and general manager John Quinn wanted it permanently in the rearview mirror.

When the 1946 season concluded the brain trust went shopping. There was a total willingness to overhaul the roster.

Once the deal to swipe Southworth from the Cardinals was complete, Perini spoke at a local luncheon predicting great things for the Braves' future. "We've got our manager," Perini said. "Now we'll try to give him players of similar ability."[68]

The Braves invested $180,000 in purchasing players that seemed to better suit Southworth. They bought Johnny Hopp, Eddie Joost, Dick Litwhiler, Ray Sanders, and Alvin Dark. They spent $50,000 for first baseman Earl Torgeson and threw in four players, too.

Torgeson wore glasses when few players did, and nobody had contact lenses. He was from Snohomish, Washington, and his nickname was "The Earl of Snohomish." The Braves thought his potential was to the moon. Some players had done good things for Southworth in St. Louis and he remembered. Ernie White once won 17 games for the Cards but was injured almost immediately in Boston and never won a game for the Braves in three seasons of trying to get healthy.

Perini bought the Milwaukee minor league team for $270,000 to use as his Double-A affiliate. That purchase proved significant later.

Whoever showed up learned quickly Southworth was a zero-tolerance manager. He had no patience for mistakes or frivolity. If someone wanted to have fun, he better have it on his own time, not Southworth's. Southworth had a 13-year major-leaguer career and hit .297 but also spent some of his playing time in the minors between 1913 and 1929. He managed for parts of 13 years.

Once, when asked the funniest thing that ever happened to him in baseball Southworth had no answer. His answer was a blank slate. "There wasn't any," he said. "There's nothing funny about a play which may mean a ballgame. Baseball has always been a serious business with me."[69]

Southworth's players probably heard that and winced. Whatever happened to baseball being a little boy's game? Not when you got paid to play.

The 1946 season was the first step in an urban renewal project, an apt metaphor for what Perini hoped to accomplish with the Braves since he was a construction magnate as well as a sporting magnate. The clubhouse door never stopped revolving as Southworth wanted to build, build, build.

Third baseman Bob Elliott was a major addition, obtained in a trade with the Pittsburgh Pirates. Elliott smacked 22 home runs, drove in 113, and batted .317 for the Braves in 1947. His was the big bat in the order. Torgeson did fine for a rookie, hitting 16 homers and driving in 78 runs with a .281 batting average. Catcher Phil Masi hit .304. Tommy Holmes didn't hit for as much power as he had but still averaged .317.

Frank McCormick was thirty-six and nearing the end of a career that saw him win a Most Valuable Player Award in 1940 for Cincinnati and earn eight All-Star selections. He appeared in 81 games and batted .354. He was a great guy to have coming off the bench although he stayed around Boston one season too long the next year, his average dropping more than 100 points to .250, which also lowered his lifetime average to .299.

While Red Barrett (11–12) and Bill Voiselle (8–7) held down places in the pitching rotation, the Braves suffered from a shortage of starters. Besides Spahn, the only other frontline starter was Johnny Sain. A bunch of other guys started some games, but no one else contributed more than six wins.

By making him a regular feature of their starting rotation, the Braves showed they had faith in Spahn to blossom right then and there. This was a guy who still had little on his resume to indicate how good he might be. Although he was eight years out of high school, Spahn was still marking his place on the roster based on potential.

For every 5,000 pitchers with promise who came along but accomplished no more or no less than Spahn in the majors, how could the Braves truly know he was the one with the golden arm? No one could guess Spahn would pitch for another two decades and would win 363 regular season games, more than any other left-handed pitcher in history.

On Wednesday, April 23, his birthday, six games into the 1947 season, Spahn started against the New York Giants in an afternoon contest at Braves Field. Illustrating the recent dire status of the Braves, just 4,074 fans were counted coming through the turnstiles.

Another reason for a low turnout was the 41-degree gametime temperature.

The chill did not bother Spahn. He pitched a complete game, surrendered 12 hits, but prevented the Giants from advancing around the bases. The final score was 5–1. Spahn, who batted left-handed, as well as throwing from that side, even got a hit that game, but more importantly, he had his first victory of the season in the bank.

The Giants were not the Giants of a few years later, but they had some scary hitters in the lineup, notably future Hall of Famer Johnny Mize and Bobby Thomson, who became legendary in 1951 for hitting one particular homer that won his team the pennant over the Dodgers.

Spahn was a quick worker on the mound. The game took just two hours, ten minutes to play. He did not dilly-dally. When the catcher threw the ball back, Spahn was ready to roll. He went into his fluid motion, that high kick helping to blind the batter, and threw with little wasted time.

Although the poetic phrase memorializing the Spahn-Sain duo did not take hold until a season later, the duo's dominance began in 1947. Sain also won 21 games that season. After his own three years away from the game, Sain had returned for the 1946 season and recorded his first 20-win year. By 1947 he was already turning twenty-nine. He was a known quantity. He was the right-handed half of the twosome few teams could conquer. Spahn and Sain were at the beginning of a beautiful partnership.

Sain was born September 25, 1917, in Havana, Arkansas, which even as recently as 2010 had just 375 people. It had 500 or so people when Sain was born. Sain is the most famous person to come out of that community, although James Huey Walkup, another pitcher, was born there in 1895 and his son,

James Elton Walkup, born in 1909, also played in the majors. The town is located in the foothills of the Ozark Mountains.

It was somewhat of a miracle Sain was noticed to be signed to Osceola of the Class D Northeast Arkansas League at age eighteen in 1936. That is starting out in pro ball as low as you can go. Sain's pay was fifty dollars a month. In 1938, Sain went 16–4 in Class D Newport in the same league and the next year finished 18–10, again for Newport. His progress upward was nil. But just as World War II began gobbling up American baseball players to serve in the military, Sain caught the eye of then–Braves manager Casey Stengel.

Nobody thought Sain had big-league speed in his arm and by 1942, there was some suggestion Sain might become an outfielder to stick in the game. The shortage of ballplayers meant Stengel was on the prowl for any new talent and he saw something he liked in Sain's arm no one else appreciated. He made the Boston club, and while compiling a 3.90 earned run average, Sain finished 4–7. Then he disappeared into the military for the 1943, 1944, and 1945 seasons.

Sain actually pitched quite a bit of ball while in the service. He realized he might never pitch in the majors again if he did not enhance his skills, so he developed a variety of off-speed throws in military leagues. That enabled him to show off new skills when he returned to the Braves for 1946 spring training.

"I wasn't blessed with velocity," Sain said, "a fastball that you'd say, 'Here it is, hit it.' I knew that I had to vary my motions and speeds and variations of breaking balls and sinkers."[70]

He was a new man. Much like Spahn, Sain had gone into the military as a baseball nobody and emerged as a fresh star. During the 1946 season, his first real year, Sain went 20–14 with a 2.21

ERA and led the National League with 24 complete games. He was the ace of the staff.

By mid-season, Sain and Spahn had teamed up. A year later, in 1947, they were both stars. Few other teams had two front-line hurlers to match their savvy, expertise, and hardcore desire to win that led to 20-victory seasons. They were perfectly complementary.

"Spahn was smooth, orthodox," Sain said. "I was all motion, change of speed, unorthodox. That's when I got interested in the mechanics of pitching. There are just as many ways to pitch as there are pitchers."[71]

In later years, after he retired as an active player, Sain made a living as a pitching coach. During his years serving several teams, he became widely known for his knowledge and is generally considered the greatest pitching coach of all time, one so superior there is a strong belief among many experts he deserves a place in the Baseball Hall of Fame for that role.

Baseball in 1947 was about to undergo the kind of upheaval the rest of the United States and the world were expecting after the war, and the Braves were in the middle of it.

Post–World War II America was in flux. Although the carnage of war had ceased, with Germany and Japan soundly thrashed, the peace that came left much of the world uneasy. Almost immediately, the Soviet Union, the West's wartime ally, loomed as a new threat, dictator Josef Stalin apparently intent on spreading communism. President Harry Truman was the leader of the free world, the successor to Franklin D. Roosevelt, who died in office in 1945. What followed was an era of tense world political posturing that was labeled the Cold War. The United States and Soviet Union never fired missiles upon each other's territory, but geopolitics was played by proxy, with chess moves made on behalf of one side or another in other sections of the world.

While Americans were easily persuaded of this "Red Menace," it was of major comfort there was no more shooting in the late 1940s (though hostilities resumed during the Korean War in the early 1950s). The US economy was on the move and so was the American psyche with the old familiar pre-war pursuits being revived.

But not everyone was content to return to the status quo. The country founded on life, liberty, and the pursuit of happiness had never quite lived up to the equality-for-all doctrine. America's greatest sin was the imposition of slavery on a large segment of the population based on skin color. Even the conclusion of the Civil War, accompanied by the Emancipation Proclamation, did not cure this evil completely.

In numerous ways, large and small, the American black was deprived of rights and opportunity. As the symbol of the ultimate in American sport, baseball was the national pastime, the true American game. Yet through unwritten rules, albeit strictly enforced, no African American had played major-league baseball since Moses Fleetwood Walker was forced off the Toledo Blue Stockings' roster in 1884.

Journalists at leading black newspapers around the country had agitated for change for years. Pressures grew on white club owners in the majors to give players from the Negro Leagues tryouts. In several cases big-name players received sham tryouts. Somehow there was no room at the inn.

Although Bill Veeck, the so-called people's owner who was later elected to the Hall of Fame, wanted to integrate baseball in the mid-1940s by purchasing the woebegone Philadelphia Phillies and stocking the roster with such Negro Leagues stars as Satchel Paige, Josh Gibson, Cool Papa Bell, and Buck Leonard, he was thwarted.

After the war, there was just one man in a position of authority who possessed convictions so firm he was willing to take risks to change the world and provide justice for the black ballplayer. Branch Rickey, vice president and general manager of the Brooklyn Dodgers, quietly set in motion a search for the right man to break the color barrier.

He settled on Jackie Robinson for a number of reasons. Robinson was college educated, played on integrated sports teams at UCLA, was married, and had a stable social life. He seemed to be strong-willed and yet of appropriate temperament to handle the grief and prejudice he was sure to face.

After playing a season in Montreal for the Dodgers' Triple-A outlet, Robinson was ready for the bigs. When he made his debut on April 15, 1947, he was already twenty-eight years old, an old rookie. For a season, as he established himself as a fiery ballplayer, Robinson endured much taunting and prejudice. As he had promised Rickey, he refrained from answering back or fighting back in what could be interpreted as any sort of inflammatory manner.

In the 1940s, the major-league season did not start until mid-April, not around the first of the month as it does now. Opening Day for the Boston Braves that season was April 15 and the opponent was the Brooklyn Dodgers, in Brooklyn.

Brooklyn won 5–3 that day at Ebbets Field with attendance listed at 26,623. This was Robinson's introduction to the majors. He started at first base and went 0-for-3, although he scored a run. The starting pitcher for Boston was Johnny Sain. Sain threw the first pitch Robinson ever faced in the majors. Spahn, Sain, and Robinson were destined to become great rivals in National League play.

Robinson hit 12 home runs with 48 runs batted in, gathered 74 walks, and hit .297 in 1947. He became the first winner of the Rookie of the Year Award. Eventually, he was named to six All-Star teams, batted .311 lifetime, and was chosen for the Hall of Fame. Much later, Major League Baseball retired his No. 42 across the board for all teams, acknowledgment of his important role as a social pioneer as well as a superb player.

Although many southern ballplayers resented Robinson's ascension to the majors and in later years even some of Spahn's teammates seemed to harbor inordinately stronger emotions than a simple rival would elicit, Spahn pretty much always appeared color-blind.

"I felt that we were the big leagues and we played a World Series," Spahn said of the arrival of Robinson in the majors. "So if we played a World Series, then we should be able to play against the best of every nation: black, white, yellow, green, or whatever. And Jackie was a good talent. He could run like a deer. What tickled me was that we heard about Jackie and that Branch Rickey picked the first black guy in baseball because of his college education and athleticism. I understand from other black people that the catcher (Josh Gibson) in the Negro Leagues was a better ballplayer than Jackie."[72]

There was truth to those opinions, but they were outdated by 1947. Gibson was past his prime and in failing health by the end of World War II, and he died at thirty-five in January of 1947. It was Monte Irvin who ranked higher in Rickey's scouting search. Irvin had been a devastating hitter in the Negro Leagues and Mexican League but went stale during his military years.

Irvin did not feel ready for the majors immediately after coming out of the service, and Rickey and Newark Eagles owner Effa Manley also squabbled over a sale price for him to the Dodgers.

Rickey bowed out, but Irvin ended up an All-Star outfielder with the New York Giants and a Hall of Famer.

What Spahn remembered hearing as Robinson established himself was that "Jackie fit the mold that Branch Rickey wanted to break the color line with. Rickey wanted to mold this person as being somebody to represent the black community."[73] Spahn's impression was on the money, as it was later explained by Rickey.

It took time for vociferous backing to come from Commissioner Albert "Happy" Chandler, the former US senator and governor from Kentucky. Eventually, Chandler spoke out against racial epithets directed at Robinson There were tensions, for sure, and Spahn did not sugarcoat those.

"You know, that's a tough role for anybody to be the first," Spahn said, "and I think Jackie handled himself pretty darned well." Once, Spahn said, he ticked off Robinson. It was some years later and Robinson had gained some weight. "I yelled out at Jackie, 'What time does the balloon go up?' because he got so big. And he threw the ball at me in the dugout. We had a friendly adversary-type relationship, but he belonged. He was a good ballplayer, and I'm proud of the fact that the National League got the first black ballplayer."[74]

8

A PENNANT FOR BOSTON

WARREN SPAHN AND Johnny Sain were never more important together than in 1948. There were several seasons when
Spahn was better than he was in '48, but Sain posted the best year
of his career that summer.

Spahn won at least 20 games in a season thirteen times, but
1948 was not one of them. It will surprise baseball fans to learn
that during this memorable Boston Braves season Spahn finished
just 15–12. Yet somehow the Braves won the National League
pennant, fulfilling the dream of owner Lou Perini and satisfying
the disciplined hand of manager Billy Southworth.

To some degree, it was an off-year for Spahn, but it did not
matter because for one of the few times during that time period the
Braves had a couple of extra guys who could buttress the two aces.

Due to the overall excellence of that 91–62 club and the emer-
gence of Spahn and Sain, the sprightly pen of newsman Gerald
V. Hern gave fans forevermore a reason to explain at least the
September run to the finish. In one of baseball's most enduring
ditties (perhaps second in memory only to the poetic embrace of
the Chicago Cubs' double play combination of the past, Tinkers

to Evers to Chance), Hern coined a famous phrase about Spahn and Sain and praying for rain.

While there was pitching help for the two stalwarts, it was neither overwhelming nor enduring and when in need Southworth always turned to a member of the "S" duo. Jotting down his thoughts about the rotation for the *Boston Post*, Hern wrote:

First we'll use Spahn, then we'll use Sain,
Then an off day, followed by rain.
Back will come Spahn, followed by Sain,
And followed, we hope, by two days of rain.[75]

Catchy phrasing it was. The poem then shrunk a bit to more succinctly be called "Spahn and Sain and pray for rain."

That was the short version of the season. The Braves, under Perini's ownership and Southworth's field leadership, turned things around swiftly, leaving those horrible years of the early 1940s to the distant past.

They rebuilt in every way. It took an improvement of just 10 wins from Southworth's first season in command, but those 10 wins were like the distance from the East Coast to the West Coast. It was an eight-team NL in those days, but the Braves shrugged off all comers. They won the pennant by 6 1/2 games over the St. Louis Cardinals, Southworth's old team that was led by the magnificent Stan Musial.

This club generated newfound excitement in Boston, raising attendance to more than 1.4 million who flooded Braves Field, the park overlooking the Charles River, and rewarding fans starved for success. The Braves had not won a pennant since 1914 when the team that came to be known as "The Miracle Braves" had won the National League crown and defeated Connie Mack's Philadelphia Athletics in the World Series. It had been a thirty-four-year wait.

In all of the years between their 1914 Series triumph and 1948, the Braves finished as high as second just one other time. Little boys from the pennant year of 1914 were middle-aged men by the time of Boston's 1948 success.

When he reflected in later years, Spahn believed the 1947 team was a useful forerunner of the 1948 team. All of those trades and player purchases the front office made led to the 1948 team's success.

"This was a great year for me personally," Spahn said of 1947, "and I also think for the Braves that this was the nucleus to the ballclub that won the pennant the following year in '48. We had a ballclub that was experienced, maybe not as fleet of foot, but knew how to play the game. We had good defense. You know, all of these things contributed to us winning in '48, that was all molded in '47."[76]

In no way were the Braves of 1948 underdogs in the manner of the Braves of 1914. Grantland Rice, one of the most famous sportswriters of all, took a look at Southworth's material in March, in spring training, and saw possibilities. Rice said of the squad beginning the pennant race, it "might easily bring the Braves to the top of the pile in September."[77]

Rice believed in Southworth's know-how, Earl Torgeson at first base, Alvin Dark at short, naturally Spahn and Sain on the mound, and also Bill Voiselle as a likely helpmate in the starting rotation.

"I can promise you we'll have a much better ballclub in 1948 than we had in 1947," Southworth said.[78]

As hoped, Southworth had given the Braves instant credibility when he took over as Boston manager. Perini was the principal owner, although his two major ownership partners, comparatively silent Guido Rugo and Joe Maney, were also construction men. Sports columnists took to calling them "The Steam Shovels" or

"The Three Steam Shovels." One of their strengths was aware-
ness of strengths and weaknesses and a willingness to delegate
handling what they were not experts in. Writer Grantland Rice
presented the team's group philosophy as, "If a man wants to
build a building, he comes to us or somebody like us. We want
to build a pennant winner. Ergo, we'll go to a man who builds
pennant winners."[79]

Southworth built them a pennant.

Right-hander Bill Voiselle, who roomed on the road with
Spahn for three years, stood 6-foot-4 and weighed 200 pounds.
By the standards of the times he was a large hurler. He was not
a star of the magnitude of Spahn or Sain despite winning 21
games in 1944. But he was a fixture as a starter, going 13–13 in
1948 with a 3.63 earned run average. He ate up innings, 215
2/3 of them.

"It was no two-man pitching staff," Voiselle said later. "They
tried to make out like it was."[80]

The fourth starter, righty Vern Bickford, had been buried in the
minors since 1939. He was on the roster of the Indianapolis minor-
league team in 1947 when the Braves bought the franchise but not
all of the players. Perini found himself involved in a dispersal
draft without knowing a thing about the available talent. As he
mulled his choice a thought came to him.

"I didn't recognize any of the names at first," he said. "But all
of a sudden, the name of Bickford rang a bell with me. I recalled
that Branch Rickey at one time had expressed an interest in him.
I figured that if Bickford was good enough for Rickey, he was
good enough for the Braves."[81]

So in 1947, Bickford became a member of the Braves' Triple-
A Milwaukee team and finished 9–5. That made him worth a
look-see despite being past his twenty-seventh birthday. Good

call by Southworth keeping him. No Bickford, no pennant. He went 11–5 with a 3.27 ERA in winning a regular job.

"I learned how to pitch in the Army," Bickford said. He learned from other big leaguers on service teams. "I always could throw hard, but it wasn't until I played with (Kirby) Higbe's outfit that I learned the change of pace. That's when I became a pitcher instead of a thrower."[82]

Bickford won 16 games the next season and 19 in 1950. He retired in 1955 because of a bone chip in his arm and died young, at thirty-nine, of cancer in 1960.

Another rookie thrower was Bob Hogue, whose nickname was "Knuckleball Bob." Like Bickford, Hogue was more familiar to travel agents than baseball managers as he switched from team to team in the minors. In 1948, Hogue was a twenty-seven-year-old rookie coming off a 16–8 season in Double-A. And also like Bickford, Hogue became a key man for Southworth. Top-notch relievers were still a rarity in the late 1940s, but Hogue provided relief for the headaches starters sometimes created. Hogue was 8–2 with a 3.23 ERA while starting just one game. He was Mr. Bullpen.

Hogue did not make a strong first impression as a fit athlete. He stood 5-foot-9 and weighed 190 pounds, making him a little round around the middle. Nor did he possess lightning in his right arm. But he loved baseball and recognized he needed to add another weapon to a limited arsenal.

"I knew it was either rassling, raking leaves, or some other business if I didn't add something to my alleged fastball and curve," Hogue said. "So I just stuck to the standard pitches and added the knuckleball."[83]

Hogue's tough attitude stemmed from his upbringing. His father Oakley was a boxing trainer, and before Hogue chose baseball he flirted with a boxing career, winning 36 of 39 amateur fights. The closest he came to going down for the count, however, was pitching for Winston-Salem against Asheville on a field so wet he slipped trying to field a bunt and "Honestly, I skidded not only off the field, but into the Asheville dugout. When I finally climbed out, the guy was on third with a triple."[84]

Southworth liked his fighting spirit. Southworth also liked guys whom he had institutional knowledge of like right-hander Red Barrett. He seemed to have a soft spot for the men who helped him succeed during World War II ball, and his acquisition of many of them, if only to provide a last chance, did not go unnoticed. Some took to calling the Braves "The Cape Cod Cardinals," as if the St. Louis bunch opened a branch office on the outskirts of Boston.

Barrett did good work for Southworth in St. Louis and had even already been a Boston Brave once before. Some managers disdain players who are not 100 percent serious, 100 percent of the time. Since Southworth was known for his seriousness, it was a bit surprising he also seemed to appreciate a guy who could keep the clubhouse loose.

Barrett was the Braves' class clown once he returned to Boston in 1947. His reputation definitely preceded him. Eddie Dyer, one of his former managers, said, "If that fellow devoted as much time to his pitching as he does to clowning and to making jokes, he would become a very fine pitcher."[85] Barrett won 11 games for Boston in 1947 and seven in 1948.

Actually, Southworth had a future ace pitcher on his roster all the time in 1948, but he was just eighteen years old and not ready for prime time. Southpaw Johnny Antonelli had a 0–0 record for Boston as a rookie while appearing in four games. Antonelli was a talent who earlier that year was signed for $52,000 out of Rochester, New York, then the largest bonus ever paid to a player. In time, he would become a 20-game winner more than once, but that time was not 1948. In those days, however, a bonus baby had to remain on the major-league roster.

That made Antonelli a spectator more than a participant for the 1948 pennant year.

"There was not all that much pressure on me," Antonelli said, "except the pressure from my pride. I threw a lot of batting practice. There were stories at the time that the veterans resented me getting that money and how Sain demanded a raise. In most cases, the Braves players were great to me."[86]

However, that did not include Spahn. Sain did get a raise, but rather than tutor a young southpaw, Antonelli contended Spahn treated him poorly and he was never sure why.

"For some reason, which I still don't understand," Antonelli said in a 2012 book about his life, "Warren Spahn resented me from the start and never stopped. I always showed him the utmost respect and have said on many occasions that he was the greatest southpaw in baseball history. But that didn't seem to matter to Warren. He always treated me with disdain, even after both of us stopped playing."[87]

Records of player salaries were much more closely held in the late 1940s and Spahn's annual major-league salary figures were not well-documented. He did say the most he made for one year in the majors was $87,500. It was a much tougher route to the top for Spahn, through his trials in the minors and risks taken during World War II, so he could well have resented Antonelli's seemingly golden path to the top.

Rochester is just 75 miles from Buffalo, Spahn's hometown, and Antonelli said he even had two uncles who went to high school with Spahn.

"I don't know if he was jealous of my bonus or felt threatened when Perini signed me, but he acted as if I had stolen money from him or had done harm to one of his loved ones," Antonelli said.[88]

It might be said bonuses came dearly in earlier days of baseball. When Mel Ott, the Hall of Fame outfielder for the New York Giants who broke into the majors as a seventeen-year-old under the legendary John McGraw in 1926, heard about Antonelli's signing amount, his comment was wry.

"John McGraw gave me $400 for signing," Ott said, "but of course a dollar went farther in those days."[89]

The 1948 Braves outscored opponents 739 runs to 584 runs. That illustrated two things. Overall, the pitching staff was pretty stingy, and the hitting was much better than it recently had been.

Bob Elliott was coming off an MVP season at third base and he kept up his steady hitting, batting .283 with 23 home runs and 100 runs batted in. Elliott had done some fine work for the Pittsburgh Pirates, but he did his best work for the Braves, especially when the team needed him most in 1947 and 1948.

When Southworth obtained Elliott, he delivered a pep talk that was remarkably prescient.

"You're a very fine ballplayer, Bob," Southworth told his new man. "You can make all the stops you're supposed to make at third base. You have an excellent arm. You run the bases well, and you are a dangerous long-ball hitter. All you need to achieve true greatness is the added sparkle of more hustle. If you hustle, I'm absolutely convinced that you will win the Most Valuable Player Award this season."[90]

Southworth knew his baseball. Against the odds, Elliott did win the MVP award in 1947. The pep talk rated a 10 on a scale of 10. And a year later Elliott helped deliver a pennant to Boston. Elliott was a six-time All-Star who six times drove in more than 100 runs in a season.

Torgeson cranked out 10 homers that year but was definitely overly hyped. The Braves gave him uniform No. 9, just like Ted Williams wore across town, and one Boston newspaperman quoted an "expert" saying of Torgeson in 1947, "He's a better hitter than Williams right now, and he has more all-around ability because he can leg it as fast as any athlete in the majors and his drag bunt gives him a third weapon." It was not later reported that the expert failed a sobriety test or that Williams laughed at the drag bunt being such a nuclear weapon it trumped his all-around game.[91]

Tommy Holmes, manning the outfield, was still smacking the ball and hit .325. Sparkplug Eddie Stanky (the correct answer to the World War II question posed to the Germans to identify themselves properly or die) came over from the Dodgers and batted .320 in 67 games.

To a later generation of baseball fans, Alvin Dark was known as the manager of the San Francisco Giants, Kansas City Athletics, Cleveland Indians, Oakland Athletics, and San Diego Padres. He managed thirteen years in the bigs, winning two pennants and a World Series title with Oakland. He was also widely known for his strong religious convictions.

Dark was born in Comanche, Oklahoma, in 1922, and was a fiery player when he broke into the majors after World War II. Dark made it into 15 games for the Braves in 1946 but was still officially a rookie in 1948 when he exploded onto the National League scene with a .322 average, winning the Rookie of the Year Award. He batted .289 and was a three-time All-Star during a 14-year playing career.

Between investing time in the Marines and attending Louisiana State, where he was a football star, Dark was an old rookie at twenty-six. He was never better than in 1948 when he was a huge contributor to the Braves' pennant.

Dark became available to the Braves after his long layoff during World War II, but they had a tough time deciding if he was worth the money he was asking. Finally, Southworth gave a thumbs-up to the deal and launched Dark's decades-long career in the sport.

A couple of years before he died in 2014 at ninety-two, Dark said, "Baseball was my business and life. I gave it all I had. I never drank, never smoked, never chewed, never anything like that. It was all against my sports upbringing. I feel very fortunate. And very happy. God blessed me."[92]

In 1948, Boston was blessed with a National League pennant, even after the Braves began the season slowly. They were 1–6 on April 25, 6–7 on May 1, and 16–17 on May 31. They were not making true believers out of those who had foreseen a pennant. The next stretch was kinder, and Boston was 34–22 on June 20. But no one else was tearing it up either. July was profitable and by mid-month the Braves led the league by eight games. Boston never fell out of first place again, although on September 1, the Braves briefly dropped into a tie for first.

During this unusually erratic season for him, Warren Spahn won his first game on April 28, a 7–0 shutout of the Phillies. It was a two-hitter. On May 15, Spahn shut out Brooklyn on four hits. Not every win was so artistic. On some days Spahn prevailed while allowing four, five, or even six runs. His normal sharpness came and went.

When Spahn topped the Dodgers, 2–1, on August 12, his record was just 9–7, but he pushed the Braves to 17 games over

.500. In another big game, with the Dodgers lurking in the standings, Spahn beat them 2–1 again on August 21. Spahn hurled another shutout, besting St. Louis, 2–0, on August 25.

As the season turned the corner into September, it seemed as if Spahn or Sain, who was experiencing his finest season, pitched all the time for the Braves. That's when the rhyme kicked in. Together they started 78 of Boston's 154 games in 1948.

However, neither was on the mound when the pennant was clinched September 26. Vern Bickford got the win, going seven innings in a 3–2 victory over the New York Giants. Nelson Potter pitched the last two innings in relief. That was Potter's shining moment, but the season belonged to Spahn and Sain.

Infielder Sibby Sisti said Spahn and Sain together in the rotation generally meant there was no job for a relief pitcher on those days. "They were both great competitors. . . . The thing I remember about John and Warren is that neither one of them ever wanted to come out of a game."[93]

The pennant arrived on September 26, and Spahn's son Greg arrived on October 1. Although his 3.71 earned run average, the highest of his career, was nothing to celebrate, Spahn did enjoy the other developments. He also long remembered how the "Spahn and Sain" thing got started.

"As you well know, in New England in September and in late August there is a lot of rain, and there were a lot of off days put in the schedule because of that," Spahn said. "Well, it just so happened that during a course of three or four weeks Sain would pitch, I would pitch, and then it would rain. Vern Bickford was a great pitcher and he didn't get a chance to pitch. So we were pitching every other game, John Sain and I. I thought it was a great tribute."[94]

9

THE BRAVES' WORLD SERIES

UP UNTIL ABOUT the last hour of the regular season it seemed there might be an all-Boston World Series in 1948, the Boston Braves against the Boston Red Sox.

During the first half of the twentieth century, baseball fans were used to the always-there New York Yankees playing in the World Series, and often enough they faced off against the New York Giants or Brooklyn Dodgers.

Despite decades of baseball played in Beantown, Boston had never experienced the success the New York–based teams had. For one thing, prior to 1948 the only time the Braves had ever won the National League pennant was 1914. The Red Sox were an early American League power, winning world titles five times between 1903 and 1918—and not again. However, the Red Sox were recent visitors to the Series, losing in seven games in 1946.

Although there were distinctly different groups of supporters for the Red Sox at Fenway Park and the Braves at Braves Field, there were a large number of just baseball fans and civic leaders who would have been delighted to witness an all-Boston championship round.

Vern Bickford clinched the pennant with a week left in the regular season. The Braves took care of business through Sunday, October 3. Much like the Braves, the Red Sox began the season with a mediocre pace of play. On June 12, the Red Sox were 11 games out of first place, sitting sixth in the standings. It took them until July 25 to move into a first-place tie. As the end of August neared, the Red Sox were in front, and they spent most of the rest of the month trying to fend off the Cleveland Indians.

By far the best Boston player—and perhaps the greatest of all time—was left fielder Ted Williams. The Splendid Splinter's hitting sometimes defied physics. His eyesight was so good he could see a curveball curve and other pitches dip. Williams hit .369 as the batting champion that year and led the American League in doubles and walks. Most astounding—and this was an unappreciated statistic during his career—his on-base percentage was a ridiculous .497.

The Red Sox had some other bats. Billy Goodman hit .310 and Dom DiMaggio, a marvelous fielder, hit .285 with 87 runs batted in. While five Boston pitchers won at least 10 games that season, they did not have a dominating ace. Southpaw Mel Parnell was the best. When the regular season ended on October 3, the Red Sox were 96–58. But so were the Indians.

This was a pretty special place for the Indians to reside, too. It was not as if the Cleveland club, playing under such nicknames as the Naps and Spiders, as well as Indians, had much October baseball on its resume either. Only once, in 1920, had the Indians won a World Series.

These were no Cinderella Indians, though. Not only did they have an appealing owner in Bill Veeck, like the Braves' Lou Perini, but the talent level was off the charts. Looking back at the names on that roster, the Indians seemed almost Yankee-esque.

Lou Boudreau, the shortstop and player-manager, Larry Doby, the first African American to play in the American League, and second baseman Joe Gordon all went into the Hall of Fame. So did Veeck. So did pitchers Bob Feller, Bob Lemon, and Satchel Paige.

Tied after 154 games, the Red Sox and Indians played one more. The game was at Fenway Park on October 4, a day after the conclusion of the regular season. Boston manager Joe McCarthy—another future Hall of Famer—chose to start Denny Galehouse on the mound and has been second-guessed by Boston fans ever since. The Indians scored four runs in the fourth inning and won 8–3. Gene Bearden won his 20th game for Cleveland.

The Braves thought it would have been neat to have an all-Boston World Series, but the main thing was getting there. Every professional athlete wants to play for a championship and win a championship. Athletes live for those moments and those among them who are the toughest competitors crave the big stage even more.

"Every year we were chasing the Dodgers," Spahn said.[95]

Well, this time the Braves caught the Dodgers and surpassed them. They got to see what happens up close after a pennant race ends.

"I didn't have a real good year that year," Spahn said. "I won 15 and lost 12. But I pitched in a lot of ballgames where I was pinch-hit for or was relieved in the later part of the game. We were in a pennant fight. We had a good defensive ballclub, a double-play combination, in center field, pitching, and we were in a lot of ballgames we weren't the year before."[96]

It had been so long between World Series for the Braves and for the Indians, it was a toss-up which fan base reveled more in the first-in-decades chance to play. With Cleveland's 80,000-seat Municipal Stadium as the Indians' home park, the team drew a major-league-record 2,620,627 fans to regular season games. As recently as 1944, the Braves' attendance had been 208,691 for the whole season. The Braves topped a million fans for the first time in 1947 and in 1948 set the Boston Braves record of 1,455,439.

Lou Perini, general manager John Quinn, Billy Southworth, Warren Spahn, and Johnny Sain had made the Braves baseball fan care again.

The 1948 World Series opened in Boston on October 6. Braves Field was crammed with full-throated partisans, 40,135 of them. Billy Southworth's starter was Johnny Sain, winner of 24 games, going up against Cleveland's Bob Feller. The matchup screamed pitcher's duel. Spahn was scheduled for the second game, and who knew, maybe Rain was slated to start Game Three for Boston.

That was later. This game was a doozy. It turned into the masterful pitching exhibition people had predicted. Neither team could score for the first seven innings. Sain sent the Indians down in the top of the eighth as well. By this point in the game, it was obvious any baserunner was precious. Boston catcher Bill Salkeld worked Feller for a walk and Southworth pinch-ran Boston's other catcher, Phil Masi.

Mike McCormick set down a sacrifice bunt, sending Masi to second. Both managers were playing chase by now. Eddie Stanky was intentionally walked by Feller and Sibbi Sisti pinch-ran for him. So the Braves had runners on first and second as Feller surprised Boston when he spun around and tried to pick Masi off second. The throw went to Boudreau who tagged Masi. Boudreau was sure the subterfuge worked and Masi was out. But Masi was called safe and promptly scored on a single by Tommy Holmes.

That was the game's only run, with Boston winning 1–0. The controversy over whether Masi was out or safe lingered in baseball lore for years until Masi, who died in 1990, reported in his will he believed he was out. That was a bit late for Cleveland to play the game under protest.

After the game, Sain, who had fulfilled an ambition by winning a World Series game while limiting the Indians to just four hits, was repeatedly asked to pose for pictures by news photographers and urged to smile. Sain couldn't work up a smile despite the circumstances and to match what he said. "It was just the greatest thrill of my life beating Bob Feller and the Cleveland Indians 1–0 in the opening game of the 1948 World Series. But ballplayers can't get as excited as I was. They'd never be able to get their work done."[97]

Game Two was another super pitching match, Spahn versus Bob Lemon, again in Boston, just a day later at 1 p.m. Television was in its infancy, but in a successful experiment, the Baltimore and Ohio Railroad managed to show the game live on a train run between Washington, DC, and New York City. Live streaming was not a phrase at the time.

Spahn had waited a lifetime for this Series opportunity, but it did not provide a lifetime of good memories. Boston staked him to a 1–0 lead in the first inning, but the Indians pecked away at his less-than-stellar stuff on this day. He wasn't battered but gave up two runs in the top of the fourth inning and another in the fifth. Cleveland added one more run in the ninth, but the Braves never touched Lemon again. The final score was 4–1 Cleveland and Spahn was the loser in his first World Series game.

The Indians did not shell Spahn, but Southworth did not feel as if he was in command and lifted the southpaw after completing 4 1/3 innings, allowing six hits and three earned runs. Spahn was a disappointed man when Red Barrett replaced him on the mound and he returned to the dugout.

"A few inches the other way and a couple of those hits would have been outs," Sain said in an effort to console him. "You gave it a good try." Spahn wasn't hearing those good wishes. "A good try isn't enough for me, Johnny. I pitch to win them all, same as you."[98]

It was one of those games when a pitcher goes out to the mound feeling good, believing he is ready for anything and seems to have all of his pitches working, only to discover that the batters' bats are one step quicker on that day.

Unlike Feller, whose fastball was always rated as being among the fastest ever alongside Walter Johnson's, Smoky Joe Wood's, and Nolan Ryan's, Lemon was more of an off-speed specialist, somewhat like Spahn. When Lemon was on—and he was on frequently given that he won 20 or more games seven times—he was hard to beat.

"Lemon looked so easy to hit," Spahn said. "But he had a good sinker and we hit a lot of ground balls and didn't score very much off him."[99]

In the 1940s, baseball schedulers did not make much allowance for player weariness. They jammed the World Series into as few days as could be arranged. There were no West Coast teams yet. All sixteen teams were geographically crammed into an area of the United States between Boston to the north and St. Louis to the south and west. It was easy to get there from here and teams traveled by train.

So Game Three was set for October 8 in Cleveland. If players wanted to rest rather than play cards or drink beer, it was on them to sleep on the train, but there was going to be an afternoon game scheduled whenever they arrived. On the other hand, they did not have to work hard for long. The Indians drew 70,306 fans to Municipal Stadium for a game that was over in one hour, thirty-six minutes.

Boudreau sent out Gene Bearden, the knuckleballer from nowhere who had flummoxed the American League all summer as Rookie of the Year and with a record of 20–7. In spring training, Bearden was not even expected to make the final roster. The only reason he had not pitched in the Series to this point was that he was recovering from winning the playoff game over Boston to send the Indians ahead.

Bearden's big-league career started late (he was twenty-six that season) and it ended early (after just seven seasons), and 1948 was the only year he approached this level of magnificence. But that year belonged to Bearden. He showed why in Game Three when he overwhelmed the Braves, 2–0, on just five hits. Vern Bickford, Bill Voiselle, and Red Barrett all pitched for Boston and surrendered just one earned run. Yet that wasn't good enough.

Cleveland became even more excited with the Indians ahead 2–1 in games, and attendance soared to 81,897 for Game Four. At the time that was the largest crowd ever for a World Series game.

Right-hander Steve Gromek was not nearly as famous as some of the other Cleveland pitchers in the rotation. He went 9–3 in 1948, a couple of years removed from his best-ever 19–9 season. Gromek may have appeared to be a weak link in the rotation for Braves batters to take advantage of, but things did not work out that way.

Sain was his usual estimable self for the Braves, and he permitted just two runs on five hits. Gromek was even better, however, and Cleveland won, 2–1. Cleveland's second run scored on a Larry Doby home run. Doby, the American League's first African American player, had suffered through insults and discrimination as a rookie in 1947. However, in the clubhouse, after the Indians won, Gromek unabashedly hugged Doby and the photograph of the white man and black man warmly celebrating flashed around the world. Doby said he always treasured the picture. In Gromek's 2002 *New York Times* obituary, mention of the photograph was as prominent as his baseball career.

The Braves were in a precarious position as the Series moved to a fifth game, still in Cleveland and again with no rest between games. Attendance in Municipal Stadium set a new record with 86,288 fans counted coming in the building. That remains the fourth-highest attendance for a World Series game. All three of the top marks were set in 1959 when the Los Angeles Dodgers hosted the Chicago White Sox in the capacious Los Angeles Coliseum.

Warren Spahn did not care how many people were in the stadium rooting for his opponents. He wanted to win a World Series game and keep alive his team's chances. Cleveland led, 3–1, in the best four-out-of-seven Series. He was not even scheduled to pitch on October 10.

Bob Feller, perhaps even hungrier than Spahn to capture a World Series victory, was the Cleveland starter. But he was off right from the beginning, permitting three runs in the top of the first. Nelson Potter started for Boston, and he was not sharp either. Feller lasted 6 1/3 innings but gave up seven runs to the Braves, whose batters had been itching to break out. This was a major opportunity for Boston, catching Feller on a down day. Yet Potter allowed five runs in 3 1/3 innings, so the Braves seemed to be trying to give back the lead.

When Potter got into trouble, Southworth called to Spahn, ready in the bullpen. Over 21 seasons, Spahn pitched in 750 regular-season games and started 665 of those, so the number of his relief appearances was limited. This was the most important one of his life.

Potter exited in the fourth inning after walking Joe Gordon, giving up a single to Ken Keltner, a single to Wally Judnich, and a three-run homer to Jim Hegan. By the time Spahn appeared at the scene of the crime, the Indians had turned a 4–1 deficit into a 5–4 lead.

Catcher Salkeld greeted him with a pep talk.

"Just fog 'em in there, Spahnie, these guys can't hit," Salkeld said.[100]

Spahn was at his best. Over 5 2/3 innings, as his teammates rejuvenated the offense, the lefty gave up just one hit and struck out seven. Except for a Lou Boudreau double, Cleveland was baffled by his pitches. The Braves piled on the runs, including six in the seventh inning to win 11–5. Spahn had his World Series victory, and the Braves sent the Series back to Boston. Tucked into the middle of the action was the appearance of Satchel Paige throwing two-thirds of an inning in relief for Cleveland. The forty-two-year-old rookie, so long exiled to the Negro Leagues, became the first African American to pitch in a World Series game.

Again there was no off-day as the teams rushed to Boston and Braves Field to beat the 40,103 fans. Bob Lemon went against Bill Voiselle, and both had good stuff. Lemon was in a groove, going 7 1/3 innings while allowing three runs. Voiselle outshined his previous showing, also allowing three runs in seven innings.

In the eighth inning, Boudreau turned to Bearden in the bullpen. It had been a magical season for the young man, and the Indians hoped he still had some fairy dust left in his arm. When Southworth needed aid, he wasn't sure where to turn. Spahn had just thrown more than five innings less than twenty-four hours earlier.

Boston needed help. Southworth pinch-hit for Voiselle, removing him from the game with the score 3–3 and no obvious pitching replacement in mind. He sat down in the dugout next to Spahn and did not say anything at first. Then he asked, "Think you can go in there?" What pitcher is going to turn down his manager at crunch time? "I'll give it all I've got," Spahn answered.[101]

So the warrior accepted the assignment and walked to the mound in front of the hostile multitudes with everything on the line: the inning, the game, the season, the championship.

This time, whether he was too tired from too many pitches the day before or Cleveland just figured out Spahn's repertoire, he could not hold the Indians. In the eighth inning of Game Six, Spahn gave up three straight singles, and although he picked Thurman Tucker off of first base, the Indians punched home a run to lead 4–1.

In the bottom of the inning, Clint Conatser pinch-hit and blasted a deep fly to left-center. Tucker ran it down, making a superb catch, holding Conatser to a sacrifice fly as the Braves closed to 4–3.

Conatser said Tucker "made a great play," and if he had missed the ball, the Braves would have won the game, gone to a seventh game, and taken advantage of Cleveland being short on pitching. "We should have won the World Series."[102]

Spahn was irritated by the run he allowed in the eighth and brought his feelings to the mound in the top of the ninth, striking out the side. But Bearden protected the lead, and the Indians won the Series when Holmes made the last out on a fly ball.

"I pitched the second game," Spahn said, "and I pitched again in the fourth game. I threw the ball better in the fourth game than I did in the second game. But we got beat in six games. Oh, Bearden, that son of a gun, couldn't do any wrong."[103]

10

PENNANT HANGOVER

IN 1949 WARREN Spahn, disenchanted by his 15–12 season and a World Series loss, was replaced by the Spahn who had emerged as a star hurler in 1947.

Every pennant-winner shows up the following spring training proud of the accomplishment of the preceding season but convinced it can take the last step, win another pennant, and also capture the World Series. The Braves were no different.

Spahn won 21 games in 1949, leading the National League in victories for the first time. He pitched a league-leading 302 1/3 innings, started a league-leading 38 times, and completed a league-leading 25 games. He won his first strikeout title with 151 Ks, although that was a low number to be a league king.

The leader of the staff and the leader of the team, Spahn was magnificent. Only the Braves collapsed. They had revamped the roster a bit, but adding newcomers added nothing. Worse, the top position players of 1948 all had comparatively off-years hitting the next season. The decline was surprising in its thoroughness. So many things went wrong in 1949 that went right in 1948 it is difficult to quantify the most damaging.

One could start with Johnny Sain. The right-handed comple-ment to the left-handed Spahn, who outdid Spahn during the pennant run with his finest season, turned in just about his worst season. Fans weren't praying for Sain in 1949. They preferred rain. His 24 wins was a National League best one minute and he was a demoralizing 10–17 the next. Sain's earned run average jumped more than two runs, going up from 2.60 to 4.81.

The 24-win campaign was the apex of Sain's career. Only once more did he win 20 games. Sain's slump was a big problem for the Braves in 1949. The starting rotation was thin enough in 1948 with Spahn and Sain, but the new secondary ace was Vern Bickford. He went 16–11, which was helpful, but it would have been better for the Braves if Bickford was the third option. Bill Voiselle, 7–8, was the fourth starter. Two other guys won just six games.

Through 1948 the Braves charted an upward course under manager Billy Southworth. Southworth's magic wore off in 1949. On their way to a 75–79 finish, a dramatic turnaround in the wrong direction, Southworth took much of the blame.

Some players felt Southworth claimed too much credit for the pennant and the Braves no longer had a happy clubhouse. A bad attitude, coupled with losing games and jealousy of the manager, does not make for a positive atmosphere.

One might think Southworth would come to spring training the year after guiding the team to a pennant with more confi-dence and good cheer. But Southworth, who prided himself on the seriousness of his approach to the game, worked his players even harder. They endured some six-hour workouts. Worse, boasting by the front office that it had pulled off a coup in bringing Southworth to Boston alienated players. They were irritated by the notion Southworth pulled all the right strings and they were merely puppets hopping along doing his bidding.

"Southworth won the pennant," management broadcast. "You didn't. You should thank Lou Perini for bringing you here to play for such a great manager."[104] That outlook did not play very well, especially in the context of contract negotiations.

The feel-good residue of a wonderful season evaporated swiftly, and the same players who performed so well played poorly. Where were the sluggers when the Braves needed them? Striking out or grounding out instead of hitting balls over the Braves Field wall.

If players resented Southworth's imperious attitude, he was still digesting praise for the previous season more than a month into the new one. A feature article appeared well into May in *Look* magazine by a Boston sportswriter with the headline, "Billy Southworth, The Pennant Man." The story began with an anecdote about how Southworth had long before determined if he ever became a manager he would "treat players the way they wanted to be treated. He'd handle them like human beings."[105]

Somehow that thought must have gotten lost in the sands of time because the players definitely did not feel that was how Southworth administered clubhouse justice.

Third baseman Bob Elliott's numbers were still good but did not approach his previous two years' production. Elliott hit 17 home runs with 76 runs batted in and a .280 batting average. Tommy Holmes dropped from .325 to .266. Alvin Dark fell from .322 to .276.

In a somewhat stalled-out National League race the Braves were actually in first place by two games on June 2 with a 25–17 record. Things unraveled from there and September was brutal. Before finishing with two victories in October to end the regular season, Boston went from 67–60 to 73–79 during September. It was a 6–19 stretch.

By then the hallowed Southworth wasn't even with the team. Tensed up, distraught over the losing, supposedly drinking too much, he stepped aside with the team at 55–54, a leave of absence chalked up to health reasons. Some felt he was on the verge of a nervous breakdown.

Coach Johnny Cooney guided the team to a 20–25 finish. Perhaps still riding a high from the year before and still believing the team could rally, the Braves did draw one million people to their home games. But this follow-up season was a major flop.

Cooney played twenty years in the majors between 1921 and 1944, some seasons rarely seeing action, others playing nearly full-time. He was a center fielder, first baseman, and even pitched while compiling a .286 lifetime average. He was a solid baseball man, but except for one game filling in for Al Lopez with the Chicago White Sox later, this was his only turn as a big-league manager.

Cooney knew the game, and he obtained one piece of advice early from Casey Stengel. "Casey showed me the advantage of hitting down the foul lines, first and third," Cooney said. "He pointed out that there is only one man to get the ball by at third and first, whereas if you hit through the middle there are three men who have a chance to retire you—the pitcher, shortstop, and second baseman."[106]

If the Braves had adopted the same philosophy, they might have won more often in 1949.

Outfielder Jeff Heath, who hit .319 in 1948 before getting injured in September, broke his ankle and only played in 36 games the next season, spending much of the summer on the disabled list. First baseman Earl Torgeson separated a shoulder early in the 1949 season and broke a thumb later.

It is difficult to think of many examples of other teams coming off a championship falling so thoroughly apart and performing so dismally and dysfunctionally.

One plus that season was the arrival of Del Crandall, who took over the catching job and became one of the finest catchers in Braves history. He was smart, a good fielder, called a good game, and was a solid hitter. Crandall was just nineteen that season, a .263 hitter in 67 games. He had the right build for a receiver at 6-foot-1 and 180 pounds and was runner-up for NL Rookie of the Year. Crandall played 16 major-league seasons, mostly for the Braves, and was an 11-time All-Star. No doubt excited to be joining a pennant winner, Crandall might have been too young to be disturbed by the mess he wandered into that season.

Especially before free agency when owners controlled players and their futures, the easiest way to antagonize a player was through his pocketbook. The Braves were grumbling as early as spring training. Pitcher Red Barrett, who was about to embark on his own lousy season, going 1–1 with a 5.68 earned average in 23 appearances, tried to play peacemaker with his teammates. Barrett was thirty-four and didn't know it, but 1949 would be his final season. At the least he knew he did not want to waste it.

He urged, while playing diplomat even as he acknowledged grievances, that the players regroup, gather themselves, and play good baseball. Even if they were mad at the front office and unhappy with Southworth, they should do it for themselves.

"I suggest we forget about what's done and can't be helped, and go out and win another pennant," Barrett said. "I didn't hear anyone complain last year about getting that extra $4,500 from the World Series."[107]

Barrett's message did not take. Word of player revolt seeped out of the clubhouse and into the newspapers. Barrett tried to muster a vote of confidence for Southworth so players could tell the sportswriters. He couldn't get support to take the vote. Spahn, the most esteemed player on the team, wasn't even around. He was holding out back home on his new ranch in Hartshorne, Oklahoma, the spread that became his decades-long off-season home. That told the players even their best player viewed the front office as cheap.

The Braves sent Spahn a new contract in January, but he believed they were low-balling him. He felt his 15–12 record, while hardly his best, masked his team contributions. He did what dissatisfied players did in an era before agents represented them in negotiations. Spahn mailed the unsigned contract back to Boston.

Spring training was underway in Florida with Spahn sitting in Oklahoma when GM John Quinn telephoned him in an attempt to strike a deal. In Spahn's mind the two sides were not close to agreement.

"You come down a little and we'll go up a little," Quinn said. "We've always treated you right, Warren."[108]

It was amazing how often management used that patter on players. Sometimes smooth talk helped, and sometimes it did not make a dent. Spahn was not pacified or soothed.

"I'll come down a little," he said. "But you'll have to come up a lot. My record deserves better."[109]

This is when Quinn emphasized the 15–12, not the big wins that helped clinch the pennant and how much the Braves relied on Spahn. As turmoil raged in the Boston clubhouse, Quinn was concerned not having his top pitcher aboard. It took until March 5 for the sides to publicly announce a contract agreement.

Southworth, the boss of the dugout, and on the sidelines, watching the salary debate, knew he wanted Spahn on his side that season. He immediately began flattering him and buttering him up.

"He's one of the best left-handers in the league, if not the best," Southworth proclaimed. "It may have been my fault that Spahn didn't repeat his 1947 success last season. [Where was Southworth whispering that into Quinn's ear while Spahn and the general manager were arguing?] It may be that I neglected him too much, took too much for granted."[110]

Southworth predicted Spahn would become a 20-game winner for the second time.

Spahn was twenty-eight years old for the 1949 season, by most definitions in his prime, even though he had a late start to his major-league career. His team was very much counting on him, and he rose above the chaos to return to his higher level of pitching of 1947.

The season began on April 18 against the Philadelphia Phillies and Sain got the start, appropriate given his 24-win season of the year before. He got beat, 4–0, unfortunately foreshadowing his trials to come.

Spahn started the next day, threw eight innings, and gave up six hits and three runs. But the Braves rallied to win late and reliever Nelson Potter got the victory. Still, this showed that even when Spahn wasn't superb, he was very, very good. Well, most of the time. In his next outing, four days later, Spahn was shelled by the New York Giants.

It was more-like-it-time when Spahn next twirled against the Phillies, winning 2–0 with a three-hitter and five strikeouts. He got back at the Giants May 1, going the distance, allowing 10 hits and five runs, but winning 6–5. When you had a horse, you rode him, and managers stuck with their starters often until their tongues hung out from exhaustion. Starting pitchers were expected to finish the game if at all possible and they took pride in doing so.

This was very much the era of the complete game, not the bullpen reliever, the closer. In the second decade of the twenty-first century it is a big deal for starting pitchers, who are in a rotation with four others, not three others, and who pitch on five days rest, not four, to top 200 innings in a season. For 17 seasons in a row Spahn threw a minimum of 245 2/3 innings and mixed in were two seasons of more than 300 innings and four others of at least 290.

Spahn did have five days rest before his next outing because the Braves had a day off for travel between series. When he raised his record to 3–1, Spahn bested Cincinnati, 6–1 on four hits. He struck out eight. This was the Spahn way: Trot out to the mound every fourth day and give it your all, rear back with that big kick and fool batsman after batsman.

"He was the greatest left-hander to ever put on a uniform," said Johnny Logan, later a longtime teammate of Spahn's. "His success was knowing the opponents' weaknesses."[111]

Spahn kept winning in 1949. The Braves started out OK, but began to fade as the heat picked up during the summer and during the pennant race. After a while, Spahn was the only consistent winner on the staff.

That late May *Look* magazine article appeared after the Braves had begun to swoon, and viewed in perspective with the knowledge players were on the edge of rebellion and the team was about to go down the tubes, there are some revealing anecdotes.

The writer watched Southworth ream out the team creatively because of players' habits of missing signs. He gathered the group together and said, "The Phillies won't steal a single sign

WARREN SPAHN

from us today, men. I've fixed it so no team will ever steal one of our signs again." This intrigued the players, who wanted to know how this would come to pass. "I'm not using any!" he shouted. "Why should I? Nobody but the Phillies paid any attention to them yesterday."[112]

Since most Braves looked at Southworth as a dictator, they must have gotten a chuckle out of the place in the story where it read he solicited input from all of them and managed more by committee. Southworth said, "There are twenty-five managers on my team. I welcome and get plenty of suggestions from the players. If I think one of their ideas will help us win more games, I try it out."[113]

Maybe Southworth did occasionally employ a suggestion. But twenty-five managers? Right, over his dead carcass.

Whether in later years nobody wanted to admit the goings-on in the clubhouse or they had selective memories, Sibby Sisti said relations with the manager did not account for the down year. Sisti was an old friend of Spahn's from Buffalo. The hometown papers used to keep close track of both of them. Spahn was the Hall of Famer in the making, Sisti a 1,000-game utility man. In fact, he played seven positions for the Braves in 1949.

Many years later, when provoked to talk about the 1949 debacle, Sisti was brief. "A lot of people said we had a lot of dissension on the team. But that wasn't so. We just didn't play as well as we did the year before."[114]

Next question.

Sisti was more voluble at other times. He had his own theory of how Spahn managed to throw so many complete games or remain in games longer than other pitchers. "Warren Spahn was always a good hitter, so he often stayed in the game in late innings."[115]

Excepting three years in military service, from the time he was eighteen in 1939 until the team wrapped up its stay in Boston in 1952, Sisti was always a Brave. While batting .244 lifetime and hitting that figure right on the nose in 1949, Sisti's greatest contribution to Braves history and to Boston and its sports history was an event that occurred during the 1948 pennant year off the field.

Sisti, Southworth, and some other players visited a patient at Boston Children's Hospital after a radio broadcast drew attention to a boy named "Jimmy" suffering from cancer and who said he wanted a television to watch his favorite team, the Braves. From that short visit grew the Jimmy Fund. A plea for money collected $200,000 as donations to cancer research at the Dana Farber Cancer Institute. The true identity of "Jimmy," who recovered, was kept secret for fifty years.

Braves owner Lou Perini took a lead role in promoting the Jimmy Fund, and when the Braves left town, he gained assurances from Boston Red Sox owner Tom Yawkey his team would keep up the baseball connection. The Red Sox partnership with the Jimmy Fund began in 1953 and has never waned.

The Braves plodded through the 1949 season with a black cloud over their heads and Southworth slowly disintegrating as the team crumbled. Spahn was the major exception. Outside of Vern Bickford, nobody else was winning. For the second time in three years, Spahn broke the 20-game winning mark, winning 21. Ironically—and this was something Sibby Sisti noticed and remembered—Spahn wore No. 21 on his uniform and eight times in a season he won 21 games.

Clint Conatser, an outfielder on those Braves teams of 1948 and 1949 and who played only those two seasons in the majors while batting .271 lifetime, always marveled at Spahn's abilities.

"He was an outstanding pitcher," Conatser said. "He was so smooth. He'd work the hitters in and out. He'd put a little spin on it here and a little there like a musician."[116]

Spahn realized opposing hitters could not name that tune.

11

THE COLLAPSE

HOW QUICKLY THE Boston Braves declined after the 1948 American League pennant. The 1949 season was a disaster for just about everyone except Warren Spahn.

The question was what to do next, how to repair the engine. Lou Perini was thrilled in 1948, downcast in 1949. The season actually ended with a losing record and his high-paid, savior manager at home in Ohio. Johnny Cooney was a good coach, but not the long-term answer. Worse, Billy Southworth, the manager on the sidelines, had a long-term contract and was then making $50,000 a year.

Before the Braves could address the personnel issue on the field they had to figure out who was going to lead the team. Nobody wanted to endure behind-the-scenes tension for another year.

Surprisingly, Perini and general manager John Quinn, who had proclaimed Southworth the greatest leader since George Washington, stuck to their original outlook and brought Southworth back to run the dugout. Once that move was in place the roster had to be dealt with and that meant some house cleaning, not solely based on performance.

There were several major differences in the everyday lineup for the 1950 season. Al Dark and Eddie Stanky, so important in their roles as middle infielders, were exiled because of the friction with Southworth. Earl Torgeson, who missed so much playing time in 1949 because of injury, was back at first base. Soon after the season began, an aging but still able Walker Cooper, came over from the Cincinnati Reds to catch. Cooper, thirty-five, batted .329 and served as a mentor to still-young Del Crandall. Roy Hartsfield (second base) and Buddy Kerr (short) were the new middle infielders.

Sid Gordon and Willard Marshall were acquired. Also, Sam Jethroe, the Braves' first African American player, became an outfield starter. Now that is an overhaul. There were thirteen new players on the roster.

Dark and Stanky were shipped to the New York Giants for Marshall, Gordon, Kerr, and pitcher Sam Webb, who did not make the team. Spahn had proved once before that he was a good soldier, and when he spoke of the trade, which brought in older and slower players in place of two key energetic infielders, he praised it.

"Both Gordon and Marshall were rough hitters for me," Spahn said of the pleasure he would derive from avoiding facing them and having them on his side chasing down the fly balls he allowed. "And they're good outfielders, too."[117]

Gordon was a very good hitter. In 1950, he batted .304 with 27 home runs and 103 runs batted in. He did an excellent job for Southworth. Marshall hit just .235.

Yet for all of that—and this could be read more than one way— no key changes occurred in the pitching rotation. There was faith that Johnny Sain would rebound, and he did. The top three were Warren Spahn, Sain, and Vern Bickford. The big problem is that there was no number four starter, nor a real fill-in number five. It was now Spahn and Sain, pray for rain, and Flick Your Bick. This was the thinnest starting pitching rotation since the Deadball Era when teams often only bothered with three.

Spahn and Bickford each started 39 games, and Sain started 37. Bickford threw 311 2/3 innings, Spahn 293, and Sain 278 1/3. Spahn won 21 games, Sain 20, and Bickford 19.

If there was a fourth starter it was lefty Bob Chipman. Chipman started 12 games, finished 7–7, but had a 4.43 earned run average over 124 innings. Bobby Hogue appeared in 36 games, all but one in relief. Max Surkont threw 55 2/3 innings and went 5–2.

On August 11, 1950, at Braves Field before 29,008 fans, Bickford tossed a no-hitter, shutting out the Brooklyn Dodgers, 7–0, with four walks. This was no slouch team Bickford halted. That day the Dodgers had Pee Wee Reese, Duke Snider, Jackie Robinson, Roy Campanella, and Gil Hodges in the lineup, four Hall of Famers and one player (Hodges) some believe should be in the Hall.

The Braves' big fielding play was Marshall's grab of a third-inning popup struck by Joe Hatten. Whether it was a sign of his late-game edginess or not, two of Bickford's walks came in the ninth inning when Brooklyn was trying to break up the no-hitter. But the game ended on a double play, Snider making the last out.

For all of the shuffling, wheeling and dealing, and breaking in of new faces, the Braves were quite respectable at 83–71. At 944,391, attendance was so-so. The glow had worn off from 1948, and 1949 left a bitter taste in some mouths, but 1950 showed management was trying.

Spahn was now established as one of the best pitchers in baseball. It is said of some hurlers that they throw aspirins. Those are the real fastball pitchers who shrink the baseball to such a small size it can barely be seen as it approaches the batter's box. Of others, especially when slumping and giving up home runs, it might be said they were throwing grapefruits up there. When it came to Spahn, his long fingers allowing him to manipulate the ball and make it dance, the ball was more like an orange. It was that size, but it did not travel in a straight line when he threw it.

A peculiarity of Spahn's career stood out during this period. Walter Johnson was nicknamed "Big Train" because his fastball came at hitters so fast it reminded them of a speeding choo-choo. Bob Feller and Nolan Ryan were supersonic throwers who made batters cringe. Spahn did not have rocket speed. He outthought batters more often than intimidated them. Spahn more often made fools of them, though in more subtle fashion than a knuckleballer.

Yet in 1949 Spahn led the National League in strikeouts with 151. In 1950, his total was a career-high 191 strikeouts, again leading the league. He did it again in 1951 with 164 Ks and in 1952 with 183 strikeouts. For four straight years Spahn led the league in strikeouts—and never again.

Sportswriters were enthralled Spahn could do this. He was using his noodle as much as his arm, outthinking, outsmarting batters. His admirable control was his strength. Even his fastball had good movement.

"When a pitcher faces a batter, it's his timing against yours," Spahn said. "Throw him the same thing every time and he'll soon get set for it. Every good pitcher has a pitch which he likes and controls better than any other, but he also has variety. Even the fastball pitchers do. He must have it or he loses the battle of timing."[118]

Certainly, many pitchers get a charge out of punching out hitters with the blazing fastball, giving them a sense of superiority. Since Spahn never possessed the gift of overwhelming speed he never got caught up in that. It was almost counterintuitive that he led the league in strikeouts four straight years.

Once, Spahn even spoke on the inefficiency of going after strikeouts instead of compiling one-pitch outs while also recognizing neither would happen on every play.

"It would be a pushover if every batter hit the first pitch," Spahn said. "Why, you could finish a ballgame with 27 pitches. But when you have to strike guys out you have to throw an absolute minimum to each man, and between called balls and two-strike fouls you can pile up a lot more."[119]

That was all basic baseball logic. Unlike in current-day baseball, when Spahn was pitching nobody really kept track of the number of pitches he or other starters threw. The entire concept of pitch counts would have been foreign to the throwers of the 1940s and 1950s. The idea of a manager trudging to the mound to lift them from a game because they had reached 110 pitches would have been laughable. If a pitcher was winning 2–0 in the seventh and the manager came out to yank him, he might well have thrown (pitch 111) the ball through him.

During the 1950 season, Bickford threw 27 complete games, and Spahn and Sain threw 25 each. If Southworth was looking for exercise, he didn't get it walking from the dugout to the mound.

When Jackie Robinson played first base for the Brooklyn Dodgers on April 15, 1947, he became a social pioneer as well as a major-league baseball player. No African American had competed in the majors since the 1880s. Once the Dodgers and Robinson broke the color line other teams signed African American talent, some more quickly than others, some at a slower pace than was desirable.

Although Robinson's was at first a lonely fight, within months some other teams integrated, and ten other African Americans were in the bigs before 1950. Robinson was joined on the Dodgers by Dan Bankhead, who was the first African American pitcher in the majors in the twentieth century. Catcher Roy Campanella joined the Dodgers in 1948 and pitcher Don Newcombe in 1949.

Outfielder Larry Doby became the first African American barrier-breaker in the American League with the Cleveland Indians later in 1947. The inimitable Satchel Paige played for Cleveland in 1948 and Luke Easter did so in 1949. Minnie Minoso, a black Cuban, broke in with Cleveland in 1949 before becoming the Chicago White Sox's color-barrier breaker in 1951.

Hank Thompson and Willard Brown joined the St. Louis Browns only weeks after Doby suited up for Cleveland. In 1949, Monte Irvin integrated the New York Giants.

By the time the Boston Braves signed Sam Jethroe nearly a dozen black players had competed in the majors, and that was only the beginning of long-overdue integration.

Jethroe also had an unsettling backstory stemming from 1945. In April of that year, Jethroe had what was later construed to be a fake tryout with Boston—the Boston Red Sox. The tryout was held because of media pressure that had been growing in the black press from top sportswriters and from an influential Boston African American city councilman.

Five years before he won the National League Rookie of the Year Award, Jethroe appeared at Fenway Park with Jackie Robinson and another Negro Leagues player named Marvin Williams, and none were offered contracts. In 1959, when the Red Sox suited up infielder Pumpsie Green, they were the last team to integrate, twelve years post-Robinson.

"I don't think it dawned on any of us that we might be going to the major leagues," was what Jethroe said years later about tryout day. In the 1990s, he said, "I talk to young (African American) guys now and I tell them they don't know how tough times can be. It's nothing compared to how tough it was for those guys in the Negro Leagues."[120]

Jethroe arrived with a reputation after spending a hot season at Triple-A Montreal in the Dodgers' chain and being purchased for $150,000. Between 1942 and 1948 he played for the Buckeyes in the Negro Leagues, which moved between Cincinnati and Cleveland, while leading his league in stolen bases three times and winning two batting titles. His club won the Negro Leagues World Series in 1945.

Born in East St. Louis, Illinois in 1918, at thirty-two Jethroe was old for a big-league rookie, but the Braves were not looking to develop him. They hoped they had obtained a ready-made regular. Known for his speed, Jethroe was a switch-hitter. Given some of the stories of the earliest days of Robinson's trials with the Dodgers, it can be seen as ironic that a Braves team characterized by dissension in 1949 experienced more harmony in 1950 integrating a still-somewhat rare black man in baseball into the lineup. The real debate was whether Jethroe was as good as advertised.

In March of 1950, during a spring training swing through St. Petersburg, Florida, there were worries that when the Braves with Jethroe met the New York Yankees and St. Louis Cardinals local officials might object. There had been issues there before, but not this time, and Jethroe became the first African American major leaguer to play at Al Lang Field. One New York sportswriter wrote, "Little by little, racial tension is being eliminated in the South, insofar as appearances of big-league players are concerned."[121] That was optimistic, but perhaps for that brief slice of time in that situation it was an accurate observation.

Jethroe was promptly acknowledged as the fastest runner in baseball, nicknamed "Jet," and he could hit well enough (.273 with 18 homers and an NL-leading 35 stolen bases in 1950). But he had a below-average outfielder's arm and his fielding was suspect.

Although in the 1970s and 1980s forced busing to integrate public schools set off protests and rioting in Boston, there was no strong reaction to Jethroe integrating the Braves. He was a popular player and said he enjoyed his three seasons in Boston.

"I felt a small amount of racism," Jethroe said in 1994. "At that particular time a lot of that was eliminated. In Boston, I was well-liked and there was no trouble whatsoever there."[122]

Despite dodging any kind of incident in St. Petersburg, and though Jethroe talked about "a small amount of racism" in baseball, he did encounter that virulent disease in the South during spring training.

In Bradenton, Florida, Jethroe was shipped out to stay overnight at a private home rather in the team hotel. In Atlanta, he was not allowed to dress in the team locker room at Ponce de Leon Park and changed into his uniform at a black hotel. He was not allowed to stay in white hotels in St. Louis and sometimes in Chicago. A hotel manager called him "Sambo." But his first impression of Boston was all positive. "The people in Boston were crazy about me," he said. "Everyone crowded around for autographs after my first game. There was this woman who wanted to take me to dinner. A white woman."[123] He did not accept that invitation.

Jethroe spent 1950 to 1952 with the Braves and then played one season with the Pirates in 1954 when he was thirty-six. He remains the oldest player to win a Rookie of the Year Award. Still flashing that speed, Jethroe won a second stolen-base title in 1951, again with 35 thefts. He again slugged 18 home runs and hit .280.

Buck O'Neil, the one-time Negro Leagues All-Star and manager of the Kansas City Monarchs before becoming the majors' first African American scout, confirmed Jethroe was an extremely swift runner, if not as fast as Cool Papa Bell. "But real fast," O'Neil said, fast enough that teams had to draw in the infield "or you'd never throw him out."[124]

If there was discontent on the Braves because of race that season it was not noticeable. Spahn had become a team leader. He was respected, a star player, an example for everyone to work hard, and cared above all about winning. He may have been a prankster, but he did not stir up trouble, make major speeches, or give the writers controversial material to put in the papers.

On the team and around the league Spahn was known as a nice guy and a gentleman. Starting in spring training he embraced the arrival of Jethroe, by example if not anything else. When the most admired player on the team comes up to you to extend a hand of friendship, everyone is aware of it.

Jethroe learned plenty about Spahn from their initial meetings. Spahn proposed they play pepper and they did so regularly, batting the ball back and forth. He did not have to reach out to a rookie, but did. However, when Spahn felt it was time to stop, he ceased playing and always declared victory, a minor tell about his compulsion to win.

"That man Spahn," Jethroe said. "He doesn't know how to count, so he never loses."[125]

Even if he was the best, Spahn did lose sometimes. Spahn beat the New York Giants 11–4 on Opening Day and he was 3–0 by the end of April. In that third victory, Spahn went 10 innings to get the 2–1 win, again over the Giants. In the present-day climate, he probably would have been removed in the sixth inning and it would take four more guys to finish the game. Spahn was able to win 363 games partly by sticking around.

Things didn't go as smoothly in May when Spahn lost four times, and they were not all gems that got away from him. Foes scored about six runs a game in those defeats. By the end of June Spahn was just 9–8, but he gained strength after July to finish 21–17. For the Braves, it was a fairly good season, finishing 12 games above .500 at 83–71. It was neither a great season like 1948 when they copped a pennant or like the lousy losing one in 1949.

Clearly, a renovation was in order for 1951, but maybe not wholesale house cleaning as occurred after the 1949 season. The 1951 Braves had some pop in the lineup. Bob Elliott was still hitting respectably, with 15 homers and 70 runs batted in. Although his batting average was average, Earl Torgeson stroked 24 homers, drove in 92 runs, walked 102 times, and stole 20 bases. Sid Gordon was even better with 29 home runs and 109 RBIs. Longtime outfielder Tommy Holmes retired before the season but stayed in the organization as manager of a minor-league club in Hartford, Connecticut.

The core of the rotation of Spahn, Sain, and Bickford was still intact. Contributions in the way of an 11–8 record were made by a rookie named Chet Nichols, who spent more of his major-league career with the Boston Red Sox than the Boston Braves. And Max Surkont became a starter who won 12 games.

Surkont was an interesting case. From Rhode Island, Surkont attracted scouts' attention when he was fifteen, still in the ninth grade. His fastball was so fast they blinked when he threw it. They figured he would get bigger and stronger and faster—and of course become much more intimidating on the mound. There is no such thing as a sure thing, and although Surkont did grow to be 6-foot-1 and 195 pounds, it took until he was twenty-seven to break into the majors with the Chicago White Sox. He stuck around the majors for nine seasons but finished with a losing record.

Surkont was known for his practical jokes, which gave him a kinship with Spahn. For some reason—Surkont blames a deprived youth since he turned pro so young—he had a fascination with firecrackers. He deployed them in situations where some people may have suggested he showed poor judgment. Once, while playing in the Pacific Coast League, his Sacramento Solons were staying in a hotel where not long before there had been a shooting case. Surkont stuffed firecrackers into cigarettes and left them in the lobby men's room. When things went boom, police officers swarmed the place, and he got a big laugh out of it.

Another time Surkont's pyrotechnics led to the temporary abandonment of the Brooklyn Dodgers' dugout. This kind of stuff tickled Spahn. Surkont was in the Navy during World War II, serving in the Pacific. "We had some big firecrackers out there," he said.[126]

A few years into his Braves stay Surkont had one exceptional moment of glory. In a May 1953 game against the Cincinnati Reds, he struck out eight batters in a row for a then-major-league record. In 1951, Surkont went 12–16 for the Braves, but that was the second most wins on the club to Spahn.

The shock was the collapse of Johnny Sain. Sain finished 5–13. He was thirty-three and the Braves figured he was done, as well as overpaid at about $25,000 a year. On August 29, the team traded Sain to the Yankees. At first that seemed like a desperate move. In the long run it turned into a fantastic swap for Boston. The player they obtained, Lew Burdette, was a right-handed pitcher who became the perfect replacement for Sain and one of Warren Spahn's best friends.

By then, manager Billy Southworth was gone, too. Southworth never recaptured the 1948 touch. Although many bet against the likelihood of him even returning after his previous health-reasons vacation, Southworth made it through 59 games in 1951, going 28–31. His replacement was the good company man Tommy Holmes. A nice guy who was pals with many of the players, Holmes had not acquired much managerial experience in two-thirds of a season in Connecticut.

Aware of the doubts about his personality being right for the clubhouse, Holmes said, "I've got to be firm. Everything depends on it. It'll be a tough job."[127]

Under Holmes, the Braves went 48–47 and finished fourth in the National League standings with a 76–78 record. Holmes was extended into the next season.

Most alarming from a management standpoint was that the Braves had lost the fans. Just a few years earlier attendance neared 1.5 million people. In 1951, home attendance was 487,475, last in the league.

Where had all the people gone? Where had all the wins gone? The two questions were linked. It seemed if not for Warren Spahn's reliable left arm there wouldn't be any wins.

12

LAST DAYS IN BOSTON

AN INABILITY TO score runs topped the list of problems the 1952 Boston Braves faced. Pretty simple, really.

Because the Braves could not hit they finished with a terrible 64–89 record. Because the Braves could not hit, manager Tommy Holmes was fired with a 13–22 record and replaced by Charlie Grimm. Because the Braves could not hit, Warren Spahn could not win despite a 2.98 earned run average. Because the Braves could not hit, none of their other top pitchers could win either.

And because the Braves could not hit or win, the fans stopped coming to Braves Field. The team attracted just 281,278 fans for the whole season. That translated into a loss of nearly $600,000.

The 1952 season was a multi-pronged disaster for the Braves. For one thing, the team sold just 420 season tickets by March, a month before the season. That was almost surreal.

Sid Gordon was the best hitter on the club, smacking 25 home runs with 75 runs batted in and recording a .289 batting average. There were newcomers moving into the lineup who would shine in later years, but they were only here-and-there helpful this season. Third baseman Eddie Mathews, a future Hall of Famer, broke in with 25 home runs and 58 RBIs, but he was only twenty and his career was in front of him. Shortstop Johnny Logan took over that position, hit .283, and held it for years.

These were useful additions. Logan was a fiery player, although it had taken him most of five years to get out of the minors. This was one gripe some players had against Billy Southworth. They believed Logan should have been up with the big club a couple of years sooner. In contrast, as good as he was, Mathews probably could have used another season in the minors. He was supremely talented, but raw, and his maturity was questioned when he blew his top frequently. Some days he looked very ready to play at the top level of the game and at times some wanted to dump a bucket of cold water over his head to tame him.

There was another new name on the 1952 team who had an intriguing background. Big George Crowe did not quite dislodge Earl Torgeson at first, but he appeared in 73 games while batting .258. A left-hander in the field and at bat, Crowe was already thirty-one years old. He stood 6-foot-2 and weighed 210 pounds.

Growing up in Indiana, Crowe's first sport was basketball. Despite being an African American during a time of great prejudice in that state, he was such a fine player in 1939 he was named the first Indiana Mr. Basketball—the state's best high school player. After graduating from Franklin High he attended Indiana Central College where he played both basketball and baseball. Later he toured with the New York Renaissance basketball team and played baseball for the Negro League's New York Black Yankees.

Before the Braves brought Crowe up, he had virtually destroyed pitching at every level of the minors on behalf of the organization between 1949 and early 1952, hitting .354, .353, .339, and .351.

Although he was old by rookie standards, that made Crowe hard to ignore. He never really played regularly for the Braves, but in 1957 he belted 31 homers for the Reds, and in 1958 he was chosen for the National League All-Star team.

Crowe's athletic career, in basketball and then baseball, overlapped with the early battles over integration and he tried to remain calm in the face of prejudices, although somewhat later he helped integrate a movie theatre in his hometown.

"It didn't really bother me that much," Crowe said of being turned away from hotels and restaurants his baseball teammates patronized. "I knew that was the way it was. You knew what you were getting into."[128]

As a team, the Braves hit .233 in 1952 and individually there were some truly ugly batting averages. Second baseman Jack Dittmar hit .193, Sam Jethroe hit .232, Earl Torgeson hit .230, Sibby Sisti .212, and outfielder Jack Daniels .187. And these guys had hundreds of at-bats.

Some of the pitchers besides Spahn had half-decent earned run averages, but they got so little run support they were always throwing under great pressure. This was one of the worst years of Spahn's life. Despite holding opponents to less than three earned runs per game he finished 14–19. Max Surkont went 12–13. Vern Bickford slumped to 7–12. New arrival Lew Burdette hadn't quite settled into being Lew Burdette, a righty who would win 203 games in his career. Burdette went 6–11, although his ERA was 3.61, not too bad. Righty Jim Wilson came along as a starter at age thirty and went 12–14, the second-best record of his career. The Braves were so bad they scored just 569 runs.

Somehow, it seemed, Boston had given up on the Braves even before this season began. At no time did the Braves, who put more than 40,000 fans into Braves Field for the 1948 home World Series games, draw respectable crowds in 1952. On July 5, 13,405 fans showed up for a game against the Dodgers and that was the high point for a single day's attendance. The last home game of the season on September 21, also against the Dodgers, brought in 8,822 ticket-holders. Nobody wanted to shell out to see the Braves. That was even true on the road where many times as visitors the Braves played before crowds of less than 10,000.

Spahn was thirty-one years old, but he wasn't losing it. He was just losing for lack of run support. The 19 defeats were the most he experienced during his 21 years in the majors. His ERA showed that he could still pitch, plus he struck out 183 batters to lead the National League in that category for the fourth straight year. He even made his fifth All-Star team, which indicated other baseball observers realized he was still pitching at a high level.

On June 14, with only 3,053 fans in the stands at Braves Field, Spahn lost a 3–1 decision to the Chicago Cubs. That was after hurling all 15 innings and striking out 18 men. The Braves put together just four hits in the entire game. One of those hits, and the only run, was produced by the bat of Warren Spahn, who hit a solo homer.

During the course of the long game Spahn spun a ball in on Chicago outfielder Frankie Baumholtz and the pitch broke his hand. As if the loss was not frustrating enough, in response to the errant pitch, Spahn received an unsigned threatening letter in the days following the game. It read, "When you come back to Chicago, I'll see you and make good. This is not a crank letter, but a sorehead like you will get it from me. I'll get you somehow. You can be handled."[129]

And most people thought Al Capone was no longer in charge of the Chicago mob. The letter was turned over to authorities. The

Braves returned to Wrigley Field for a three-game series in mid-July and three police officers shadowed Spahn the whole time he was in the Windy City. That included one of the detectives seated next to him in the dugout during the games, a Major League Baseball exception to the rules prohibiting civilians on the bench.

Spahn started the July 16 game, and it was a typical 1952 outing for him. Spahn tossed 9 1/3 innings and allowed two earned runs while striking out eight. Spahn left the game in the 10th inning with Burdette replacing him in relief. Burdette gave up one run, and Chicago won in the 13th inning. No violence was attempted on Spahn's person while he was in Chicago.

It was that kind of season where just about anything that could go haywire did. Spahn had not had any difficulty with other teams reading his pitches since his rookie year. His habit of covering his mouth with his glove, his clock-like delivery with the big kick that all helped masquerade what he was throwing, had served him well for years.

He kept trying to develop new off-speed pitches as supplements for the day when his fastball would inevitably slow by a few miles per hour. Since Spahn never again led the National League in strikeouts, it is possible he sensed that day might be approaching more quickly than expected.

In 1952, Spahn began experimenting with what was then called a "palm ball," an off-speed pitch that in delivery resembles the release of a fastball with something taken off. The grip is similar to a fastball and can fool batters into thinking the pitch is coming at them faster than they think. In today's major leagues it would be characterized as a type of changeup. For a southpaw like Spahn, the ball should be grasped with the middle finger on top of the right side of the ball and the ring finger on the top left. The ball should snugly fit into the palm of the hand. The other fingers should be spread on the surface of the ball without touching a seam.

Spahn learned quickly he was not hiding his delivery as well with that pitch during a game against the New York Giants. Freddie Fitzsimmons won 217 games in a long major-league career and then became a coach. He was in the first-base coach's box for the Giants and every time Spahn was poised to throw a palm ball he heard Fitzsimmons scream, "Now!" Clearly, Spahn was tipping his pitches, and the clever and knowledgeable Fitzsimmons was reading them and trying to provide a quick heads-up to his guys.

Irritated by Fitzsimmons, Spahn paused from his usual rapid-fire delivery to the opposition. He took a step sideways, looked at Fitzsimmons, and issued an ultimatum. Since as a coach Fitzsimmons was not going to step into the batter's box, Spahn chose to deliver a message differently.

"All right, Fitz, just keep right on doing it," he said, "and one of those Giants is going to have a ball stuck right in his ear for keeps."[130]

Umpires in that era were much less inclined to interfere with brushback pitches, so Fitzsimmons took the warning seriously and ceased for a while. Spahn was not a headhunter, but he knew he had to protect himself and his livelihood any way he could. He never had to fulfill the promise, but Fitzsimmons worried him. If he could read him other coaches could, too. He needed a new plan.

Teammate Bob Chipman, another left-handed hurler for the Braves, was in the last season of his 12-year, big-league career and was a three-year Spahn teammate in Boston. He was never a big winner, going 51–46 lifetime, but Spahn respected his mind and his baseball savvy. Spahn sought Chipman out for advice after the incident with Fitzsimmons. Since Chipman was not a fastball pitcher he had to employ off-speed pitches to survive.

"There's something I can't cover up with the pitch," Spahn told Chipman. "Those coaches see me lift a couple of fingers off the ball just as I get ready to throw it. What do I do?"[131]

Chipman suggested Spahn take another approach and not rely on his fingers so much.

"It's all in the wrist," Chipman said. "It's like you throw a screwball, a little push and a reverse move."[132]

Spahn adapted and the pitch helped him immensely by the end of the season and for years afterward. So the lefty was fine as the 1952 season ended, certainly looking forward to a better 1953 and beyond.

The Braves management, too, was glad to have this terrible year behind the team. The next season just had to be better. What perplexed the owners and general manager John Quinn was how to make it happen fast and regain the interest of the Boston fans.

At the very tail end of the season rumors began spreading the Braves might become the first franchise in more than fifty years to move to another city. Given that the club had been stationed in Boston since 1876, this was astonishing and it was not clear how many fans (however many there were) believed this idea. Boston newspapermen were sniffing hard.

One of the original Boston owners was now out of the picture and main owner Lou Perini was reportedly buying up most of the stock that was out there. Since 1903, two years after the American League established itself as another major league alongside the National League, there had been eight teams in each league with several cities operating two franchises. The

Federal League had come along for a couple of seasons just before World War I, but none of the stable AL or NL teams had yielded.

The sixteen teams from 1903 on were rocks, locked into place, permanent features in Major League Baseball. Post–World War II American society was in transition in several ways, from television sets taking over living rooms to seemingly every household (at least those not in downtown centers) owning automobiles. The country was on the move, baseball remained the pre-eminent sport, and some growing cities wanted the designation of being viewed as big-league.

Bill Veeck was owner of the Cleveland Indians when the team won the World Series in 1948 with record-setting attendance. He was a maverick with creative ideas, and he regularly tweaked staid ownership. He had to sell off the Indians but soon was back in baseball as the owner of the St. Louis Browns. Veeck took over in 1951 but soon realized he was running a failing operation, one that could not compete with the St. Louis Cardinals.

Veeck had been a wildly popular owner of the minor-league Milwaukee franchise during World War II. City fathers in Milwaukee, desperate to attract a major-league team, built a ballpark, County Stadium, on spec, hoping the ready-made building would help convince a team to shift to Milwaukee. Veeck was ready. There was one key obstacle, however, besides the other owners' vote. The Boston Braves owned the minor-league team at that time and therefore owned the rights to the territory.

Milwaukee wanted Veeck to come, but city officials weren't that fussy as long as they landed a team. Boston refused to surrender its rights to the area without a payment of $500,000.

Most of these goings-on percolated somewhat in the background. When the Braves concluded their 1952 losing season with the city mostly ignoring the team, there were no outward discussions about the Braves not being back in Boston for 1953. The players scattered to their offseason homes and offseason jobs.

As far as anyone knew, all of the attention focused on Milwaukee's desire to obtain a major-league club was just talk.

13

THE BRAVES MOVE TO MILWAUKEE

WARREN SPAHN HAD a new baseball address in 1953. So did all of his teammates. Following the gloomy 1952 season, owner Lou Perini negotiated with Milwaukee officials who were clamoring for a major-league team.

Discussions went on all winter and into spring training and still the Braves were scheduled to open the season representing Boston. And then it became official. A deal was struck and the Braves, so long a Boston institution, were headed to the Midwest, superseding a longtime successful minor-league team and shaking up the National League.

The Boston franchise moved to Milwaukee, giving up baked beans and clam chowder for beer and Wisconsin cheese. No major-league team had abandoned a city in the previous half-century of American League and National League play. The 1950s would become the decade of change and realignment for the big leagues. Soon enough the St. Louis Browns located to Baltimore. The Philadelphia Athletics moved to Kansas City. Suddenly, New York, always a three-team major-league city, was dumped by the Brooklyn

Dodgers, on to Los Angeles, and the New York Giants, who became the San Francisco Giants.

All of these teams were suffering in the shadow of another alpha team in their home city, unable to keep up or learning there were not enough baseball fans to split up. The Browns could not compete financially with the Cardinals. The Athletics were simply living on the edge of their financial means. The Dodgers and Giants chased West Coast gold. The country's population was growing, and Los Angeles and San Francisco were definitely big-league cities. Dodgers owner Walter O'Malley looked westward, as if following Horace Greeley's advice to a young man, and believed he was latching onto a rainbow. Horace Stoneham's Giant fans in New York were aging and not being replenished. For travel reasons, there had to be two West Coast teams to make the entire situation work. California was big enough to accommodate two, even if they were 400 miles rather than a borough apart.

Milwaukee started the dominoes falling. The city was hungry for major-league ball and not that picky about whether or not the team that chose to hang its shingle next to Miller High Life beer signs was a good one or a bad one. The Braves were no bargain on the field in 1952 despite having several attractive talented players, either established or on the way up. That did not matter in the short run. All the Braves were asked to be was present. All Milwaukee—and regional—baseball fans wanted at first was to be able to reach out and touch the merchandise to ascertain it was real, as long as the occasional autograph was thrown in, too.

Perini was born and grew up in Boston and had always been loyal to his city's ballclubs. He was fortunate enough to inherit a construction company that made him rich enough to become the key member of the ownership group that purchased the Braves. Above all he wanted the Braves to be a success—and in 1948 helped deliver the organization's first pennant in thirty-four years—and just as hungrily he wanted the Braves to be a popular and financial success, in Boston.

But the total indifference shown to his team in 1952 was astonishing and put him in a bind. To draw just 281,000 fans for an entire season was such a blow it wobbled the underpinnings of the franchise. It made Perini susceptible to sweet talk from Milwaukee suitors. Much of the discussion about the Braves switching allegiances from Boston to Milwaukee took place out of the public eye. Essentially, Perini was being jilted by Boston, being told by his wife that he was not needed anymore. He was being pointed in the direction of divorce court, although it was up to him to file the papers.

As is typical of the breakup of any major relationship, one party is more aggrieved than the other. Perini did not want a divorce. He wanted to make things work. Yet he had no solution for how to convince the other side to remain devoted. He had blown through his entreaties and was running on empty. Even so, he was reluctant to take an irrevocable step. Despite the one-in-the-hand offer from Milwaukee, Perini wanted to wait and see for another year in Boston.

As the owner of Milwaukee's minor-league team, the Brewers, Perini had first dibs on the territory, a poker hand that trumped anyone else if he chose to exercise his power. Bill Veeck, the popular owner of the St. Louis Browns, who had a residue of good will in Milwaukee from his 1940s operations of the minor-league club, wanted to move to Milwaukee and make everyone's dreams come true—his, the city of Milwaukee, and the Wisconsin baseball fan.

The Browns outdrew the Braves in 1952, with 518,796 clicking the turnstiles, although that was still last in the American League. The team's record of 64–90 didn't help matters, but the attendance was nearly twice as good as the Browns' numbers of 1951. Veeck believed if he remained in St. Louis, the Cardinals and their big-stick bank account wielded by new owners Anheuser-Busch would crush him.

Veeck struck out on Milwaukee but was still in a bind. So he proposed moving the team to Baltimore, replacing the longtime minor-league affiliation there and renewing the harbor town's affiliation with big-league ball for the first time since 1903 when the Orioles became the New York Highlanders, who became the New York Yankees.

But Veeck needed the approval of the other American League owners, who as a group disliked him. He was a rabble-rouser, and they were staid conservatives. He insulted them. So now that he needed those same guys to bail him out, there was no sympathy for this devil and they blocked any move that would rescue Veeck. They would be glad to see him go. As a result, Veeck sold the Browns and only then did the American League move into Baltimore.

So as a by-product of Perini's slow-moving talks with Milwaukee, Veeck was out of the picture. Perini finally decided to pull the plug on Boston, and he sought a hearing before the other owners to make a quick move. It was so late, so close to the early April start of the season, Commissioner Ford Frick tried to put everything on hold.

Perini called a press conference in Florida on March 14 to make an announcement. He had waited so long into the offseason that Boston sportswriters thought he was about to announce a player trade rather than something of this magnitude. He startled all when he said, "This was a difficult decision to make, but we've made up our minds to take the team into Milwaukee."[133]

This was jaw-dropping news and not popular with the Boston papers and however many Braves fans there still were in Boston. Perini said he had only made up his mind to take the plunge a couple of days earlier. Frick said he had not heard anything was in the works until two days before. Apparently, though, Perini had been sounding out the other owners who were against Veeck's move to see where they might stand on his. It was like working the back hallways of Congress before legislation reached the floor for a vote.

Frick was not happy about the developments, but after reading the fine print in his contract and baseball rule books, and probably getting advice from the Supreme Court, he realized he had no power to intercede and order the Braves to stay in Boston. Frick did not actually oppose the move in theory, but only in practice because it was such a rush job so near to the start of the season. He had used the same reasoning with Veeck's hope to move to Baltimore for the 1953 season.

"And I oppose this move by Perini because of its untimeliness," Frick said. "Not for the good of baseball, mind you, since I think this has to happen in the new alignment of baseball. I have no power to do anything unless there is a disagreement among the owners."[134]

At about that time Perini called the Braves together for a meeting in the locker room at spring training and told them what he was up to and why.

"You know, you fellows come in looking for more money and we couldn't give it," he said. "I have picked up a check for over $1 million since owning the Braves. I think you will have a better outlook if we get our franchise moved to Milwaukee."[135]

It was said the players applauded. If so, they were clapping for their future prospects, a belief they would be paid higher salaries in a more welcoming environment. It did not seem as if any Braves were nostalgic about leaving Boston.

After the refusal of the American League owners to permit Veeck to move to Baltimore immediately and Frick's stance against a quick shift, some sportswriters were handicapping Perini's chances of getting the approval he needed to move right away as 60–40. They, along with many baseball observers, especially those in New England, were surprised when the owners gave their unanimous assent and the Boston Braves were no longer.

The Braves were in the middle of an exhibition game against the New York Yankees in St. Petersburg on March 18 when word trickled down to the dugout the deal had been sealed. A *New York Times* columnist on the scene wrote, "Somewhere around the fifth inning of today's game with the Yankees, the Boston Braves learned they were wearing the wrong uniforms. The Boston lettering on their shirt fronts was in error. They had just become the Milwaukee Braves. It was almost as if Plymouth Rock had been uprooted and moved out to Wisconsin."[136] No doubt that would have provoked more ire and angst than the Braves' departure did.

Charlie Grimm had taken over as Braves manager from Tommy Holmes during the 1952 season. Known as "Jolly Cholly" because of his outgoing personality, Grimm was a baseball lifer with considerable allegiance to the Chicago Cubs over the decades. During the 1940s, when Veeck owned the Milwaukee minor-league team, Grimm managed it and was an extremely popular fellow in town.

Upon hearing the Braves were headed to his old stomping grounds, Grimm was pleased, saying, "Those Dutchmen out there are the greatest fans in the world. Give them a bottle of beer and a good ballgame and they'll stay happy."[137]

Grimm was right about that, too.

Perini was better liked than his peers than Veeck was by his and was able to persuade the NL owners of his need to go. By 1953, Branch Rickey had shifted from the Dodgers to the Pittsburgh Pirates, which he sought to rebuild and he looked at the big picture when supporting Perini.

"I hope it's a good move," Rickey said. "The welfare of baseball at large is more important than that of any one club."[138]

It may have been a good move for baseball, but the timing was definitely questionable for Warren Spahn's financial health. Many prominent athletes have invested in partnerships where their names adorn restaurants as a selling point. Spahn had just poured $30,000 into a restaurant located across the street from Braves Field when he learned the Braves would no longer be playing there and he would no longer be the best-known occupant of the ballpark. It was going to be tougher for him to lure business to the restaurant from 1,000 miles away.

For a guy whose nickname was "Hook" and who was on the hook for this deal, Spahn chose to publicly control his reaction when approached by sportswriters.

"If the business [the restaurant] is there, it will go," he said. "My partner called me the minute he got the news and we talked it over. I can't step out now. I'll have to be his partner long-distance." Teammates aware of Spahn's new business venture teased him about the change in the situation, saying, "If it's on wheels, you can roll it out to Milwaukee."[139]

Braves players were more shocked than dismayed. They tried to digest the team shift by putting it in personal terms of whether or not it would be better for them. They really weren't sure because few of them had much acquaintanceship with Milwaukee other than as a minor-league stop. Even if the players had passed through with the Brewers, or played there against them, none of the players had played at County Stadium.

County Stadium was the community ace, the building built to show Major League Baseball it was serious about obtaining a big-league club. That is a tremendous commitment for a city to make and it paid off for Milwaukee. The new ballpark was owned by the county and the cost to construct it was $4,843,000, financed by a bond issue.

The Braves would be the main tenant, but Milwaukee hoped to lure the Green Bay Packers to town, too. For many years the Packers did play some home games each year at County Stadium, but the team never abandoned its Green Bay roots and eventually gave up playing any home games out of town. When the stadium opened it was designed to hold 35,701 but carried the boast that it could be expanded to 76,000 seats eventually. That never occurred. There was going to be a shortage of parking from the get-go with 7,000 spaces available. But Milwaukee was already looking into overflow parking arrangements.

Young Eddie Mathews, the team's promising third baseman who broke in at twenty in 1952, had passed through the Triple-A Milwaukee team in 1951, though he played just 12 games there. "I don't know if this is good or bad," Mathews said of the announced move. "I'll just have to keep swinging, I guess."[140] That was always the best policy for the slugger who retired with 512 career home runs.

Sibby Sisti, who first appeared in a Braves uniform representing Boston in 1939 at age eighteen, thought he had seen it all until this earth-shaking change. "I outlasted a lot of ballplayers, managers, coaches, sportswriters, umpires in Boston. Now I've outlasted the town."[141]

Perini agonized over his decision. He was a Bostonian through and through. Now he was going to be perceived as Benedict Arnold by many. As soon as word spread about the move Perini began receiving telegraphed pleas from Boston's mayor and Massachusetts's governor. But he had already thought things through on his lonesome without sentimental begging. He had reduced his circumstances to business, to a dollars and cents equation. He built buildings, and he had built on the family fortune. He had no desire to swing a wrecking ball at either office buildings or the family bank account.

"Somebody has to tell me why this isn't a good move," Perini said. "I'm sick of pounding my head against a stone wall. This is no sudden thing. I've known for two years this was inevitable. Boston is simply not a two-club city."[142]

It was not accurate to say Perini had known he was going to move the Braves to Milwaukee for two years. Maybe for two months. He might have had an inkling he was going to have to move the Braves somewhere to survive. He had concluded Boston could not support the Red Sox and the Braves. He knew fans liked Fenway Park better than Braves Field, and he knew the Red Sox had Ted Williams in the lineup. As long as No. 9 was draped over his back and not a retired number on the wall of the Green Monster, the Braves would never outdraw the Red Sox.

Might that have changed? Perini did wonder. He knew his team was improving and was going to be better in 1953 than it had been in 1952. Neither his scouts nor his crystal ball was accurate enough to tell him that in 1954 (still two long seasons away), he too would have on his roster one of the greatest ballplayers of all time. But

Henry Aaron's rookie year was in the future and Perini needed cash now.

Perini did not even consult with his family or let his wife and children know he was contemplating such a major change.

"Oh, there were so many things," Perini said. "This move affects a lot of people. But remember, it affected me first. My family, my friends up in New England. That's why I waited so long to move. It was a weighty problem."[143]

There was gloom in Boston but delirium in Milwaukee. Major League Baseball stamped Milwaukee as a big-league city. This was tremendously satisfying to the egos of those who threw so much energy behind the effort and gambled by ponying up the money for County Stadium. It wasn't as if Milwaukee was tiny. In the 1950 census, the population was 637,392 and it was still growing. For as cosmopolitan as the United States's largest cities could be, they could be very provincial in attitude. Many sophisticated New Yorkers probably could not locate Milwaukee on the map because it did not seem worth the effort to try. That superior sensibility led to them thinking anyone who lived west of the Hudson River and south of Washington, DC, was probably a hick.

Indeed, the big-city newspapermen, not only those in Boston, rallied behind Beantown by hurling insults at Milwaukee as a "bush" town. That was the ultimate insult in Wisconsin. Because the city had no major-league track record, it was dismissed before the Braves even showed up.

One thing Milwaukee was known for was good beer, and beer did play a role in wooing the Braves west. Fred Miller, who owned Miller Brewing, played the sponsorship card that helped Perini make up his mind.

When the Braves traveled north from spring training they did not know what awaited them in Milwaukee. They were stunned when an estimated 60,000 to 80,000 people greeted them as the train pulled into town. Players transferred to convertibles and paraded through the city to downtown as fans cheered wildly. Comparisons were made to ticker-tape parades for World Series champs. The Braves were 0–0. This was wild stuff, and the players were blown away. Their first impression of their new fans was off the charts. Spahn and other players were besieged for autographs. Talk about a feeling of being welcomed home—to a new home.

"I'm gambling on Milwaukee becoming a great Major League city," Perini said.[144]

The season was scheduled to open April 14 at County Stadium versus the St. Louis Cardinals. About 29,000 tickets were sold in advance and then 7,500 bleacher tickets went on sale a week before the game. The line snaked through the parking lot, and when the box office opened at 9 a.m. workers were overwhelmed, selling out the remaining seats.

Showing up for the parade was free. Buying tickets for Opening Day cost. It seemed this love for the Braves would translate into attendance at the ballpark.

Did these burst-upon-the-scene erstwhile Boston Braves make Milwaukee residents feel big league after all? You bet it did, before the parade was even over.

"The team satisfies the ego of our population," said Mayor Frank Zeidler, and the team likely satisfied the mayor's ego as well. "We have long felt we are capable people, but because of our peculiar geography, tucked away as we are behind Lake Michigan, our voice has not been heard in the land. This is a means of letting people know we exist."[145]

14

THE LOVE AFFAIR BEGINS

THE ABSOLUTE, BLIND adoration directed toward the Braves by Milwaukee baseball fans bordered on lunacy. There is infatuation. There is love. And there is flat-out complete devotion.

Publicly, Warren Spahn, who was the Braves' best player, was diplomatic about the team's exit from Boston. He was no doubt lamenting the effect on his restaurant more than he let on. But he liked the place just fine. Although he and wife LoRene had a home in Oklahoma, they also had accommodations in Boston during the season and that season lasted half of the year.

"I broke into the majors in Boston, and LoRene and I had an apartment up there which we used during the season," Spahn said. "I guess I have kind of a sentimental attachment for the place."[146]

That was a fairly low-key emotional response. There was nothing low-key about the way Milwaukee adopted the Braves. Although Braves players did not know what to expect from their new city, they did have a basis for comparison. Boston's almost complete indifference to the team during the 1952 season was the equivalent of a six-month-long nap. Milwaukee's embrace was so enthusiastic it could be compared to receiving a long-lost relative known previously only by reputation.

The players were supplied with cases of beer by their lockers, something appreciated by many of the hard-drinking players. They were recognized everywhere they went. If a Braves player was spotted in a bar he was treated to drinks. If he walked into a restaurant he was treated to a meal. Free clothing was provided at men's stores. It was as if everyone's birthday was every day.

These days it would seem ludicrous for fans to shower players with gifts since every member of the team, including the least compensated of the twenty-five players, is making at least a half-million dollars per season and most of the players much more than that. But in the early 1950s some players made $7,000 a year, and the richest players were probably being paid $25,000 or so. Actually, Spahn made $30,000 in 1952, but when he posted his losing record, his salary was cut by $5,000 for the 1953 season.

Beyond the monetary value, the welcome-to-Milwaukee gifts were symbolic. It was almost as if the Braves were a liberating army, so pleased was the populace to see them parading down the street in those convertibles. The mobs of fans cheering at the sight of the Braves represented an announcement: We've been waiting for you, and we're glad you're here.

The reception was so overwhelming the Braves were taken aback. They felt they hadn't done anything to deserve this worship. They hadn't played a game yet and they were beloved. So amazed were the players they felt they had an obligation to win, or at least put on a good show. The baseball fans were so supportive it seemed they had been wandering in the desert for forty years like Moses, just waiting for big-league ball to come to town.

Even the most joyful of expansion cities that followed did not manage such enthusiastic welcomes. From the beginning, obtaining

Braves tickets was almost like purchasing a winning lottery ticket. Demand was so high County Stadium was jammed from the beginning of the season on. This wasn't a show-me town. This was a seller's market. Lou Perini had a product his customers were so hot to buy they probably would have filled a stadium twice as large, a Cleveland Municipal Stadium–sized ballpark, the one in the projected plans that dreamed of expansion to 76,000.

It should also be recalled Milwaukee was getting a loser, a 64–89 team. The Braves of 1952 were a lousy team with a roster burdened with so many shortcomings that not much could be expected of its year-later successor. Warren Spahn was an established pitching star, but even he was coming off his worst year, that 14–19 mark. Lew Burdette was about to become somebody, but nobody could be sure of that. Third baseman Eddie Mathews was headed for the Hall of Fame, but at twenty that was not yet apparent. Shortstop Johnny Logan was a firebrand. Sid Gordon was still around hitting well.

Manager Charlie Grimm was a good front man for the club with his built-in following in Milwaukee. Charlie could talk up a storm, and he would have been excellent at selling beach-front property in Florida. Boy, those Milwaukee fans wanted to believe him, but really, what was he selling coming off 1952? We're going to be better, Grimm, Perini, and general manager John Quinn kept saying. But it was an article of faith until the season began.

On paper there were pluses. Del Crandall was now in as the permanent catcher. Outfielder Billy Bruton, a superb fielder and baserunner, was up from the minors and he already had friends in Milwaukee. Bruton had played for the Brewers in 1952 and batted .325. Slugging first baseman Joe Adcock was acquired from Cincinnati and his best years were ahead of him. Outfielder Andy Pafko was past thirty, but he had made four All-Star teams for the Chicago Cubs before a brief stint with the Dodgers. There was no question the everyday lineup should be better.

The Braves foresaw a bright future for Mathews, but they needed another strong bat near him in the order and coveted Pafko. For a time it seemed possible Quinn was going to do the unthinkable and trade Spahn to Brooklyn for Pafko, primarily because the GM was spooked by Spahn's 14–19 mark. Rumors were rampant throughout the baseball world the Braves were going to part ways with the southpaw. The *Sporting News* mentioned it.

It was said not only Pafko but solid-hitting outfielder Carl Furillo, third baseman Bobby Cox, and $500,000 would go from Brooklyn to the Braves for Spahn, who at that time over the winter were still located in Boston.

Spahn heard the talk and when he ran into Dodger manager Charlie Dressen at one of those formerly ubiquitous winter baseball dinners, he asked him point-blank if he was headed to his team.

"Don't look like it," Dressen said. "We offered them half the ballclub for you and they wanted the uniforms, too."[147]

Likewise, the pitching rotation seemed likely to improve. Spahn was not going to have another off-year. Bonus baby Johnny Antonelli won 12 games. Burdette did indeed demonstrate the Yankees had made a silly mistake by letting him go, and he won 15 games. Newcomer Bob Buhl broke in at age twenty-four with a 13–8 record and was about to spend the next decade of his life representing the Braves in Milwaukee. Oh, and Max Surkont was actually better than ever that debut season in the Midwest, going 11–5.

This was very much a revamped team. No one could be sure these guys would perform at such a high level, but they amazed the National League with their reversal of team fortune, going from 64 victories to 92. The Braves were in the pennant hunt. Milwaukee fans got what they paid for. If the Braves won the pennant, the happy mayor's head probably would have exploded.

Initially, the relationship between the fans and the Braves was one-sided. The fans offered unconditional love. The Braves responded with wide-eyed wonder. The rewards began when the season began.

The Braves started the 1953 season with a single game on the road at Cincinnati. Surkont pitched a complete-game, three-hitter as the Braves won 2–0 at Crosley Field in less than two hours. Bruton, Gordon, and Surkont himself each knocked out two hits.

Milwaukee's party began the next day with the home opener at County Stadium. It was a day game and all 34,357 tickets were sold. Befitting the atmosphere and the special nature of the occasion, the Braves kept on selling tickets anyway and it was estimated standing room brought the crowd to 45,000. That year box seats cost $3.50 and grandstand tickets cost $1.50. Getting them was the big problem. The average American's income was $3,139.

Appropriately, Spahn was handed the ball by Grimm to face the St. Louis Cardinals' steady Gerry Staley who was about to embark on his best season of 18–9 at age thirty-two. The right-handed Staley was on his game this day and so was Spahn.

"I was so anxious to make good for those people that if the tension were any more terrific I'd have blown my top," Spahn said. "If these people can't make a guy win, I don't know what will."[148]

A good fastball and curve always helped and Spahn had his stuff working fine that day. Also, as he learned in 1952, it was handy to have teammates push across some runs if you wanted to win. Despite the karma in the air, despite Spahn pitching well, despite how important it felt to win the first game in Milwaukee, victory did not come easily.

The Braves scored one run in the bottom of the second. Adcock singled, and when Crandall singled and the play was compounded by Cards third baseman Ray Jablonski's error, Milwaukee was on the board. The Cardinals touched Spahn for a run in the fifth. Future Hall of Fame outfielder Enos Slaughter walked. Slaughter was a good runner. Spahn had him picked off first but threw the ball away for an error, sending Slaughter to second base. Jablonski singled, and Slaughter sped around to score. That made it 1–1.

Milwaukee scratched out another run in the bottom of the eighth for a 2–1 lead. Bruton tripled, and Gordon drove him home a few batters later. Things were looking good for the happy crowd until St. Louis fought back again with a run in the top of the ninth inning. There were two outs when Jablonski stroked a single. Pitcher Harvey Haddix pinch-ran for Jablonski, and Peanuts Lowery pinch-hit for outfielder Ray Repulski. St. Louis's manager was old Braves friend Eddie Stanky, whose strategy worked.

Staley set down three Braves in order in the bottom of the ninth sending the game into extra innings. Neither starting pitcher was wilting, and they both stayed in the game for the extra frame. Staley led off the 10th and singled off Spahn, but he died on the bases. Spahn was the leadoff man for the Braves in their half of the inning, and he tried bunting for a hit but was thrown out. Bruton came up at the top of the order and *boom!* He blasted a home run out of the park on the right-field side for the winning run.

Braves 3, St. Louis 2. Spahn went 10 innings while permitting just six hits and two earned runs. Staley went 9 1/3 and also gave up just six hits. Three of those hits were produced by Bruton's bat. Bruton did not hit another home run all season.

Spahn had done a yeoman's job on the mound, performing at a high level by anyone's standards, but he knew the Braves fans were behind him from the time he threw his first pitch ever at County Stadium to St. Louis leadoff man Solly Hemus. That pitch was a strike and it was one of the most admired strikes of all time.

"I threw the first pitch," Spahn said, "and a tremendous roar came from the crowd. I looked up to see what was going on and then I stepped off the rubber and looked behind me." Sometimes a pitcher will get distracted by some kind of fan action, a rhubarb in the stands, or something of that ilk. Spahn did not notice anything out of the ordinary going on. "Then I realized that all they were screaming about was the called strike."[149]

It was like that all of the time for the Braves, the heroes who could do no wrong, even when they did lose a game or strike out. Fan enthusiasm would have raised the roof if County Stadium had one like the subsequent Milwaukee stadium, Miller Park, named for the local beer company.

Spahn had bickered with Perini over his contract in the previous offseason. He was disappointed when asked to take the pay cut. Perini countered with an unusual offer. He said Spahn should either take the $25,000 or take a risk of pitching for 10 cents for every customer who bought a ticket. As pitifully as the Braves drew in 1952 with that approximately 281,000 figure it would have translated to $28,000. Spahn still said no.

That was all before the announcement the team was moving to Milwaukee, an unknown in itself. It did not take long for Spahn to realize he had made a miscalculation. The Braves were on their way to drawing 1,826,397 fans, a National League–leading total. That would have been a heck of a raise for Spahn.

That standing-room-only crowd for the opener impressed the Braves, with Sibby Sisti cracking that he didn't think the Braves drew that many fans all year at Braves Field. Logan observed that the heat was on the Braves to win.

"Better imagine what it'll be like if we lose a few," he said. "They're liable to tear us limb from limb and ship us back to Boston."[150]

That was the one thing Milwaukee was not going to do given how much angst, sweat, and effort went into obtaining a major-league team.

Sam Jethroe, the first African American player for the Braves and who integrated the team in Boston, was no longer with the club. George Crowe continued to play for the Braves in Milwaukee as a backup and was one of two African Americans on the team—along with Billy Bruton—in a very white community. By all accounts, Milwaukee was a racially tolerant city, especially if you were affiliated with the Braves. Milwaukee and the state of Wisconsin were predominantly white, and the black players may have been curiosities as much as anything. But if they were good enough for the Braves they were good enough for the people of Milwaukee.

As did many players of the era, Bruton, who first lived in Alabama and then Delaware, got a late start in pro ball because of World War II service. He was spotted as a prospect by Judy Johnson, the Negro Leagues Hall of Famer, whose daughter he married and in whose home he later lived after Johnson died in 1989.

When he was a youth, especially in segregated Alabama, Bruton aspired to play pro ball, but Major League Baseball was also segregated then. Much later, with the Braves, Bruton was on the road for a public relations appearance with the team's media relations director Bob Allen and they shared a hotel room.

Allen was surprised when Bruton climbed out of bed, dropped to his knees, and said his prayers.

"He told me that when he was a kid he was a good ballplayer and he'd always wished he could play in the major leagues, but that he knew it'd never happen," Allen said. Bruton added, "Now I play beside Hank Aaron and Warren Spahn and I make a lot of money. So every night I thank the Good Lord for being so kind to me and my family."[151]

Bruton stood 6 feet tall but barely weighed 170 pounds. He batted left-handed but was no slugger. He was a brilliant gloveman in center field and hard to cut down on the bases. Between 1953 and 1955, the Braves' first three seasons in Milwaukee, Bruton led the NL in stolen bases all three times. He swiped 26, 34, and 25 and kept opposing pitchers jittery. He knew his strength was in his legs, not his wrists.

"A home run didn't use my speed," Bruton said. "It left the bases empty. I could intimidate the pitcher more by being on base. They knew I would run, but they didn't know when. That kept them from total concentration on the next hitters."[152]

As a rookie, Grimm was generous with Bruton's freedom to take off. He recognized Bruton, who was already twenty-seven, was no neophyte and Grimm himself was no whiz on the basepaths as a player. Grimm could hit, but he stole just 57 bases in a 20-year playing career.

"You're in the majors," Grimm told Bruton. "You should know when to steal and when not to. You know the pitcher better than I do."[153] So Grimm let Bruton fly at will.

Bruton did bat .273 lifetime in twelve years in the majors, but it was difficult to tell if he took more pride in his patrolling of center or his impact on the bases.

"It used to gall me to see those little bloopers fall in there," he said, "when the batter gets fooled and holds up his swing and then nubs the ball over the infield. I played the position as good as anybody."[154]

Bruton cracked two hits in the opener at Cincinnati and in addition to the game-winning, walk-off homer at County Stadium the next day he added two more hits. When he was first asked by a scribe what he enjoyed most about those two days, Bruton tried to go down the path of explaining what a charge he got out of catching fly balls. But then he took the listener through the home run at-bat.

"Staley threw a knuckler," Bruton said, "and it seemed to hang in there, straight at me. So I swung."[155]

And immediately became a good friend of Warren Spahn.

Another big addition—and big works here in more than one way—was Adcock, the 6-foot-4, 210-pound first baseman. Adcock made the majors in 1950 and played three seasons for the Cincinnati Reds.

He did a good job, but Ted Kluszewski, a Reds legend, had a stranglehold on first base. Adcock knew he was a natural first baseman and did not enjoy playing the outfield. He did not really break out as a star until becoming a full-time starter at first base for the Braves in 1953. That year he became a major plus in Milwaukee by bashing 18 home runs with 80 runs batted in and a .285 batting average. He was just settling in, too, and soon enough improved on those career-best numbers. What is often overlooked about Adcock is that he was also a superior fielder. Over 16 seasons, Adcock faced 13,968 chances and made just 83 errors for a career fielding percentage of .994, one of the best ever.

The most remarkable thing about Adcock's baseball career was that it did not even begin until he entered Louisiana State

University, the flagship college in his home state. The town of Coushatta, population 500, offered no baseball play for its boys. Basketball was the game, and Adcock was good enough at that sport to be offered a scholarship by LSU. Adcock was a terrific basketball player, and the New York Knicks of the young NBA requested his services. But he liked baseball better. There was good reason to think so since he collected six hits in seven at-bats in his first college doubleheader.

Adcock, who owned a notable southern drawl, said he turned his mother and sister into baseball fans because of his success, but he often had to translate the symbols in a box score for them. In baseball's offseason Adcock was an outdoorsman, especially fond of hunting. He once told a sportswriter a story that sounded just like a country song's lyrics. "My bird dog got run over by a car just last Saturday. Sure hated to lose him. He was a good one. You sure can get attached to those dogs. I guess I'll have to get me another one."[156]

Adcock solidified his reputation as the wielder of a big bat early in the Braves' first season in Milwaukee. The team was on the road at the Polo Grounds just two weeks into the campaign on April 29 when Adcock added his name to the old park's lore. Spahn was on the mound in a tense game versus the Giants. Jim Hearn was on the mound for the Giants.

In the third inning, Adcock came up with Andy Pafko on base and launched a two-run homer. The ball was the first ever hit into the center field bleachers in a ballpark that had been around for decades. If the stands had not intervened the ball might have been spotted going into orbit around the moon by astronomers' telescopes. Milwaukee—and Spahn—won that game 3–2.

Spahn had won at least 21 games for the Braves three times in Boston. The 1952 season represented a stumble, but he knew he could be as good as ever as long as he had hitting support. After the game-winning home run by Bruton, Spahn asked him where had he been the year before.

On May 30, the Braves' record was 24–12 and they were leading the National League standings. They had been flirting with first place for weeks and of course the Milwaukee fans responded, drawing more people to County Stadium by far nearly every game than they did on their best days in Boston.

"I've got to watch out they don't smother us with kindness, beer, and sauerbraten," Grimm said.[157]

15

A SURPRISE PENNANT RACE

THE PEOPLE OF Milwaukee just wanted a team. They didn't care what kind of major-league team or where it came from. If it was going to be a team transferring from another city then they had to expect it would be a loser. The prospects were the St. Louis Browns and the Boston Braves, and they were among the worst teams in baseball in 1952.

So when the Braves turned out to be good, with no rebuilding period, no warning really, it was all a bonus. The 1953 Milwaukee Braves were the surprise of the sport. Basically overnight the Braves went from a team flirting with last place to one flirting with first place.

The year before Warren Spahn could muster just a 14–19 record despite an earned average of 2.98. The Braves did not score runs for him. In 1953, Spahn was brilliant and the Braves scored bushels of runs. The combination produced fabulous results. Spahn went 23–7 with a 2.10 earned run average, the finest single-season record of his career.

The Braves pounded the horsehair off of the ball, bashing so many home runs people had to duck when sluggers came to the plate. The balls descended from the sky with such rapidity it was like hail.

In 1952, Eddie Mathews was an exciting prospect. In 1953, he was one of the most terrorizing hitters in the game. The Braves bombardment started with him. That season he clubbed 47 home runs and drove in 135 runs. But he was one of only six players in the starting lineup who clubbed double-figure amounts of homers. Sid Gordon again came through, bashing 19 home runs. Joe Adcock hit 18. Andy Pafko smacked 17. Del Crandall contributed 15 and even Johnny Logan ripped 11. The offense manufactured about 150 more runs than the pitching staff allowed.

Spahn started the season 8–1, benefiting from the luxury of good run support, as well as his own sharpness. The abrupt transformation of the Braves' lineup made all of the difference. He could actually afford to give up a run here and there. Mathews's maturation at twenty-one was a huge factor. He hit .301 that season, as well as leading the National League in homers, and made his first All-Star team. Mathews had been a nice addition in 1952, but he was one of the best players in the league in 1953 with his level left-handed stroke just smoking the ball. If not flying out of the park, the ball was leaving dents in outfield walls.

"Poor Warren Spahn," Mathews called the pitcher of 1952. "Charlie Grimm didn't pitch him at the end of the season because they didn't want a 20-game loser. But it had nothing to do with Spahn. It was the terrible ball club we had."[158]

Although it was not literally the case, it almost seemed as if Mathews decided to fix the run-scoring problem all by his lonesome. This was a guy who became a nine-time All-Star, broke the 500-homer barrier, and five times drove in more than 100 runs in a 17-year career. This season he was still learning what it was all about.

Accounts of Mathews's early behavior in Milwaukee suggested the college-aged young man was just like a college kid. He reveled in his athletic success and spent his free time drinking beer. Apparently, the younger Mathews had quite a temper, too, and didn't mind mixing it up with fisticuffs anywhere anyone would oblige. Maturity and better fielding, which would come, lay over the horizon. But at 6-foot-1 and 190 pounds, he definitely had a man's muscles.

The better the Braves played the more delirious the already-delirious fans got about them. Mathews recalled not being able to pay for anything in town, with cars assigned to players, clothing given to them, restaurant meals covered. Many of the players stayed in a downtown hotel and the local beer companies, not only Miller, kept sending over their products. Not only could the Braves never run out, they couldn't run low.

"We had to rent another room just for the beer," Mathews said, "because besides Miller there were other breweries—Blatz, Schlitz, Pabst."[159]

This wasn't just a fast start, momentum out of the gate, for the Braves. They sustained their winning pace, hovering in or around first place. As of July 12, the beginning of the All-Star break, the Braves' record was 49–33 and they were in second place, 1 1/2 games behind the Brooklyn Dodgers.

The All-Star Game was played on July 14 at Crosley Field in Cincinnati. Braves selections on the team were Spahn, Mathews, and catcher Del Crandall. Mathews started, while Spahn was in the bullpen. The Phillies' Robin Roberts started and went three innings for the National League. Billy Pierce started for the American League, but after he was lifted, the NL batters touched Allie Reynolds, Mike Garcia, and Satchel Paige for runs.

Spahn came into the game after Roberts, starting the fourth inning. He stuck around for two innings without giving up a hit or a run and walking just one batter, Mickey Mantle. Spahn got the win for the National League in the 5–1 game.

He kept rolling along that summer, each outing seemingly sharper than the one before. The atmosphere for home games was totally exuberant. Each day was an adventure at County Stadium. The Braves played well and while they played well on the road, too, the contrast in mood compared to Milwaukee devotion was distinct.

On August 1, the Braves were playing Philadelphia. The Phillies were involved in a solid 83–71 season, led by Hall of Fame outfielder Richie Ashburn, Del Ennis, and Granville Hamner. Spahn was on the mound before 23,791 County Stadium witnesses. Philadelphia's starter was Jim Konstanty who in 1950 had carried the Phillies to the pennant with his 16–7 record and remarkable performance when he pitched in 74 games, finished 62 of them, and notched 22 saves.

Right from the opening pitch this had the makings of a Spahn career day. His throws were crisp and he and Crandall were communicating well about what to throw next. Whatever he threw, the Phillies could not figure it out. As the Braves were ripping 12 hits, three by Andy Pafko, and including Mathews's 33rd home run, to pile up five runs, Philadelphia was flailing. Konstanty was gone after four, replaced by Karl Crews. But Spahn was in the zone.

It was three up, three down in the first for Philadelphia with Spahn collecting two strikeouts. It was nothing-doing in the second with two fly balls and a groundout. Philly went down on a foul popup and two groundouts in the third. In the fourth inning Ashburn hit a bounding ball to Braves shortstop Jim Pendleton. The fleet Ashburn was declared safe at first for an infield hit.

After the inning ended, Crandall teased Spahn by saying, "Well, there goes your no-hitter." Spahn replied, "Yeah, and a perfect game, too." The banter was light-hearted because at that early stage of a ballgame major-league pitchers are not thinking about a no-hitter.[160]

However, that was the only hit Spahn did allow the Phillies that day. Also, he did not walk a single batter. He finished with a one-hit, 5–0 triumph, complete with eight strikeouts. Ashburn's infield hit was the only thing that stood between Spahn and a perfect game that day.

Post-mortems dissected the Ashburn grounder from all angles. Ashburn was just about the fastest runner in the league, so that was bad luck for Spahn. The handling of the ball by Pendleton, filling in for Johnny Logan that day, including his throw, did not leave any room for an official scoring decision of an error. The only item for debate was whether Ashburn really beat the throw or the ball beat him to first baseman Joe Adcock.

"It probably could have been called either way," Spahn said, "but as long as he was safe, he had to get a hit."[161]

Sportswriters checked in with the first base umpire Larry Goetz for his view.

"The play was very close," Goetz said. "Pendleton hesitated just a little too long before he threw to first."[162]

Some speculated if Logan was in that day he would have made the play. But the situation seemed more like just one of those things that can't be controlled, everyone aware that high choppers frequently take a long time to come down.

Although the discussions looked more foolish by the day the way Spahn was pitching—14–4 after the one-hitter—the reason why the Braves talked about trading their ace was to provide protection in the batting order for Mathews. Braves officials feared he would be neutralized by teams intentionally walking him if he did not have other power hitters in the order around him.

Pafko was the main target in the Dodger trade talks, but he ended up in a Braves uniform without the high price of Spahn being involved. The Braves swapped second baseman Roy Hartsfield, plus $50,000, for Pafko. Although any member of the Braves had to do to become popular in Milwaukee was exist, the always gentlemanly Pafko was a popular player wherever he competed.

A lifetime .285 hitter and an outstanding fielder, Pafko played for four National League pennant winners in three cities: Brooklyn, Chicago, and Milwaukee. He was the Dodgers left fielder when New York's Bobby Thomson bashed his "Shot Heard 'Round the World" homer to swipe the pennant from under Brooklyn's noses at the Polo Grounds in 1951. All Pafko could do as he stood forlorn against the wall was watch the ball sail out of reach.

Braves front office executives were correct that Pafko was a good fit. He often batted next to Mathews in the order and turned in seven seasons for the club, his best one the first in 1953. Pafko joined the Braves just in time for the Milwaukee move and was blown away by the fan reception.

"Chicago gave me a start in the big leagues, a World Series check and the Pruschkettes, as loyal a fan club as you can find anywhere," Pafko said. "The Brooklyn Dodgers also passed me a fat World Series dividend. And nowhere in baseball will you see fans more rabid or more colorful than in Brooklyn. But I'll take Milwaukee.

"Coming to Milwaukee was the greatest thing that has happened to me in more than 10 years in the majors. Most of us Braves think Milwaukee is one of the best things that's happened to baseball."[163]

One thing magnified Pafko's connection to the new Braves and their new home: He was born in Wisconsin. He grew up on a farm in Boyceville, a town of about 1,000 people 280 miles northwest of

Milwaukee. Pafko knew his cheeses. Pafko said when a scout showed up to sign him to a Class D minor league deal at age nineteen it took him five minutes to abandon his dad's threshing machine and jump in the car for Eau Claire.

That first season for the Braves in Milwaukee Pafko was voted the fans' favorite player. He may have had a head start with that Boyceville background, but he was as grateful for the outpouring of support as any of the players were.

Pafko cited incident after incident of fan generosity and ardor from that first season. One day he encountered an elderly woman who waited an hour for an autograph by his car. He was barraged by fan mail, not only from Milwaukee and Wisconsin, but from many other states and other countries. He was most amused by personally written notes from little boys whose penmanship was of beginner quality, also frequently accompanied by misspellings, proof they wrote the letters themselves.

"They usually write fan mail in printed letters so large they hardly get a dozen words on a page," Pafko said. "It's fun to arrive in a town that hasn't had major-league ball for fifty-four years and to be deluged with mail from the youngsters—even when they write 'You are my favorit player and the Braves my favorit teem. Please send me some basballs bats and a picture. Also a glove.'"[164]

Pafko said he eventually answered all his fan mail except marriage proposals. He let his wife Ellen handle those.

During that first season in Milwaukee, Pafko said he and his wife received two automobiles to use. For a while they paid to park one at a gas station until the owner realized he was a member of the team and dropped the fee. Other people supplied free gasoline. The craziness of freebies only escalated from there. Gifts kept on coming. He was given a wheelbarrow full of flowers, a new suit with all of the accompanying clothing items, a pound of butter as one farmer to another (the fan aware of his background), and a tremendous mix of sausage and cheeses. But wait, there was more, including a television set, a clothes dryer, an outboard motor, and a power lawnmower. It was as if he won on a television game show.

"I think the groundskeeper at County Stadium is eyeing that power mower," Pafko said. "That's how big it is."[165]

The environment was so welcoming at the ballpark, it was not unlike going to your own birthday party every day. Pafko called the tractor given to Spahn for his Oklahoma ranch "about the size of a Greyhound bus. All of these gifts were wonderful, but not as wonderful as the spirit that prompted them."[166]

While all of this was going on in Milwaukee, sportswriters in Boston, New York, and Washington, DC were picking away at the place, insulting Milwaukee as a bush league town that didn't belong in the exalted National League. If visiting players only realized the Braves were being treated as royalty, they would have been jealous and all requested trades to Milwaukee.

On the afternoon of the home opener, a special ceremony was conducted at County Stadium, a day Pafko remembered as being chilly enough to require players to wear team jackets until game-time and fans to wrap up in blankets. The players were on the field for the National Anthem. Officials kept the American flag at half staff while "Taps" was played on behalf of the Boston Braves and then a thirty-five-piece band played the anthem. The players were moved, impressed, and reacted emotionally. Pafko said Spahn told him, "Andy, this is the biggest moment I've had in baseball. Bigger than playing the Indians in the World Series."[167]

The addition of the big boppers in the lineup was huge for the Braves, but at least as important was the influx of some new arms and the evolution of one pitcher in particular.

Twenty-four-year-old right-hander Bob Buhl was one of the new additions, a tough pitcher who never believed in giving a batter an extra inch of the plate and didn't mind knocking down any hitter who overstepped his rightful territory to cheat on the inside pitch. Buhl's philosophy was that if he hit the guy, he hit him, and maybe he would know better next time.

As a rookie Buhl went 13–8 with a 2.97 earned run average after toiling through some tough times in the minors and earlier in life. Buhl was from Saginaw, Michigan and had to go to work when he was a senior in high school after his father died. That delayed his graduation and being signed by the Chicago White Sox. After Buhl won 19 games his first year in the minors, he figured he was on a straight yellow brick road to success. But he stumbled with losing records for a couple of years after that. Buhl's arrangement with the White Sox was voided by Commissioner Happy Chandler because it was ruled he had signed prematurely. Buhl became a free agent and signed with the Braves.

Buhl was just what the Braves needed to buttress the pitching staff. He definitely brought attitude to the rotation. "I was mean on the mound," he said.[168]

In contrast to Spahn, Buhl's delivery to the plate did not look smooth. He even called his own motion herky-jerky. That contributed to his periodic wildness, but it also scared batters. Knowing Buhl would just as soon hit them with a pitch made some hitters shaky in the batter's box. Buhl possessed neither sympathy nor much understanding of hitters. His fastball was mighty good, but his performance as a batter was awful, one of the worst ever. He could hit a batter with the ball, but he couldn't hit the ball with a bat.

In 457 big-league games and 857 official at-bats, Buhl put together a lifetime average of .089. In 1962, when the Braves traded Buhl to the Chicago Cubs, he left Milwaukee on an 0-for-17 streak. He then went 0-for-70 for the Cubs. Buhl's all-time hot streak was going 5-for-25 for a .200 mark in 1958 in just 11 games. In a full season, he once hit as high as .163. In several others he was below .100. The designated hitter was invented to prevent players like Bob Buhl from ever coming to bat again.

When Charlie Dressen was managing the Braves he insisted every one of his players, including pitchers, practice sliding. He thought enhancement of that skill would pay off with runs. When Dressen challenged Buhl with the question of just how competent a slider he was, Eddie Mathews, Buhl's roommate and close friend interrupted and said, "How would he know? He never gets on base."[169]

Buhl was in the majors for three seasons before he struck a base hit, a double. A couple of years later he smacked another double. It is not true that any pitcher who ever surrendered a hit to Buhl was sent directly to the minors. "But let's face it, I'm a bad hitter," Buhl said.[170]

Buhl was getting paid to pitch and was a difference-maker for the Braves his first year. What the Braves may not have realized that year was that Ace No. 2 behind Spahn was already on the staff.

The man born Selva Lewis Burdette Jr. had a sparkling season for the 1953 Braves, going 15–5, although he started just 13 games. Throughout his career, sportswriters and others alternately referred to Burdette as either "Lew" or "Lou." They seemed to have used "Lou" because it was the more popular spelling, but the "Lew" spelling actually came from Burdette's middle name. The funniest part of the long-running confusion about Burdette's name is that when directly asked which way was the right way to spell it, Burdette said he didn't care.

Burdette was from Nitro, West Virginia, a community founded as the home for an explosives plant due to a gunpowder shortage for the United States when it entered World War I. It quickly but temporarily grew to house 35,000 people. About a century later the population was around 7,000 people. The New York Yankees found Burdette and signed him in 1947 after his World War II service, and he played for three different minor-league clubs that season as a twenty-year-old. He briefly appeared in two games for the Yankees in 1950 with a 0–0 record, but manager Casey Stengel sent him back to the minors.

Burdette was traded to the Boston Braves in 1951 and was used in just three games. In 1952, Burdette saw a lot of relief action, although his record was just 6–11. In 1953, everything was different for Burdette, just as it was for the Braves. He became an important member of the pitching staff.

The 6-foot-2, 180-pound Burdette who seemed to wear a military-style crew-cut for most of his life, was a cranky pitcher. He had a temper, and much like Buhl was not at all chary of brushing back hitters. He seemed to take it personally if a batter crowded the plate.

Burdette developed into one of the best pitchers in the National League in the 1950s and into the 1960s, most of that time as the right-hand complement to Spahn's left-handed throwing. In 1957, Burdette would become the biggest World Series hero in Milwaukee baseball history. But along the way he made enemies and it was always rumored Burdette's bread-and-butter pitch was the outlawed spitball. He had a knack for infuriating opposing managers, some of whom were desperate to catch him in the act of throwing the spitter. Some hitters decried his effectiveness as the work of a cheater.

That first season in Milwaukee, the Braves and Brooklyn Dodgers were fierce rivals. The Dodgers had been the top team in the NL for a while. They were loaded with stars like Jackie Robinson, Roy Campanella, and Duke Snider. The feud boiled over in an August 3 game at County Stadium.

It was a rainy night and the game would eventually be terminated after seven innings. Early in the game Burdette decided to push Campanella away from the plate. He threw close, and Campanella hit the dirt. In the dugout, Spahn, whom had apparently played this game before, announced as if he was an Olympic judge. Campanella's dive, he exclaimed, was worthy of a nine score. Darned if Burdette didn't knock Campanella down again and this time Spahn graded the dive a ten.

A steaming Campanella struck out. He turned away from the Dodgers' dugout and with bat still in his hand made for the mound, apparently going after Burdette. Others intervened and there was no fight. Burdette claimed Campanella yelled something at him that he didn't hear. Campanella became even more infuriated.

"I didn't say a word to him, not one word," Campanella said. Campanella said Burdette yelled at him, but before he could utter what he heard, Robinson jumped in and said, "He called Campy a blankety-blank nigger." Robinson said Burdette had previously reverted to that type of name-calling, as well. Burdette denied all of that, especially the inflammatory racial epithet. Burdette said he didn't call Campanella anything but defiantly stated he intended to keep pitching inside.[171] When Dodger manager Charlie Dressen also complained about Burdette's behavior, the pitcher responded, "He must think that baseball is a tea party."[172]

Whatever really happened, home plate umpire Tom Gorman said he did not hear either Burdette or Campanella call out names to one another.

Due to the rainy conditions, the game ended after seven innings and Dodger pitcher Russ Meyer out-threw Burdette, gaining a 1–0 win.

This game may have represented an extreme situation, but Burdette was feisty throughout his career, a determined thrower for whom winning meant everything. If that required decking batters, so be it. If that required either throwing a spitter or just convincing hitters he threw one to play games with their heads, that was fine.

The Braves put together a marvelous season, playing way above expectations. They finished 92–62 and in second place in the NL. The hated Dodgers, however, ran away with the flag, finishing 13 games ahead in the standings with a sterling 105–49 record.

Burdette and Spahn had bonded and evidenced great respect for each other's pitching talents. Burdette referred to Spahn in print as "the best friend I ever had."[173]

It was at the end of the 1953 season, when Burdette had proved himself with his excellent 15–5 year and Spahn had completed his best-ever 23–7 season, that the duet realized that working together could well bring a pennant to Milwaukee.

"If anyone could pass the test of greatness," Burdette said to Spahn, "you're down in my books as the greatest pitcher in baseball today. And I'm proud and happy to call you my friend."[174]

Spahn was equally complimentary of how Burdette had performed, and they made a pact to move the team from second to first in 1954.

"Well friend, what do you say we really go all the way next year and win the pennant?" Spahn said.[175]

16

HENRY AARON

THE YEAR 1954 belonged to Henry Aaron.

These Milwaukee Braves leap-frogged much of the National League during the 1953 season, their first year in the new city that loved them so much it was as if they were a newborn home from the hospital.

And now they would be better because Henry Aaron was better than anyone the Braves already had, even the great Warren Spahn, even the great Eddie Mathews. For those who believed Willie Mays was a once-in-a-lifetime player, only three years later baseball observers were anointing Aaron the next Willie Mays.

The reality was he was the first and only Henry Aaron, but for the moment favorable comparisons to the Say-Hey Kid would do. Aaron was twenty years old, and he appeared in 122 games. He was still learning what he could do at the top level of the game and his teammates were finding out what he could do as well. Aaron's arrival was splashy, if not statistically overwhelming—that would come later. But once they analyzed his skills, everyone knew Aaron was going to be around for a long time.

Aaron was born in February of 1934 in Mobile, Alabama. People tend to forget, but many of the best ballplayers of all time came out of Alabama, including Aaron, Mays, Satchel Paige, Monte Irvin, Heinie Manush, Willie McCovey, Ozzie Smith, Don Sutton, Billy Williams, and Early Wynn—Hall of Famers all. Aaron played left field his first season. In center was Bill Bruton, also born in Alabama.

At eighteen, Aaron accepted his first minor-league assignment, and it took him to Eau Claire, Wisconsin. No problem with that. But the next season, playing for Class A Jacksonville, Florida in the South Atlantic League, or Sally League, Aaron endured much racial abuse. He also batted .362 to earn his promotion to Braves spring training in 1954.

"Which city was the worst?" Aaron said of his time in the Sally League. "You couldn't say, because they were all bad."[176]

Besides Jacksonville, other teams were in Montgomery, Alabama; Savannah, Georgia; Macon, Georgia; and a couple in South Carolina, all like-minded previously in favor of the Confederacy.

Jim Frey, later a major-league manager for the Kansas City Royals and Chicago Cubs, was an Aaron teammate with the Jacksonville Braves.

"It was just terrible what he was subjected to," Frey said of Aaron's season. "And he just took it all and hit. Baseball is a hard enough game when everyone is rooting for you. You cannot believe what it must have been to be like Henry Aaron in 1953. It was a heartbreaking thing to watch."[177]

Felix Mantilla was another black man, from Puerto Rico, on that team, and he was subjected to the same taunting and insults as Aaron. Mantilla also made the big leagues, but he did not rise to the Braves roster until 1956. He also carried a long memory of the disturbing season in Jacksonville.

Once, after winning a big game, Mantilla and Aaron were walking out of the home park when a white fan came running up to them from behind to offer his version of a compliment, saying, "I just wanted to say that you niggers played a hell of a game." Mantilla was even more naïve than Aaron, and English was not his first language. "It was Hank who always kept me away from the things that could have gotten me in trouble [such as segregated movie theatres]. Hank and I relied on each other. We tried not to let the other out of our sight."[178]

People also sometimes overlook that Aaron, at seventeen, left home to play for the Indianapolis Clowns in the Negro Leagues. That was his first real taste of being on the road and playing ball with men. Growing up in the segregated South, experiencing what it was like to play on an all-black team, and then spending a year as one of few African Americans on a southern team in a southern league, it was no wonder Aaron kept to himself a lot, described himself as quiet. It was not always safe to open his mouth.

His natural reticence, coupled with his bruising experiences, led Aaron to adopt the same wary outlook when he got to Milwaukee. Friend or foe? Aaron wondered whom he could trust and who really cared about him.

One important someone who did was Braves owner Lou Perini. He recognized Aaron was a special talent, a franchise player who plugged into the lineup could help uplift the team all by himself. Perini also recognized young Aaron was still a work in progress, not fully formed in 1954, but a ballplayer whose abilities were so outstanding Perini did not want him to be rushed. He also seemed to realize Aaron's psyche was probably fragile.

Perini, who could have kept his distance from the dugout and clubhouse scene, instead offered friendship to many players, but especially so to Aaron, asking him if he was doing OK, talking about his family: in other words, treating the young man like a person, something lacking much of the time on Aaron's minor-league tour.

Were things perfect in Milwaukee? Not quite. Although the city was mostly white, there was a small African American neighborhood called Bronzeville. Once, manager Charlie Grimm referred to Aaron as "Stepin Fetchit" because "he just keeps shuffling along."[179] Aaron did move with economy of motion. Stepin Fetchit was the 1930s stage and film persona of actor Lincoln Perry, probably the most successful African American actor of his time. However, the character was known as "the laziest man in the world." Aaron was not lazy, but he was unfairly labeled that way by some. In later years if a white manager called a player "Stepin Fetchit" it would be considered a racial slur and possibly get him fired.

Aaron was still making his way. He might not have made the final roster after spring training if Bobby Thomson hadn't broken his ankle. Aaron took his job and Thomson only played in about one-third of the games that year.

If Aaron and Mantilla hung together in Jacksonville, Bill Bruton played a protective role in the majors. Bruton was twenty-eight that season, eight years older than Aaron.

"If it weren't for Bill Bruton, I don't know if I would have made it those early years," Aaron said. "He was like a big brother and a father to me, all at the same time. He showed me the way."[180]

Aaron did not need to be shown the way at the plate. Charlie Grimm did not want to play him too often because he did not think he was ready, but when some players with notable pedigrees glimpsed him during exhibition play, they thought differently.

Ty Cobb, the leading hitter of all time with a lifetime .367 average, immediately took to Aaron's approach at the plate. "His mannerisms at the plate really impressed me," said Cobb, who said Grimm would be foolish not to play Aaron.

Red Sox star Ted Williams, who retired with a .344 average, was a student of good hitting and sometimes responded to the sound of the ball leaving a bat. "There was this crack of the bat," Williams said. "Someone hit that one on the nose. There was this skinny kid I had never seen before in the batter's box. It was my introduction to Henry Aaron."[181]

Milwaukee opened the season April 13 and lost to the Cincinnati Reds, 9–8. Aaron went 0-for-5. "It was a pretty ugly beginning," Aaron said.[182]

The next day the Braves and Warren Spahn went 11 innings to top Pittsburgh, 7–6. Aaron stroked two hits and although Spahn gave up all of the runs he got the win.

By then Spahn was the kingpin of the clubhouse. He had his reputation as a prankster and sometimes teased other players. He was thirteen years older than Aaron, a man of a different generation. He understood just how skilled Aaron was and Aaron realized just how good Spahn was. They needed one another. But they were not particularly pals.

"Spahn and I, we had our problems," Aaron said much later—not overtly serious ones where they could not share a clubhouse, but they were of very different personalities.[183]

Spahn, Lew Burdette, Bob Buhl, and Eddie Mathews were close friends and drank together. They were Braves who appreciated the easy access to beer through the team and the town. Aaron did not drink much at all. As a youngster, Spahn's son Greg was a clubhouse kid for the Braves and years later he remembered giving Cokes to Aaron to quench his thirst. One of Aaron's first impressions of Milwaukee when he came to town revolved around alcoholic beverages. He thought there was a saloon on every corner.

Aaron recovered rather quickly from his 0-fer start. Being a big leaguer was mostly about not having to take buses around those small towns in the South. Aaron was a bit jarred when he still ran into hotel and restaurant discrimination in St. Louis and Cincinnati, but overall his quality of life on the road was much improved. "Once I got acclimated, I found that playing in the big leagues wasn't as hard as getting there," Aaron said.[184]

That first season Aaron cranked out 131 hits. He smacked 13 home runs and drove in 69 runs while batting .280. They were good numbers but not astonishing stats. Mostly, observers marveled at the snap in his wrists, his unruffled manner, and the ease with which he went through his paces. Aaron was good right away, but everyone felt he soon would be great. Aaron was only fourth in National League Rookie of the Year voting, and he did not really dispute that.

"I had a decent rookie year, but I wasn't the one the fans came to watch," he said, "which was why I could walk to the ballpark without being recognized."[185]

Given the fanaticism of the fans and how they set a new NL attendance mark by turning out 2,133,388 strong, it is difficult to believe Braves followers did not recognize Aaron strolling to work.

In 1954, there were still a limited number of African American players in the majors. Mays had joined the New York Giants a couple of years earlier, and he was a superb all-around player. It didn't take long for sportswriters to examine the two players' traits and compare.

"Mays was at the top of his game when I broke into baseball," Aaron said, "and from the very beginning he was the guy I was measured against. It went on for as long as we played in the same league—20 years and then some."[186]

Spahn remained the boss of the rotation in 1954. He went 21–12 with a 3.14 earned run average while starting 39 games and pitching 283 1/3 innings. This was Spahn's sixth season of winning at least 21 games. Although the lineup was stronger, the Braves really weren't going anywhere without the left-hander's production.

Burdette again won 15 games, this time with a 2.76 ERA, and mostly as a starter. When the Braves pitching faltered, Bob Buhl was often on the mound. After winning 13 games as a rookie he finished a disastrous 2–7 the next year. The Braves might have finished much better with a steadier Buhl season, but they did add an excellent new pitcher who would have been the perfect fourth starter.

The new guy was the always-fascinating Gene Conley. Conley was one of the best all-around athletes of the 1950s and also was appreciated for his fun-loving nature and comedic delivery. Conley showed up with the Boston Braves in 1952 at twenty-one and went 0–3. It was a very different story in 1954 when Conley reappeared in the majors with a 14–9 record, a 2.96 earned run average, and was chosen for the first of his four All-Star teams.

All of which was good enough if that was all Conley did. However, at 6-foot-8 he was a terrific basketball player and also in demand by the National Basketball Association. A high school star in baseball and basketball in Washington, he was also a state champion high jumper. The professional seasons were shorter, and it was barely possible to squeeze in major-league baseball and professional basketball with the acquiescence of owners and coaches.

Conley was drafted by the Boston Celtics in 1952. This made the Braves unhappy. For a while the baseball team paid Conley not to play basketball. Still, he reasoned other players were working offseason jobs, so why shouldn't he be able to, even if his job was in another sport? After a half-decade break, Conley rejoined the Celtics. Eventually, mostly as Bill Russell's backup at center, Conley won three world championship rings in basketball and a World Series ring in baseball.

Along with football star Otto Graham, who won an NBA championship with the Rochester Royals, and catcher Del Rice, a teammate with the Braves and a teammate of Graham's in hoops, Conley is one of three athletes to win titles in two major American sports.

Conley had a winning fastball and winning personality and ended up on the All-Star team his debut season. Alas for him, he also ended up the losing pitcher in the 11–9 American League win. He allowed three hits and three runs in one-third of an inning. Not that Spahn was much better in the same game, giving up four hits and one run in two-thirds of an inning. Conley retained his sense of humor despite his weak showing.

"Boy, was I lousy," Conley said. "Anyhow, fifty years from now I can show my grandchildren my name in the box score of an All-Star game."[187]

Conley could be a hard loser other times but tried to avoid taking his work home. His wife Katie once told of how he was back at their apartment by 8:45 p.m. when he was scheduled to pitch.

"I thought you were pitching tonight," she said.

The opposing Philadelphia Phillies shelled Conley. He adjourned to the clubhouse, showered, dressed, and went home. Conley didn't want to talk about it, instead suggesting they take their kids to a drive-in movie. He stayed in a good mood around the family. "But I didn't dare ask him what happened," she said. "If I had, he'd have blown his top. When everything works out, he tells me about it. But when anything goes wrong, either he won't mention it or he tries to cover up his disappointment with a gag."[188]

Spahn liked the way Conley looked on the mound. Ewell Blackwell was a 6-foot-6 right-hander who had a solid career between 1942 and 1955, mostly with Cincinnati, for whom he led the NL with 22 wins in 1947.

"I guess Blackwell's the basis of comparison whenever a tall, thin, long-armed pitcher with whip-like delivery comes along," Spahn said. "Conley's the first one I've seen who looks like he'll outlast Blackwell because he's got better control than Blackie." Of all things, Braves general manager called Conley "our right-handed Warren Spahn."[189]

There were no other southpaw Warren Spahns, and it was a reach to call anyone a right-handed Spahn. Spahn was a notch above just about everyone around.

In midsummer, first baseman Joe Adcock recorded one of the greatest hitting days of all time. The Braves faced the Brooklyn Dodgers at Ebbets Field on July 31. Adock smashed four home runs that day, which matches the major-league, single-game homer record shared by many. But he also doubled in Milwaukee's 15--7 win for 18 total bases, a record that stood for forty-eight years. "I hit a fastball for the first homer, a slider for the second, a curve for the third, and a fastball for the fourth," Adcock said.[190]

A day later, Clem Labine of the Dodgers hit Adcock on the left side of his head with a pitch. Adcock was wearing a batting helmet, which was not mandatory at the time, or even that common.

"When they throw at me high and tight, I can duck, but when they throw behind your head, they mean business," Adcock said.[191]

Many baseball people, Braves players included, believed they could win the 1954 National League pennant. But the team finished third with an 89–65 record. That mark didn't look bad, but the Dodgers finished with 92 wins in second place and the New York Giants, driven by Most Valuable Player Willie Mays, won 97 games. Of course, no one thought the NL winner had a chance in the World Series because the Cleveland Indians won a then–American League record 111 games. Not only did the Indians fail to win, the Giants swept them in four straight games.

When the Braves defeated Cincinnati, 6–2, on September 20, Spahn won his 20th game of the season despite surrendering 10 hits. As was almost commonplace for him, he pitched a complete game.

Four days later, September 24, Spahn took his turn in the rotation and beat the St. Louis Cardinals, 4–2. That was his 21st victory of the season, again a complete game.

Winning 21 games was a fitting and remarkable achievement for Spahn in 1954. Few people knew he had been having knee trouble that sometimes threw his form off. Early on he had stumbled in some games, but by gritting his teeth through pain and through tough labor he got back to his usual self. For so many years, since his dad Ed taught him, Spahn had never deviated from his ingrained form. This time around he had to relearn it because everything was out of kilter for a while.

Spahn confided in battery mate Del Crandall that he needed his expertise to get back on track. He told Crandall, "I don't know a good pitch from a bad one anymore. You gotta help me. When I throw one that's good, really good, you come right out and tell me. And don't kid me. That's the only way I'm going to find out how to throw again."[192]

A major-league pitcher cannot show signs of weakness or the wolf-like predators in the batter's box will eat him alive. Somehow Spahn worked through his woes without revealing too much and ended up with 20 wins once more.

The Warren Spahn the writers knew was almost always accessible. He held court at his locker, offering an explanation, win or lose, though he was more thoughtful, insightful, and entertaining after a victory. He had a good rapport with the Milwaukee writers, and he gave them plenty of time. Teammates who were not in as much demand might shower, dress, and depart before Spahn finished his postgame talk.

He always kept in mind the people of Milwaukee loved the players and he, as elder statesman, more than any other player, was the front man, the face of the franchise.

17

BRAVES TRYING TO TAKE OVER

THE MILWAUKEE BRAVES were stuck on good.
That meant they were a threat to win the pennant at the start of each season, something that would bring tremendous joy to Milwaukee, but it also meant they kept coming up just shy of being the best in the National League.

In 1955, there was some shuffling of the daily lineup, some replacements of the previous top guys at their positions for one reason or another. The starting rotation seemed set with the right guys, and it appeared the Braves even had five potential useful starters. But for the most part none of them, Warren Spahn included, pitched their best that season.

Henry Aaron and Eddie Mathews continued to improve and those young guys scared the speed off of many opponents' fastballs. Foes had to tiptoe past their spots in the order and exhale only when they survived without the ball being hit off the wall or over it.

The fans still came out two million strong, faith still in place, as the Braves finished second with an 85–69 mark.

For a change, Spahn did not win 20 games. Any hint of decline in a pitcher who is thirty-four years old is alarming to management. Is it the beginning of the end, or simply an off-year? Not that 1955 was completely off. Spahn finished 17–14 with a 3.26 earned run average.

Spahn recognized he would be required to be cleverer than ever with his slower stuff and his location. The best athletes adapt as they age and Spahn was working hard to stay in the game at a top level, though his knees seemed to be wearing out. He worked hard on his conditioning because it is often said the legs go first in a pitcher.

After the 1954 season, Spahn underwent knee surgery to clean out some cartilage. He was optimistic he had fixed his problems, but when he began the 1955 season his knee regularly swelled up. He was 7–9 at the All-Star break and worried how his season was unfolding. There were definitely troubling signs. This year was not Spahn's best and he learned if had a chance of continuing as one of the top pitchers in the NL he had to adjust.

It took quite a while—into the next season, actually—but Spahn found an answer. He began quietly working on a sinker, a pitch that stayed low and for most hitters avoided their power strength. Spahn practiced on his own, throwing and throwing, long before he threw one sinker during a game. It surprised catcher Del Crandall.

"Ho, ho, what have we here?" Crandall asked. He quizzed Spahn about his seriousness with the pitch, and Spahn told him he was not fooling around. "It's going to be my best pitch."[193]

The 1955 team talked pennant but never spent a day in first place. That was despite winning the opening game on April 12, a 4–2 victory over the Cincinnati Reds. Spahn pitched eight innings and gave up two runs, for a change not going the distance. Reliever

Dave Jolly threw the ninth. Spahn moved to 2–0 with another win over the Reds five days later, this one a complete game.

After that Spahn and the Braves dipped to records around the .500 mark. Buhl rebounded from his ugly 2–7 season of 1954 to finish 13–11, so that was a plus. Lew Burdette went 13–8, although his ERA mushroomed to 4.03. That was not a plus.

April was not kind to the Braves. Mathews was twenty-three and coming off two seasons of clubbing more than 40 home runs. He was entering his prime and seemed likely to be a major star for years. That is why he was disturbed by his slow start. He did not hit a single home run during the season's opening stretch and moved on to May batting .216. Then he underwent an emergency appendicitis operation. However, the slump didn't last, and Mathews began hitting the way everyone knew he could. He was on his way to a 41-homer season and a 100-RBI year.

Gene Conley looked even better than he had as a rookie, starting 7–1. But he was unable to keep it up and finished 11–7. Joe Adcock was hit by a pitch that broke his wrist and appeared in just 84 games. George Crowe took over first base duties and batted .281 with 15 homers, an admirable fill-in job. The problem was guys were either not matching their previous bests or getting injured, so several fill-ins were necessary.

Andy Pafko made it into just 34 games, and Bobby Thomson became a starter once more. Thomson hit 12 homers. Manager Charlie Grimm was like the little Dutch boy in fairy tales trying to plug holes in a dike with his fingers.

Since neither Spahn nor Burdette were tip-top, Grimm was heartened by newcomer Chet Nichols. Nichols made his splash in 1951 with 11 victories and a league-winning 2.88 earned run average. Even before he showed well during that rookie year, manager Billy Southworth gushed about Nichols. "He's my boy. That Nichols kid is one of the most natural kid pitchers I've ever seen. He still has a few things to learn, but he's going to be one of the best left-handers in the National League. He can't miss."[194]

Back when he was a rookie, Nichols came into a game in relief against the Dodgers. Gil Hodges, Jackie Robinson, and Duke Snider were the first scheduled hitters, a fearsome group indeed. Nichols was twenty and naïve. He walked Robinson but retired the other two seemingly effortlessly, prompting Spahn to ask if he had been nervous.

"Why should I be worried?" Nichols replied. "They tie their shoes the same way I do, don't they?" Maybe not, actually. Spahn said, "Nice going, Squirrel. You're a true left-hander. You don't have to be crazy to pitch up there, but it doesn't hurt."[195]

Of course, Southworth was wrong and Nichols did miss—but for good reason. After that promising first season, Nichols, who was runner-up for the Rookie of the Year Award to Willie Mays (certainly no shame in that) then spent the next two years in the Army during the Korean War.

Being sidetracked like that did not help Nichols's career. He never had a season as good as his first one. Nichols stood 6-foot-1, but he weighed just 165 pounds, which made him a lightweight. Another left-hander besides Spahn, when he began to win Nichols did give Grimm options.

So did Henry Aaron. In his second season in the majors, Aaron played at a much higher, more consistent level than he had as a rookie. There was major improvement in all of his main offensive numbers. Aaron slugged 27 homers in 1955, drove in 106 runs, and batted .314. His 37 doubles led the NL and was selected for his first All-Star team. Aaron learned fast and so did the league about him. Rather than viewing him as a promising rookie, baseball people saw him as a breakout star dangerous at the plate in all situations.

Aaron became known as a player who did not talk much and some considered him slow, both in thinking and footspeed. First baseman Joe Adcock coined the derogatory nickname "Snowshoes" for Aaron. Worse for Aaron, manager Charlie Grimm bought into the image and used the term, too. Aaron believed this was inappropriate but remained mum, not criticizing the manager, even if he was unhappy with this depiction and believed it unfair.

"Because I was black and I never moved faster than I had to, and because I didn't speak Ivy League English, I came into the league with an image of a backward country kid who could swing the bat and was lucky he didn't have to think too much," Aaron said. "Along the way, there were plenty of stories that played along with the image. A lot of them came from Charlie Grimm. Charlie never meant anybody any harm. He was just an entertainer." The stories, Aaron added, portrayed him as "just a simple colored boy."[196]

In 1955, Aaron was chosen as the Braves' MVP, despite Mathews's huge power numbers, and it was reported that in a rare show of emotion he was thrilled to gain the honor. It turned out Aaron always thought he should have won Rookie of the Year in 1954. Winner Wally Moon of the Dodgers batted .304, some 24 points higher.

Other top rookies in 1954 included the Cubs' Ernie Banks, also at the beginning of a Hall of Fame career. Banks played in all 154 games and hit 19 homers while batting .275. Cincinnati pitcher Brooks Lawrence, who was already twenty-nine and had a shorter career than the two sluggers, won 15 games in 1954. Aaron's season was halted early because he broke an ankle.

Later, Aaron said, he was "disappointed at not winning. I just thought I could have done better. I figured if he could hit .300, I could, too."[197] From then on, Aaron did do better and soon enough also hit .300.

Aaron worried he was going to be drafted into the Army before he could play in the 1955 season. Having a cast on his leg may have precluded that from happening.

"I admit I wasn't too crazy about the thought of being in the Army," Aaron said. "When you grow up as a black kid in a Jim Crow city, you somehow don't feel a great urgency to serve your country." The Braves' traveling secretary Donald Davidson accompanied Aaron to the draft board to register. "And we got in line behind about 200 other guys. I told Donald we could leave because it looked like they had enough. I don't think he appreciated my humor."[198]

As Aaron matured at the plate, becoming the batter nobody wanted to face in a clutch situation, he was really improving as an all-around player. Many years later, Bill Bruton, who played alongside Aaron in the Braves' outfield, said fielding was often an overlooked attribute of Aaron's play and was better than most people thought.

"Nobody talks about Aaron's fielding," Bruton said. "He had good speed, good hands, a strong arm, and could make the plays. He had the instinct to put his head down and get to where the ball was going. He didn't look graceful doing it, but he got there."[199]

Several regulars and backups on the 1955 team did not hit nearly as well as Aaron and Mathews. Second baseman Danny O'Connell hit .225. Del Crandall hit just .236 that season. Backup catcher Del Rice batted just .197. Rookie Chuck Tanner batted .247 and was later more famous for leading the Pittsburgh Pirates to a World Series championship as a manager.

Warren Spahn is the winningest left-handed pitcher of all-time, capturing 363 victories. *(National Baseball Hall of Fame Museum, Cooperstown, NY)*

Known for a big kick in his delivery to the plate, distracting to batters, Spahn won at least 20 games in a season 13 times. *(National Baseball Hall of Fame Museum, Cooperstown, NY)*

Warren Spahn (left) and his right-handed counterpart Johnny
Sain, were the aces of the 1948 Boston Braves' National League
pennant-winning team. A sportswriter wrote a famous poem about
the duo's success, "Spahn and Sain and pray for rain." *(AP Images)*

A happy Spahn (center) after beating the Cleveland Indians in Game
Five of the 1948 World Series. Spahn celebrates with teammates with
Bob Elliott (left) and Tommy Holmes. *(AP Images)*

During the heyday of th Milwaukee Braves in th 1950s, Lew Burdette wa the right-handed comple ment to lefty Warre Spahn as a fearsome moun package. *(National Base ball Hall of Fame Museum Cooperstown, NY)*

Throughout the decade of the 1950s Del Cran- dall, an 11-time All-Star and four-time Gold Glove winner, was Warren Spahn's primary catcher. *(National Baseball Hall of Fame Museum, Cooperstown, NY)*

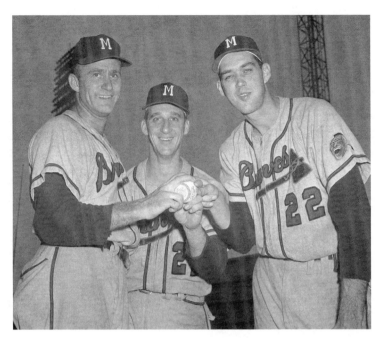

Stalwarts of the Milwaukee Braves' pitching staff in 1957 (left to right), Lew Burdette, Warren Spahn, and Gene Conley. *(AP Images)*

Legendary Hall of Famer Ty Cobb is the center of Braves players' attention Frank Torre, Warren Spahn, and Bobby Thomson during a visit to their Milwaukee clubhouse in 1957. *(AP Images)*

The 1957 World Series champion Milwaukee Braves at County Stadium, their home ballpark. *(AP Images)*

The 1958 National League pennant-winning Milwaukee Braves posed a home County Stadium. *(AP Images)*

A pair of All-Stars and future Hall of Famers. Southpaws Warren Spahn of the Braves and Whitey Ford of the Yankees the day before the start of the 1958 World Series. *(AP Images)*

Spahn talking baseball with old friend Sibby Sisti, also from Buffalo. *(National Baseball Hall of Fame Museum, Cooperstown, NY)*

Spahn edits the handmade sign acknowledging his 20th victory of the 1960 season, adding the bonus information that it was also a no-hitter. *(AP Images)*

Spahn celebrating 1961 post-season honors with Mickey Mantle (left) and Stan Musial (center) at a dinner in Houston. *(AP Images)*

On a trip to the Polo Grounds in New York, Spahn is surrounded by autograph-seeking kids. *(AP Images)*

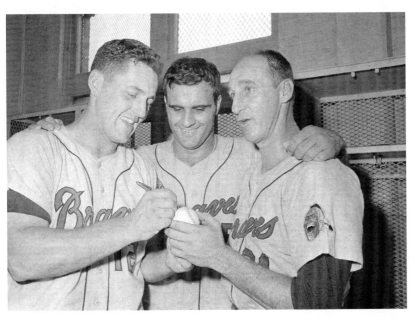

Gene Oliver signs an autograph for Warren Spahn after his home run gave the lefty his 20th victory of the 1963 season, as catcher Joe Torre looks on. *(AP Images)*

Going into his trademark big windup, Warren Spahn is ready to deliver pitch against the New York Mets in a 1964 game. *(Spread images: AP Image*

Nearing the end of his pitching days, Spahn thought he might want to become an actor. Even though the idea did not pan out long term he did have a role on the popular TV show *Combat* for an episode in 1963. *(AP Images)*

Using a hand grenade, during the filming of the TV show *Combat*, Warren Spahn demonstrates to actors Vic Morrow (left) and Rick Jason his form in throwing the curveball. *(AP Images)*

After splitting with his career-long partner Braves, Warren Spahn spent two-thirds of a season with the New York Mets in 1965. *(National Baseball Hall of Fame Museum, Cooperstown, NY)*

After his Major League career ended, Warren Spahn briefly pitched in Mexico, where he was also a coach. *(AP Images)*

Long-time teammate Hank Aaron broke Babe Ruth's career home-run record after the Braves moved to Atlanta. *(National Baseball Hall of Fame Museum, Cooperstown, NY)*

Third baseman Eddie Mathews w another staple of the Braves' lineup wh Warren Spahn pitched, and was also his way to the Hall of Fame. *(Natio Baseball Hall of Fame Museum, Coop stown, NY)*

All dressed up in tuxedos instead of Braves uniforms, Hank Aaron (left) Warren Spahn and Eddie Mathews appear at the 1969 dinner of the Milwaukee Chapter of the Baseball Writers Association of America. *(AP Images)*

pahn serving as pitching coach of the Cleveland Indians in 1972. *(AP Images)*

Holding his Baseball Hall of Fame plaque, Warren Spahn at the 1973 induction ceremony in Cooperstown, New York. Seated by him is Vera Clemente, widow of Pittsburgh Pirates star Roberto Clemente, and next is Monte Irvin. Both were also inducted at the time. *(AP Images)*

Braves Hall of Famers together (left to right), Hank Aaron, Eddie Mathews, Phil Niekro, and Warren Spahn for a special event at Turner Field in Atlanta in 1999. *(AP Images)*

The Warren Spahn statue at Turner Field on October 2, 2016, the date of the last home game before the Braves moved into a new home stadium for the 2017 season. *(AP Images)*

There was a new pitcher on the scene who made a splash in spring training in 1955, and the Braves hoped he would be a useful addition. Humberto Robinson was a right-hander and the first player born in Panama to appear in a major-league game. There was every reason for the Braves to be excited. In 1954, Robinson won 23 games for the Jacksonville Braves in the Sally League. He carried over that superb showing to spring training and made the Milwaukee Braves' roster.

Although standing 6-foot-1, Robinson weighed just 155 pounds. Milwaukee pitching coach Bucky Walters sought to allay any worries about Robinson's weight.

"That kid looks like a real athlete," Walters said. "As a matter of fact [Hall of Famer] Lefty Gomez was hardly any heavier and he had a lot of mileage on him. It's nothing unusual for a kid with a slender physique to make the grade in the big leagues. I've seen that type of player last a long time up here."[200]

Robinson did help Milwaukee in 1955 with a 3–1 record and a 3.08 earned run average in 13 games. But Walters was wrong about him, and that was his peak. He pitched parts of five seasons in the majors and finished with an 8–13 record.

The throwers who excelled for the Braves the year before struggled somewhat in 1955, with some good moments and then some not very special moments. Teams go through these stretches. When everyone is on his "A" game, teams win pennants. When the same players are a bit off, they might drop a couple of notches in the standings. Those were the Braves of 1955. It is doubtful any of the other players worried about his showing as much as Warren Spahn, because Spahn was concerned age might be creeping up on him. He was thirty-four that season and reveled in his All-Star status and the belief he was the best pitcher in the National League. That year he did not perform that way.

Spahn did not want to admit his fastball was gone, but in his heart he was sure the miles-per-hour reduction he sensed in many games was a permanent thing. Adding the sinker was supposed to add years to Spahn's career. For most of the year he was not his usual self, but he rallied in the closing months of the 1955 season, going 10–4 down the stretch. That was a heartening showing.

"I won 17 with my fastball on my knee," Spahn said.[201]

For Spahn, the real question was whether or not he could win 20, the mark of singular success for any pitcher regardless of age and regardless of what combination of pitches he threw.

Spahn was hearing, or reading, that he might be washed up, too old to remain the ace of the staff in 1956 when he was going to be thirty-five years old. Out of sight over the winter at his Oklahoma ranch, Spahn exercised rigorously, seeking to revive his youth by reporting to spring training in fabulous shape. He wasn't too sure if his creaky knees would hold up despite the rest of him being in firm condition. But when he began throwing in Florida he was pleased by the results. He was sure he still had it.

"I think the fastball has left my knee," Spahn said. "With a little luck, I could be the best pitcher with the worst knees in all baseball."[202]

He would settle for that during the 1956 season, as long as he could also pitch the Milwaukee Braves to a pennant.

18

ON THE CUSP

IT WAS NOT as if the Braves did not value Warren Spahn and Lew Burdette at the top of their rotation, but they felt Gene Conley gave them some security.

From the moment the Braves honchos signed Conley coming out of Washington State in 1952 when the club was still in Boston, they loved him. They appreciated his 6-foot-8 size and probably felt being a big guy gave his fastball extra oomph.

Although Conley went 0–3 as a twenty-one-year-old in 1952, he was still classified as a rookie in 1954 when he won those 14 games. Conley, in fact, was one of the players who finished ahead of Henry Aaron in the Rookie of the Year voting. Although he had a bit of a dropoff with 11 wins in 1955, Conley was part of the foundation, a piece needed if the Braves were going to capture a pennant.

Conley was the tallest player in the majors, and whatever sport he was playing he brought along a sense of humor and light-heartedness. When a sportswriter asked him the size of his feet and learned he wore 14-C, Conley added there was no problem finding them for sale.

"They're not too hard to find in the stores," Conley said. "I got this pair at Spokane without any trouble. But you have to shine them yourself. I wouldn't dare go into a shine parlor and ask a boy to put a gleam on them. Too much work."[203]

Conley had very long arms. Using the arm that threw his fastball, he was able to reach over the counter at the Braves' spring training hotel to grab his mail without asking the clerk for assistance. Besides the quiz on his shoe size, Conley was also asked if had to dip to fit beneath a door jamb.

"I measure my height by the doors at home," he said. "The standard door is 6-feet-8 by 2 feet. I can still make it without stooping."[204] That actually made his height more like 6-foot-7 ¾, but the measurement of basketball players has always been fudged a little bit.

While the Braves were probably content to hear Conley was able to obtain comfortable shoes, they were more interested in the condition of his arm. General manager John Quinn said Conley had a $100,000 arm and for that reason, he did not want him to play professional basketball in the offseason. "You might fall and get hurt," Quinn said.[205]

Conley did lay off NBA ball for a while but kept returning to it over the years. Some players sold cars in the offseason. Others sold insurance. Conley dunked basketballs. Conley joined the Boston Celtics for the 1952-53 season, but the next season the Braves began twisting his non-pitching arm to convince him not to play during their offseason.

"I played with the Celtics last year because I needed the money," Conley said, "and I have to play again this year for the same very good reason. 'Well,' they said, 'if you won't play we'll give you a thousand dollars.' I thought that was pretty nice. Same as getting a thousand-dollar bonus."[206] Conley continued to not play in the

NBA into 1958 when he changed his mind and resumed his basketball career.

Whether he was active at hoops or not, Conley was always good for a basketball story. During the 1955 baseball season he regaled writers with the tale of how in 1948 he was kidnapped by University of Idaho fans trying to prevent him from joining Washington State. Conley's older brother Roy attended Washington State and that's where he was headed.

The way Conley told it, he was asleep in a Washington State dormitory room on a visit when he was awakened by three people in the dark room who had apparently entered through an open window. They told him he was going for a ride. While not quite as sinister as this might have been if gangsters were the perpetrators (and especially since they wished to preserve Conley's good health), he was driven away in a car with five guys who proceeded to deliver a sales pitch for why he should attend Idaho to play ball instead of Washington State.

"They promised me an automobile and even a small cut in the profits from the hotel slot machines," he said. Finally, I was told to 'Sleep on it.'" He was taken to a gym for a workout and then asked for a phone call, as if he was incarcerated by the police. He telephoned his father who was extremely angry when he heard the story. While Conley spoke, the others tried to sell his father on why Gene should attend Idaho. The older Mr. Conley threatened to call the police unless Gene was promptly released. "Well, that same afternoon I finally registered at Washington State," he said.[207]

Conley suffered a decline in effectiveness during the 1955 season because of shoulder problems. Going into the 1956 season Braves observers expressed much concern for his well-being. Conley struggled even more so in 1956, and after the

Braves did too, a 24–22 start, Grimm was ousted as manager and replaced by Fred Haney.

"I recall Grimm telling me in Florida last spring, 'Conley's our make-or-break guy. He's got to win big for us, if we are to do it,'" Haney said.[208]

While Conley gave the Braves 31 appearances in 1956 with a solid 3.13 earned run average, his record was 8–9. That was not winning big.

Fred Haney was born in 1896 and broke into the majors for the Detroit Tigers in 1922. During seven seasons as a big-league third baseman he hit .275. After handling the Toledo Mud Hens in the minors, Haney made his major-league managerial debut for the St. Louis Browns in 1939, which turned out to be as much punishment as reward since the Browns finished 43–111. No pitcher won as many as 10 games for the Browns that year.

Haney's next big-league managerial chance (and that term was again applied loosely) was as boss of the 1953-to-1955 rebuilding Pittsburgh Pirates. The Pirates went 50–104, 53–101, and 60–94 on Haney's watch. Many of those games were hard to watch. To that point the teams Haney helmed might not have been able to reach .500, never mind win a pennant, if he managed with a tag team of John McGraw and Connie Mack helping out.

Branch Rickey was running the Pirates in those days, brought in to revive a moribund franchise and hopefully provide the zest and success he oversaw with the Brooklyn Dodgers after signing Jackie Robinson, Roy Campanella, and Don Newcombe to break baseball's color barrier. Rickey's foresight and pioneering spirit, combined with his player personnel acumen, was his crowning achievement in a long baseball career and earned him everlasting respect in the game. It was hoped his wisdom would rub off on the Pirates.

Haney said Rickey once summoned him for a discussion and asked, "Why are we so bad?" Haney's reply was forthright, if not mysterious. "I told him it's because we have a lot of lousy ballplayers," Haney said. "Rickey told me I was right and he was to blame because he was stocking the team."[209]

When Haney was fired from the Pirates he signed as a coach for the Braves beginning with the 1956 season. When Grimm's slow start got him canned, this time Haney was in the right place at the right time. He had a team loaded with talent that was a contender if he could straighten it out. The Braves made their early-season change after 46 games to juice up the team. Haney was the prince-in-waiting, anxious to demonstrate he could win if he had good players, and he was expected to win immediately.

He may have been in the staid Midwest, but Haney brought a touch of Hollywood with him. Although born in New Mexico, Haney grew up in Los Angeles, and when he wasn't playing in the majors, he was starring in the Pacific Coast League. As a longtime .300 hitter for the Los Angeles and Hollywood teams, Haney was a well-known man-about-town. He managed the Hollywood Stars, too. That team was owned by Bob Cobb, who operated the famous Brown Derby restaurant where all the Hollywood big-wigs dined and cut deals.

For that matter, Haney was also a good friend of Ty Cobb, the legendary Hall of Famer who was probably the greatest hitter of all. Cobb was his manager in Detroit and the leading proponent of what at the time was known as scientific baseball and which later became known as small ball. Babe Ruth significantly influenced the power game, but Ty Cobb was the leading proponent of playing for one run at a time. He emphasized the hit-and-run, stealing bases, bunting, and sacrifice plays. Haney ate it up, retained that knowledge, and always retained those weapons in his arsenal.

Haney was so cocky as a young player, and such a blind adherent of the Cobb philosophy, that in one of his early major-league games in the 1920s, he tweaked Ruth.

"You better watch out, you big bum," Haney told the Sultan of Swat. "I'm going to be the new home-run king." Although Ruth did not engage Haney in banter at the time, soon enough in that game he did what he did best, smashing a ball out of the park. As he ran past third base, where Haney was stationed, Ruth said, "Well, kid, you gotta get one more to catch up."[210]

Ruth clouted 714 regular season home runs. Haney hit 8.

Haney realized being elevated to run the Braves was good fortune and also probably his final chance to show he could be a big-league winner. To that end, Haney was more of a stickler on the rules than Grimm, a player's manager.

Haney could be somewhat old fashioned. He demanded players' respect. He demanded they listen. The Braves, like many teams, had their cliques. The party animals liked to drink, home or away, especially on the road. Lew Burdette, Eddie Mathews, Bob Buhl, and to some extent Warren Spahn were key pieces of the club, but they also enjoyed themselves away from the ballpark. Haney developed some theories he imposed on road-trip roommate structure.

"I never have pitchers room together," Haney said, "and I also know how to handle the bad guys. I keep pitchers apart because they get talking and one guy figures he'll try what the other fellow is doing and the next thing you know both of them are fouled up. I'd put the problem players together because when you had two of them to a room, they were that much easier to watch."[211]

Haney was the wake-up-call manager for the Braves. Management believed Milwaukee was too good to have a record hovering around .500, so Haney was the sub for the popular Grimm, a manager who once could have dined out for free in all the best spots in town. Perhaps Haney, because of his stretches in charge of poor teams, hungered to win more than Grimm.

From his introductory press conference on, Haney came across as a square-jawed hard-ass.

"Baseball is business, big business," Haney said. Then he said almost the identical words again. "Baseball is all business."[212] Well, he made that clear. Fans might have been more intrigued if he said baseball was all about winning, but Haney's words were probably interpreted that way.

Whether Haney was looking for an opportunity to make a point or things just played out in a manner where he felt he had to act to clamp down, he issued a symbolic slam against second baseman Danny O'Connell following a 2–1 victory over the Pirates on July 16. O'Connell was the Braves' leadoff man.

In the third inning O'Connell swung at a pitch and tapped a groundball to first where Dale Long sought to scoop it up. Only O'Connell did not run very hard, so when the ball took a funny bounce and rolled up Long's arm, he was still out on the play when pitcher Ron Kline dove on the ball and made the out. If O'Connell had run all of the way through the base instead of turning off early he would likely have been safe. An incensed Haney fined O'Connell fifty dollars at first, and then lowered the fine to twenty-five dollars.

The home crowd booed O'Connell, and so did Haney.

"You didn't even run 60 feet," Haney told O'Connell. O'Connell treated the incident light-heartedly when he greeted the press, saying, "How about that? It's a 10,000-to-1 shot. I gave it the old Duke Snider turn (a habit the slugger had if he was certain he was dead-to-rights) and it had to backfire. I

never saw it happen to him." Haney did not disagree about the
odds, saying he doubted the same scenario would play out again to
anyone in ten years. "Not to O'Connell, anyway," he said.[213]

It may be that Haney lost confidence in O'Connell for good
right then. O'Connell played in 139 games that season and batted
.239. Haney saw him as a weak link in his lineup. Fifty games into
the 1957 season, O'Connell was traded to the New York Giants.

Righty Bob Buhl had flirted with becoming a top-tier pitcher
since his 1953 rookie year, although he was dismayed by his 1954
slump. His resumption of his original form in 1955 was gratifying.
But Buhl suffered a worrisome arm injury. However, Buhl adjusted
his delivery somewhat and in 1956 made a major breakthrough,
finishing 18–8.

"In 1956, I hurt my arm," Buhl said, "and it was the best thing
that happened to me in my career. It made me a pitcher, not a
thrower."[214]

The Braves were resuscitated under Haney. They took off and
went 68–40. Grimm's last game was June 14, a 5–2 victory over the
New York Giants with Spahn the winner while allowing just the
two earned runs in a complete game. To that point in the season
Spahn had not recovered from his offseason fears. He had a five-
game losing streak. Even with that Giants victory he was just 4–6.
It seemed very bad news was brewing.

As soon as Haney took over, though, the Braves swiftly went on
an 11-game winning streak, and Spahn won two more games to
reach .500. He had a good rapport with Haney.

Spahn's slow start did not continue. Maybe he was distracted at
first by babysitting.

When Spahn was dating his wife LoRene, she did not know
much about baseball. She learned to appreciate the game's finer
points and enjoyed scoring in the stands. LoRene and son Greg

attended many games at County Stadium, but on days when Spahn was between starts, LoRene insisted he take care of the boy so she could keep her box score in peace.

"Where do you suggest I keep him? In the bat rack?" Spahn asked.[215]

The Spahns solved the problem by having the seven-year-old watch games with his dad in the bullpen. Lew Burdette studied Greg throwing left-handed (though he did not throw naturally from that side due to a childhood accident) and saw that he was pitching just like his father.

"You're going to be a great pitcher like your daddy some day, aren't you Greg?" Burdette said.[216]

That great pitcher was great again. After a sloppy, erratic start, the Warren Spahn personal renovation project took hold, and at thirty-five he was refreshed. Somehow he renewed the warranty and once again began mowing down batters and winning games. Spahn, the team leader and the one most relied upon on the mound, was in the thick of it when things changed for the better.

Under Haney, the Braves were on the move on the scoreboard, even if there was some grumbling in the clubhouse about his more disciplined ways. Haney wanted to crack the whip, but also did not want to overdo it as results improved.

"They're spoiled rotten," Haney said of his team at one point, perhaps thinking of all that free beer and the blind love shown by the community. "But there's just so much I can do about it without causing serious trouble. It's different when you take charge of a team in spring training. You can get things to be the way you think they should. But in mid-season. . . ."[217]

The National League had quite the pennant race going in 1956. The Dodgers, as they had been for a decade, were the

team to beat. The upstart Cincinnati Reds were playing better than
they had in a decade and a half. The Reds were big winners in 1939
and 1940 when they won pennants two seasons in a row, but they
hadn't been a factor in the races since. The drive for the pennant
came down to the final few days of the season for the three teams.

This bunch was the best Reds team in a long time. Hitters
included Rookie of the Year Frank Robinson—who led the league
in runs scored and tied the then-rookie record of 38 homers—sluggers Ted Kluszewski and Wally Post (each with 35 home runs),
catcher Ed Bailey, Gus Bell, and Johnny Temple. Smoky Burgess
was the world's greatest pinch-hitter. That was a formidable lineup
for any pitcher to face. The Reds were a bit short on pitching,
although Brooks Lawrence won 19 games. Cincinnati won 91
games that year, but that was two games behind the Dodgers and
one behind the Braves.

Between the minor leagues and the majors, playing and
managing, Reds manager Birdie Tebbetts had drawn a baseball
paycheck since 1934. He was old school and would use anything
he could think of to help win a game. He also did not like it much
if he was outsmarted. For the last couple of years, it seemed, Braves
pitcher Lew Burdette was outsmarting him by throwing a spitter,
the banned pitch. There was never any proof Burdette used the
pitch, but Tebbetts was constantly on umpires to check him and
kvetched about it all the time. Burdette drove him nuts.

"He's a cheating spitballer," Tebbetts said. "I'm sick and tired of
him getting away with murder. Why should I complain? It hasn't
done me any good for the last three years."[218]

Burdette had a temper and generally did not react meekly to
insults or challenges. But anytime opponents claimed he employed
the spitter, he shrugged off the comments. He made it sound as if
the protests were playing into his own strategy, as if Burdette was

only getting into their heads, not fooling hitters with the illegal pitch.

"Their taunts hurt them more than it does me," Burdette said. "If I can throw hitters off stride with a little psychology, why change?"[219]

From June 20, when Gene Conley beat the Pirates, through July 1, the Braves were in first place every day. From July 13 through September 15, the Braves held on to first place. During that two months the players grew to believe they were about to bring a pennant to Milwaukee. Yes, they were in first all of that time, but they never had big leads.

On September 25, the Braves beat the Reds, 7–1, to crush Cincinnati's hopes. Spahn pitched a complete game, and it marked his 20th victory of the season, the seventh time he reached that total. That was the team's 91st win, and it gave the Braves a half-game lead in the standings over Brooklyn. After the games of September 28, the Braves were still in first by a half-game.

The next day, the next-to-last-day of the regular season, Spahn took the mound for Milwaukee against the St. Louis Cardinals, an also-ran that year. Righty Herm Wehmeier was on the mound for the Cards. Over a 13-year major-league run Wehmeier was usually good for 10 to 12 wins a year. Starting in 1955, however, he became a Braves killer, saving his best stuff for showdowns with Milwaukee.

In this September 29, 1956, Saturday night game at Busch Stadium, Wehmeier was about as good as he ever was in a big-league game. The Braves could hardly nick him after scoring a single run in the first inning. Neither could the Cardinals do much damage to Spahn. He gave up one run in the sixth inning.

Henry Aaron, then twenty-two, was about to win the batting title with a .328 average and did his mightiest to solve Wehmeier, gathering three hits. Didn't matter. Bill Bruton and Bobby Thomson added two hits each and Bruton scored the Braves run. Tied at 1–1 after nine innings, the game went on and on with Spahn and Wehmeier still in the game and in control. The ninth inning passed. So did the 10th inning. As did the 11th inning.

In the bottom of the 12th inning, St. Louis great Stan Musial came to bat with one out. The future Hall of Famer belted a double to right field. The Braves intentionally walked Ken Boyer to set up a possible double play. Outfielder Rip Repulski stepped in and slugged a double to left field. The hit ended the game, gave Spahn a 2–1 loss after pitching 11 1/3 innings, and thoroughly demoralized the Braves.

On that same day the Dodgers' Clem Labine held the Pirates to one run, and Brooklyn won, 3–1. On the last day of the season if Milwaukee won and Brooklyn lost the teams would have tied, but somehow the Braves knew after the 12-inning defeat their chances had evaporated.

There were tears among the Braves. Spahn cried. So did owner Lou Perini. So did outfielder Andy Pafko. Perini sought out Spahn and hugged him.

"We play all season for these games and then we lose 'em," Spahn said. "Let's face it. It looks like it's down the drain. I know we're a better ballclub, but we just couldn't do anything right. It's a cruel truth to face, but the fact is we didn't deserve to win."[220]

For all of the spent emotion the Braves came out to win on September 30, the last day of the season, hoping the Dodgers would falter. With men like Roberto Clemente, Bill Virdon, and Dick Groat each contributing two hits, Pittsburgh made a go of it, even against Don Newcombe, a 27-game-winner who captured the first Cy Young Award that year. Brooklyn hung on for an 8–6 win, making Lew Burdette's 4–2 victory over the Cardinals moot.

The Braves lost the pennant by one game. It was the Dodgers' last pennant in Brooklyn before moving to Los Angeles. Though the Dodgers lost to the Yankees in the 1956 World Series—which featured Don Larsen's perfect game and Jackie Robinson's final appearance—and would never represent the New York borough in the Fall Classic again, the Braves would have another chance in Milwaukee in 1957.

The Braves came close to their first World Series. Instead, they flew back to Milwaukee without celebration. Yet one might not have known who the winner was judging by the reception thrown for the team. Once again Milwaukee proved itself different than most baseball cities, turning out thousands strong to thank the team for almost winning the pennant.

"There must have been 20,000 men, women, and children, including some parents with babies in their arms," Spahn said. "Some of the people were crying. Many of them patted us on the back and told us not to worry."[221]

It was right then the Braves decided they owed the people of Milwaukee one.

19

A PENNANT FOR MILWAUKEE

THE GLOOM LIFTED over the winter.

Warren Spahn felt refreshed. He looked over the Braves' roster and proclaimed this was the year. The sting of the 1956 last-minute defeat still stung, but the tears had dried and now it was looked at as a motivator. This time the Braves would win the pennant and set off an unmatched party in Milwaukee.

Spahn was thirty-six years old at the start of the new season. He was confident in his arm and in his beefed-up repertoire. He was less sure about his knees holding out, but that was out of his control, aside from occasionally letting one of his infielders handle a play instead of fielding the ball himself. At least he did not have to make any diving catches in the outfield. He left that to Henry Aaron and the other players out near the fences.

Timed for the start of the 1957 season, Spahn spoke his mind in a first-person, as-told-to feature in the *Saturday Evening Post*, the legendary Atlanta sportswriter Furman Bisher filtering his words to the masses. The headline atop the article said it all: "I Say Milwaukee Will Win The Pennant."[222] Spahn was practically speaking in all caps.

"This year they (fans) can pick Milwaukee all the way and not go wrong," Spahn said. "The Braves will win the National League pennant. I'll go even further. The Braves will also defeat the New York Yankees in the World Series, four games to two. I've never felt so positive about a Braves team since I became a steady boarder in 1946."[223]

Spahn described the plane ride from St. Louis to Milwaukee at the end of the regular season and the disappointment at finishing one game behind Brooklyn in the pennant race. There was silence on the plane, players looking into their hearts and souls and coping with their emotions knowing the season was over and there was no trip to the World Series.

"We had blown the pennant," Spahn said in his harsh analysis of recrimination. "We had goofed. When the chips were down, we lost and Brooklyn won."[224]

Maybe Spahn was right, and maybe he was too hard on himself and his teammates. That Dodgers team was a pretty special one. But when the mobs of fans greeted the Braves at the airport anyway, the team got a jump-start on renewal.

"An experience like that," Spahn said of losing under pressure and yet still being applauded, "can either kill you or inspire you. Here was a mob of fans just as disappointed as we were and they had shown up to tell us we were forgiven."[225]

The Braves did not feel worthy. But they took the Milwaukee sentiment to heart. To Spahn it was as if the future, the next season, was preordained. Nobody would beat the Braves in 1957.

The season opened April 16 at Wrigley Field against the Chicago Cubs. Braves manager Fred Haney went with his ace— Spahn. Spahn loved Opening Day, and he had won the right to be the team's choice on that special day. He admitted he still felt the butterflies, though.

"I've been pitching 20 years," Spahn said before that Cubs game, "and I don't think I ever go out there calm, collected and cool. Once you stop getting nervous, you might as well quit, because brother, you're dead."[226]

The southpaw went the distance, throwing a four-hitter in a 4–1 victory. Spahn and others might have seen that as a good omen. Nonetheless, being 1–0 after the long winter certainly felt better than being 0–1. The 1957 season was when Spahn gave up on his fastball almost completely as a go-to pitch. He had to throw them, such as they still were, once in a while, but he was relying more on that sinker.

"My fastball is no longer my ace in the hole," Spahn said in his realistic concession to age.[227]

The Braves just killed April, winning their first five games and going 9–2 in the month. Milwaukee sat in first place in the NL through May 15. It was a good-news start, though rarely could a team play to its top potential for an entire 154-game season. Some slumps are inevitable.

Manager Fred Haney had mostly let the Braves play it their way in 1956. He was a latecomer. He missed spring training. Now he was the boss from the start of the season and he had a roster full of players who believed they were the best in the National League the year before, but hadn't proven it.

When the team arrived in Bradenton for spring training, Haney had news for them. He told the players they were going to hate his guts because he was going to work them so hard on conditioning. Though Eddie Mathews was a great power hitter, Haney wanted to improve his mediocre play at third base. So he drilled Mathews until he was worn out from fielding so many grounders.

Haney was always alert for ways to upgrade the day-to-day lineup. He was not enamored of second baseman Danny O'Connell, perhaps due to that baserunning gaffe the previous season. Andy Pafko was still dangerous at the plate, but Haney wanted one more outfielder. It turned out that man was already in the farm system. There were debates over whether or not Wes Covington was ready to take the final step to the big club, but in the end he made the team. And the bench was shored up. Joe Adcock's injury in 1956, handing first base to rookie Frank Torre, might have accounted for the one-game difference in the standings, but now Haney had two quality first basemen available.

Covington turned out to be a valuable addition. He was twenty-five in 1957 and aching to see more action. He got into 96 games and produced, with 21 homers and 65 RBIs and a .284 average from the left side of the plate. The 6-foot-1, 205-pound Covington gave the Braves another African American on the team, indicating the team was color-blind in their promotion of personnel. You didn't have to be a Henry Aaron to make the squad.

During the second half of the season Covington was one of the team's key hitters, and he kept up his pace in the postseason. He was born in Laurinburg, North Carolina, and showed he could hit at every level of the minors before the Braves brought him to Milwaukee. Covington hit .330 in Eau Claire, .326 in Jacksonville (where he led the Sally League), and as a rookie in 1956 hit .283 in 75 games.

While such commentary was a bit overblown, early on Covington drew favorable comparisons to Aaron. Still, a player could be very good and not measure up to Aaron.

Minor-league manager Ben Geraghty gave Covington his highest endorsement in the scouting report he sent to Milwaukee.

"He is hitting hard and often," Geraghty said. "Besides that, he is throwing well and he is running the bases like a veteran. There probably isn't a better player in the league."[228]

Covington was an older rookie. His first sport was football and he spent time in the Army. Covington did not even play baseball in high school. He was thinking of a pro football career. But one summer he dabbled in baseball for a semi-pro team and surprised himself. When he realized he could hit a baseball with authority he changed his sporting focus. "Hitting seemed easy," Covington said.[229]

Of course Covington eventually figured out hitting a pitched ball could be a major challenge. Playing baseball in the Army helped Covington make up for his lack of experience, and then he played winter ball in Puerto Rico. When Covington hit .314 there he seemed capable of advancing to the majors. "I wanted to play with the big boys," he said.[230]

Joe Adcock was terrific in 1956 with 38 home runs and 108 runs batted in before his season-ending injury after 137 games. He was healed and ready to go in 1957—and then suffered a new debilitating injury after 65 games, breaking his leg. That could have cost the Braves the pennant, but Frank Torre filled in ably, though definitely without as much power. And Torre played with a broken finger. The Braves were in third place when Adcock was injured in 1957, and Torre recollected fans thinking he might not be able to make up for his loss, but being proud of doing so. "That's when I felt I really belonged in the big leagues," Torre said.[231]

Torre, the older brother of Joe Torre, later a National League batting champ and Hall of Fame manager, most notably for the New York Yankees, appeared in 129 games. While he hit just five home runs, his batting average was .272. Joe, who was a high school phenom, sometimes took batting practice with the Braves before his own pro career began.

The Torres grew up in Brooklyn. Frank said the family was not well off and multiple generations crammed into small living quarters.

"I had to sleep in my crib until I was three years old because there was no place else," he said. "In those days you couldn't even breathe without your grandmother's permission." When the family moved to more spacious accommodations the home was located right near a park. "That was the break for me and my younger brother, Joe, because there was a park on the corner and we got to play some ball."[232]

Torre was ready when the Braves needed him. Much later in life, when Joe was managing the Yankees during one of their regular October postseason appearances, his older brother's heart was failing. As he prepared for a heart transplant, Frank's predicament received a tremendous amount of coverage on national television.

The 1957 season was definitely one of the most special in Torre's career, certainly from a team standpoint.

"I have my Milwaukee Braves uniform from the '57 World Series," he said forty years later. "I've been chased by collectors who try to buy it."[233]

No pickup was as important as the new second baseman, however. Fred Haney was not a big fan of Danny O'Connell and he identified that position as a weakness. Whether it was a personality thing hardly mattered, because the replacement acquisition was so far superior not even O'Connell's relatives could argue against him.

He may have been thirty-four years old, but Red Schoendienst was still a star. He played 93 games for the Braves that season and hit .310. He solidified an already formidable lineup. While Schoendienst was most closely identified with the St. Louis Cardinals during his decades-long Hall of Fame career as player, coach, manager, and front office executive, he enjoyed this extremely successful interlude with the Braves.

A ten-time All-Star, Schoendienst spent nineteen years in the majors and played in 2,219 games after breaking in with the Cardinals in 1945 at twenty-two. He was not a power hitter, but a smart hitter, a leader on the field and in the clubhouse, and although he did not want to overstep his bounds with the winning Braves after being acquired after the season began, his professionalism set an example.

The 1950s were not the Cardinals' best decade. They are one of the winningest franchises in major-league history, but that stretch of years was not a high point. St. Louis traded off Schoendienst to the New York Giants in 1956. Braves general manager John Quinn wanted him. Initially, the Giants resisted a deal because they wanted Wes Covington. Quinn did not want to part with Covington. He looked like a future star, his absence would just open up a hole in the outfield, and he was years younger than Schoendienst. Ultimately, the Giants accepted another package. The Braves shipped O'Connell, Bobby Thomson, and pitcher Ray Crone to New York.

Quinn also pulled off the deal just before the trade deadline so other teams could not do anything drastic to counter.

"Credit the Braves with being smart operators," said Pittsburgh manager Bobby Bragan. "Red will give your team the spark it has always needed. He means you've become the team to beat."[234]

Schoendienst added a fresh dynamic. Henry Aaron welcomed him as just the right guy at the right time. Haney was thrilled to have him and immediately installed Red as a team captain even though he did not want the honor because he might be seen as an interloper.

"I was pretty lucky," Schoendienst said. "I walked into a real good situation and fit right in."[235]

Along with Aaron, Spahn, and Eddie Mathews, that gave the Braves four future Hall of Famers on the field and several other players who were many-time All-Stars. Quinn had assembled quite a crew. Yet it all could have been ruined because of injuries to important players. Joe Adcock was just one. Outfielder Billy Bruton missed 75 games. Sparkplug shortstop Johnny Logan, one of the team leaders, missed 25 games.

However, the Braves had Felix Mantilla, Aaron's old Sally League cohort, in reserve for the infield. A collision with Mantilla while they chased a ball in the air is what had KO'd Bruton for the rest of the season, but the infielder emerged unhurt. Mantilla ended up playing in 71 games, coming to the plate 200 times, and although he batted just .236, his fielding was excellent. He was also the only possible fill-in for Logan in the entire organization.

Mantila was just seventeen when he first suited up for a Braves minor-league affiliate in 1952, hitting .323 in the Three-I League.

"I always wanted to be a big leaguer," Mantilla said, who was noticed by the Braves. "It was for $400, which seems paltry today, but back then, I can assure you, it was a fortune. Of course I grabbed it and signed." When someone asked him how he spent the big bucks, he added, "Are you kidding? My mother got it."[236]

Although he had been playing in the Braves' chain for a few years, Mantilla's mastery of his second language of English was not complete when he reached the majors. It was said when he first arrived on the mainland his only English words were "filet mignon." He had come a long way since but was not going to banter much with fans unless they spoke Spanish. After Mantilla slid into the first-string role, he was asked what pitch he hit for a single against the Pirates. "They pitch me fast, so I hit a fastball," Mantilla said.[237]

It was noticed around the team Mantilla had a smile on his face almost all of the time, even when situations did not necessarily call for it. That was either his true nature, or at times he was not fully cognizant of what was going on, or he was just happy to be with the big club.

"That's the way he is," manager Fred Haney said. "Maybe I can help him as a ball player, but I'm in no position to worry about his disposition. He's my shortstop. He's the guy that counts now. He's a good one. We're not worried."[238]

Mathews could take the worry out of run-scoring. Now an established All-Star, he swatted 32 homers with 94 RBIs and batted .292 in 1957. He was more confident than ever but with more maturity. Mathews had also improved his fielding. A bruiser who did not mind a good scrap, Mathews was also the self-appointed team protector. If someone threw a pitch at one of his teammates he was the first to intervene, essentially announcing, "Pick on someone your own size." Mathews always had his guys' backs.

Braves pitcher Lew Burdette was always living on the edge, tempting fate when it came to angering opponents. While Burdette also said "Bring it on" as a general rule, he was always cheered to know Mathews was going to be in the foxhole with him. Mathews actually told Burdette he didn't even need his help punching out the opposition.

"With Eddie, you never worried about anything," Burdette said. "If somebody charged the mound when you were pitching, you knew he was going to be there. Eddie used to tell me, 'Let the son of a gun charge you and get the hell out of the way.'"[239]

Mathews and Aaron were among the top handful of power hitters in baseball and no team had a better combination at that time. Aaron put together an astounding season in 1957, clubbing 44 home runs, knocking in 132 runs, and batting .322. And he was still only twenty-three.

This was a new power surge for Aaron, who hit 11 homers in June alone. Catcher Del Crandall developed a theory. He believed Aaron was so good that he could just decide to become more of a home-run hitter and do it. How could he pull off such a feat? Even the best pitchers rarely fooled Aaron. He had a level swing and snap in his wrists. Once he gained a few years of experience in the majors he seemed to realize he was basically better than just about everyone else.

"I think he made up his mind he was going to hit the ball out of the ball park," Crandall said. "I think he decided he was going to be a home-run hitter because to me Henry Aaron was the best hitter I ever saw."[240]

This was the season Aaron began to invade the pantheon of the best-ever—at least he started slipping into conversations on that topic. He was an impressive young player, had advanced to regular All-Star, and kept building on that.

"Henry reminds me of the Babe," Haney said in probably the first comparison between Aaron and Ruth. Ruth's records were in the books, while Aaron was just starting out. In twenty years, the two men's home-run numbers would be scrutinized more closely than Hollywood gossip pages.[241]

Aaron said the Braves of 1957 were a particularly determined team, still smarting from the unsatisfying manner in which the 1956 season ended. "If anything good came out of blowing the pennant in 1956, it was 1957. We didn't want it to happen again and Fred Haney intended to make sure it didn't."[242]

Aaron said during his long career he had a couple of seasons where his all-around statistics gave him a chance to win the Triple Crown, and 1957 was one of those years. He was the defending National League batting champ and this was his huge breakthrough in homers, the first of many times he topped 40 homers in a season. During this most charmed of Braves seasons, Aaron did lead the NL in homers and runs batted in. He also was named the league's Most Valuable Player.

Aware of Crandall's comments later about him purposely going for more homers, Aaron said if so, it wasn't conscious, but that maybe his teammates read him better than he read himself. Warren Spahn had a keen observation of the Aaron of this time that jibes with both a man motivated consistently by pride, as Aaron was, and what Crandall said.

"I always felt there were two competitions in Henry's life," Spahn said. "One, he wanted to hit more home runs than Mathews. I think that's why he started to pull the ball more. He gave up part of the plate when he did that and his average went down a little. The other competition was that he wanted to be a better all-around player than Willie Mays. I never heard Henry say any of this. It's just what I perceived to be the case."[243]

Mathews pretty much agreed. He said he and Aaron had their own rivalry within the team, basically to push one another to do their best. The third baseman hit 512 home runs during his career, twice leading the league and four times smacking at least 40 homers in a season. Aaron ended up breaking Babe Ruth's home-run record with 755 while leading the league four times and eight times hitting at least 40 homers in a season.

"Hank and I had a friendly rivalry," Mathews said. "He pushed me and I pushed him. He'd win the home run title one year, I might win it the next. Rivalries were important to us. We always looked for rivalries to keep us going. If we were in St. Louis, for instance, I might say to myself 'I want to beat Ken Boyer this series in every department.' Maybe we felt that way because guys like Hank and I didn't get the publicity we should have due to the fact we were playing in Milwaukee. Willie Mays, in my opinion, wasn't as good a player as Hank Aaron, but whenever Willie did something, the New York press and the skies lit up."[244]

In early June the Braves fell to fourth place. This National League season, Milwaukee, St. Louis, Brooklyn, and Cincinnati would win at least 80 games. The Dodgers were in transition. Jackie Robinson had retired. While guys like Duke Snider, Pee Wee Reese, and Roy Campanella were around, Don Newcombe suffered a major dropoff from his 27-win season of 1956, and young Sandy Koufax, 5–4, was just starting out. Don Drysdale was Brooklyn's only big winner.

Led by Frank Robinson, the Reds still had all of those power hitters. Despite disposing of Red Schoendienst, the Cardinals were on the rise. The great Stan Musial batted .351 that season, Wally Moon batted .295, Joe Cunningham hit .318, and Ken Boyer was rounding into competition for Mathews as the best third baseman in the league. Musial won his seventh National League batting title that season at age thirty-six and in his 22-year career batted .331.

During his own long career, which closely paralleled Musial's, Spahn declared the lefty swinger with the distinctive crouch in the batting box to be the best hitter he faced.

"I've got to go along with Stanley Musial," Spahn said. "He did it so many times I think the thing that amazed me about him is that for a number of years no matter what you threw Stan Musial, everything he swung at he hit on the barrel of the bat."[245]

But each of those challenging teams was flawed and could not put together pull-away winning streaks. By mid-June, after winning four straight, Milwaukee eased back into first place. On June 14, the Braves topped the Philadelphia Phillies, 10–2, and Spahn inched his record up to 7–3 with a complete-game three-hitter while allowing just one earned run.

On July 12, the Braves edged the Pirates, 5–4, with Spahn gaining his ninth win. He came out after 8 1/3 innings in favor of twenty-seven-year-old rookie Don McMahon. McMahon, who would appear in his last major-league game at age forty-four, recorded a 1.54 earned run average in 1957. He was ahead of his time as a reliever, especially that year when McMahon pitched in 32 games after getting called up in June, but accumulated just 46 2/3 innings.

"To keep sharp, I've got to pitch three times a week, at least," McMahon said. "Otherwise I get wild. Actually, I'm wild anyway and when I don't get enough work I'm really in trouble."[246]

In a tight pennant race every fan looks for omens. The Braves made their fan base very nervous on July 15 at Ebbets Field. It turned into the most embarrassing day of the season for Milwaukee when the Dodgers overpowered them, 20–4 on 16 hits. Bob Trowbridge and Ernie Johnson were battered early, Gene Conley held Brooklyn in check for three innings, but then poor Taylor Phillips gave up nine runs in the eighth inning. Worse, despised Don Drysdale got the win. Did this portend a Braves collapse? Braves fans took the loss so badly some even hung manager Haney in effigy in the streets. Milwaukee had just one day to fret over this miserable outing, however. It was Warren Spahn to the rescue.

On July 16, when Spahn won his 10th game of the season, beating the Phillies, 6–2, the Braves moved from third place and one game out to a tie for first. Patrolling right field, Andy Pafko made a show-stopping sliding catch to end the game and ignite team admiration. "It was the first time a pitcher ever hugged me," Pafko said of Spahn's reaction. "That made me feel real good."[247]

It also made the Braves feel really good. The win kicked off a stretch of seven wins in eight games. They remained in no worse than a tie for first place into August. After dropping slightly off the pace over the first few days of that month, Spahn took the mound for a 5–4 victory over Cincinnati. Spahn surrendered four runs, three of them earned, to outlast Hal Jeffcoat.

That was the second win in a Braves 10-game winning streak, and by August 15, the last day of that stretch, Milwaukee had an eight-game lead in the standings. Spahn won twice more during that streak, 9–0 over the Cardinals and 8–1 over the Reds. Spahn was on his way to a 21-win season with Bob Buhl winning 18. Burdette won 17, though pitching a little bit more unevenly than the others. Spahn's earned run average was 2.69, the 21 triumphs led the league, and he won the Cy Young Award that season. National League batters probably did not reflect much on Spahn being thirty-six years old.

The Braves were minus Logan, Adcock, and Bruton for major stretches and Pafko periodically nursed a weak back. They were loaded with other good hitters, but those injury hits were a challenge to absorb. Two-thirds of the season was over before the day-to-day replacement for Bruton emerged, and the player who made one of the greatest unexpected come-out-of-nowhere runs of excellence in baseball history did not appear in his first game for Milwaukee until August.

Left-handed-hitting outfielder Bob Hazle was born in South Carolina in 1930. Always a good hitter, he attracted attention from the Cincinnati Reds and after bestowing a $50,000 signing bonus on him in 1950 they, at last, brought him to the majors for a six-game trial in 1955 when he went 3-for-13. Some of the wait was attributable to Hazle's being borrowed by the Army for a couple of years.

Next year in spring training Hazle was expected to break into the Reds' lineup. But they seemingly lost interest, kept him at Double-A Wichita for all of 1956, and then swapped him to the Braves as part of a deal where Cincinnati obtained George Crowe. Through 92 games for Milwaukee in Triple-A in 1957 Hazle hit .279 but was favoring a lingering knee injury. When the Braves needed help after Bruton went down, again minor-league manager Ben Geraghty spoke up. Hazle could do the job, he said.

After a day getting used to the major-league clubhouse, Fred Haney inserted Hazle into a game as a pinch-hitter on July 29. Then starting a game he struck a single against the Pittsburgh Pirates. That was July 31, a 4–2 Braves win. On August 4, Hazle went 2-for-3. On August 6, he went 1-for-3. Hazle had an 0-for-1 day August 7.

Then the real craziness began. In a 13–2 victory over St. Louis (Bob Buhl's 15th win of the year) August 9, Hazle went 4-for-5. He hit his first home run off Lindy McDaniel. A day later, during a 9–0 win over the Cardinals, Hazle went 3-for-4, drove in three runs, and scored two.

Game after game, Hazle kept it up. Because he was from South Carolina and in 1954 there had been a devastating Hurricane Hazel in his home state, Hazle received the nickname "Hurricane."

After a month in the majors Hazle was batting .507 and was the sensation of the sport.

"It doesn't seem possible that anyone can keep up such a pace," Red Schoendienst said. "But right now the kid is Stan Musial, Mickey Mantle, and Ted Williams all wrapped in one."[248]

Hazle was unstoppable. The Braves thought he had to come back to earth eventually, but for the moment his fabulous hot streak was helping them win game after game.

"I didn't want to wake up," Hazle said. "Gosh, that was a good life."[249]

Between being passed over in the minors and struggling with the knee injury, Hazle revealed if he had not made it to the bigs in 1957 he was going to retire and take up another profession to support his young family.

"I thought I had had it," Hazle said. "I decided that if I didn't make the majors by '57 I would call it quits and go sell insurance or something. When I got to camp this spring and the knee still bothered me, I was ready to take the first bus back home."[250]

Instead he became one of the best-known names in the sport overnight. The 6-foot, 190-pound Hazle, whom Pafko said had some of the strongest wrists around (though perhaps not on par with Henry Aaron's), stayed hot enough to grill a steak throughout the rest of the regular season. Hazle played in 41 games, hitting seven home runs with 27 runs batted in and an average of .403 with a .477 on-base percentage.

During August, Spahn, who by then had earned the nickname "Old Folks" in some quarters, won seven games as the Braves finished the month seven games ahead in the standings. The others had dropped off. Spahn was at 17 wins and counting with a month left in the season.

There was one bizarre game in early September when the Braves mashed the Chicago Cubs, 23–10, on 26 hits. Of course, the wind was blowing out at Wrigley Field that day. Hazle and Frank Torre each stroked four hits. Aaron drove in six runs, and so did Covington. The way things started it seemed both teams might score 23 runs. Lew Burdette was chased in the third inning after giving up seven runs. Ernie Johnson went the rest of the way for the win.

The Cardinals were the last other team standing, still hoping they could mount their own miracle run in the last week-plus of the regular season. But the Braves turned the screws. Haney remained as intense as ever, and his mood dominated the clubhouse.

On September 20, a rainy day which scared away most spectators, Spahn won his 20th game of the season. The weather was bad enough the game could easily have been postponed. Paid attendance was just 4,032. But they played on a muddy field and Spahn took his turn. A five-run Braves seventh inning broke open the game, and Milwaukee won 9–3.

This was the eighth time Warren Spahn won at least 20 games in a season. Lefty Grove, who retired with a 300–141 record, was the only other left-hander to accomplish that. (Grove won 31 in a season once.)

St. Louis was on life support on September 23 when the Cardinals rolled into County Stadium, not yet mathematically eliminated. But this cold day with temperatures in the 40s might be the day the Braves could clinch. Burdette was the starter, and Spahn went public to drum up excitement—as if the people of Milwaukee needed more incentive to cheer or drink another beer.

"I want to see the people in Milwaukee tear down the stands tomorrow night!" Spahn said the night before the encounter. "And they can do it."[251]

Never mind just the goalposts, so to speak. But the Cardinals were not ready to go gently into that good night in front of 40,926 witnesses. Wilmer "Vinegar Bend" Mizell opposed Burdette on the mound. The man with perhaps the best nickname in baseball history won 90 games in a nine-year career and later served North Carolina in Congress, but this wasn't one of his best nights. He was pulled in the second inning by manager Fred Hutchinson after allowing a run on four hits.

Larry Jackson came in and shut the door. Jackson threw the next seven innings and gave up just one more run. Jackson was pretty much a face on a wanted poster for the Braves from an incident earlier in the season. Henry Aaron had labeled him public enemy number one after a pitch sailed near his head. The postgame was fiery with Hutchinson, Jackson, and coach Terry Moore on the other side.

Moore said Aaron's comments about Jackson throwing at him were "Bush League," a sensitive phrase around Milwaukee. Aaron said, "Bush League, huh? Real big-league pitchers don't throw at you, only gutless ones."[252]

The September showdown game went on. Billy Muffett, who almost never yielded home runs, replaced Jackson for St. Louis in the bottom of the ninth. Burdette lasted through 10 innings with Gene Conley subbing for him to start the 11th inning as tensions increased. Conley retired three straight.

In the bottom of the 11th, Schoendienst flied out for Milwaukee. Johnny Logan singled to center field. Eddie Mathews flied out, bringing up Aaron. Aaron slammed the ball over the fence in the deepest part of the ballpark, his third hit of the game and the most memorable hit of the 1957 season.

The Braves grasped their pennant tightly as the County Stadium organist played "Happy Days Are Here Again."

The Braves felt the Cardinals had not been very respectful of their talent. Spahn kind of rubbed the triumph in again on September 24 when he won his 21st game of the season. It was another complete-game win, a 6–1 five-hitter.

St. Louis did finish second with 87 wins to Milwaukee's 95, but as September ended the Cardinals went home for the winter. The Braves, as they long had dreamed, had a date with the New York Yankees in the World Series.

20

WORLD SERIES

THIS IS WHAT Milwaukee Braves fans had dreamed of from the moment they acquired a major-league team. Their Braves, their guys, their players, won a pennant and were bringing the World Series to the beer-swigging, cheese-producing land of Wisconsin far from Madison Avenue, far from the eastern snobs who proclaimed Milwaukee a bush town when it gained standing in the National League.

Milwaukee had celebrated when the Braves first got off the train to begin their first season in town, but this was worth ten times the emotion, the thrill, the excitement. The World Series! The apex of the sport, the chance to show the best baseball team in the country called Milwaukee home.

"Happy Days Are Here Again" indeed.

Wouldn't you know it, when the Braves were headed off to New York and Yankee Stadium to begin play in the World Series on October 2, 1957, the natives sent them on their way with another parade. The authorities estimated attendance at 80,000 for the send-off, twice the population of County Stadium at any given game.

If passion counted on the scoreboard, the Yankees were dead. Of course, everyone knew that only fools counted out the Yankees in October. From the days of Ruth and Gehrig, through the DiMaggio era of the 1930s and 1940s, to the new generation of Yankees managed by Spahn's old nemesis Casey Stengel who sent his own superstar Mickey Mantle out to the field to lead the Pinstripes, the Yankees were the only team in the sport that needed a calculator to count pennants and World Series rings, the only ones that marked epochs in franchise history with Dynasties plural.

Certainly the relieved Braves, who outran the rest of the National League through the tortuous summer months, did not lack for confidence. They had sweated not only for a season, but for several years to capture a prized pennant. They wanted to finish the job, put the whipped cream on top of the hot fudge and vanilla ice cream. And yes, add the cherry, too.

As they prepared to head out of town, the parade passed through the city, players riding in open convertibles. A fan ran up to Warren Spahn's vehicle and urged him to win a game. Spahn held up two fingers and shouted back, "Not one, two!"[253]

Spahn had always hungered to return to the World Series after his lone appearance with the Boston Braves in 1948. This was a fine year to do so. The great Cy Young, who won more games than any pitcher in history and still holds that record of 511, died in 1955. Baseball decided to honor him the next year by instituting the Cy Young Award to be given to the best pitcher in the majors each season. The Dodgers' Don Newcombe won the first award, but in 1957 it went to Warren Spahn. It was not until 1967 that a Cy Young Award was given to the top pitcher in each league.

The Braves were almost giddy about getting their chance to upend the feared Yankees. Spahn, who had been on the losing side in 1948 when the Cleveland Indians won the crown, desperately wanted to be part of a world champion.

"The series wasn't as important to me personally as it should have been," he said of 1948 and his intense desire to win this title. "They can't take it away from you."[254]

The New York Yankees won their first World Series title in 1923 when Yankee Stadium was new and Babe Ruth was the team's biggest star. They won twice more in the 1920s and won four times in a row in the 1930s and a fifth time overall in that decade. They won their share in the 1940s, including 1949, which kicked off a run of five straight titles through 1953. In 1957, they were defending champs, having dispatched the Dodgers in 1956.

Milwaukee won 95 games in grabbing the National League pennant. The Yankees won 98 to take the American League, the 23rd pennant in franchise history. New York was seen as such a formidable postseason opponent, loaded with talent and experience, the Yankees became the betting favorites. The Braves may have been sentimental favorites for baseball fans who were sick of Yankee victories, but it was always hard to argue with that New York lineup.

Mantle, the gifted switch-hitter from Oklahoma, was just twenty-five years old and very much in his prime despite owning the knees of a sixty-year-old. He found ways to cope, and in 1956 won the Triple Crown and the AL Most Valuable Player Award. In 1957, he hit 34 home runs with 94 RBIs and led the league with 121 runs and 146 walks while batting .365. He was again voted MVP.

New York's offense started with Mantle, but he was surrounded by other top hitters, most prominently future Hall of Fame catcher Yogi Berra, plus good fielders and clutch hitters like Bill Skowron, Bobby Richardson, Gil McDougald, Andy Carey, Elston Howard, and Hank Bauer. Tony Kubek, who wasn't even starting at short yet, and future Hall of Famer Enos Slaughter both came off the bench. Overall, eight Yankees were selected as AL All-Stars.

Southpaw Whitey Ford was on his way to the Hall of Fame, as well, but this wasn't one of his top years. In a limited 28-game season he finished 11–5. However, the Yanks definitely had mound depth. Six pitchers, led by Tom Sturdivant's 16–6 mark, won at least 10 games. Don Larsen went 10–4 a year after hurling the only perfect game in World Series history. Savvy Sal Maglie, aka "The Barber" for his habit of pitching inside, was acquired near the end of the season and went 2–0 with a 1.73 earned run average. Three times in his thirties, with time split between the Brooklyn Dodgers and New York Giants, Maglie pitched in the Series. The Yanks figured he could provide tips about the NL Braves.

One guy missing from the 1956 champs, and broken-hearted about it, was Billy Martin. During the summer, Martin and several of his teammates visited the famed Copacabana nightclub. Not only was it an All-Star cast of players, but many wives were in attendance, making it unlikely any trouble might break out over the champagne flowing for Martin's twenty-ninth birthday party.

However, a brawl did take place, Bauer was arrested, and a furious Yankees' management, ticked off by the blow to the team's image, sent Martin packing to the Kansas City Athletics. It was alleged some bowlers hurled racial insults at performer Sammy Davis Jr., which sparked the fight. Many stories, most not in agreement, were told about that night. The front office fined several players $1,000 each.

Berra, as only he could, took stock of the scenario and said, "Nobody did nothin' to nobody."[255]

Thirty-six-year-old Warren Spahn was chosen by manager Fred Haney to start Game One of the World Series at Yankee Stadium on October 2. Attendance was 69,476 for the afternoon game. His opponent was Whitey Ford.

Ford retired Red Schoendienst, Johnny Logan, and Eddie Mathews in order in the top of the first. In the home half of the first Spahn relinquished singles to McDougald and Mantle. Mantle's safety was an infield hit. But no one scored.

Henry Aaron led off the Braves' second with a groundout to second base. Before leaving Milwaukee, Aaron said, "Those people were so good to us. We felt like we were going to win, but we really wanted to win for those folks."[256]

That did not happen in the opener. Spahn flirted with danger in the second inning, allowing a double to Jerry Coleman, but Coleman was stranded on base. The game remained scoreless into the bottom of the fifth when Coleman touched Spahn for a leadoff single. Two outs later, Bauer sent Coleman home with a double to center. Milwaukee could not get anything going against Ford. In the sixth, Spahn allowed a single to Howard and walked Berra. There were two men on when Fred Haney walked to the mound to chat with Spahn. It was unlikely he discussed candlesticks as a potential wedding present like the scene spoofing mound conferences in the movie *Bull Durham*. Haney had the bullpen warming.

"How you feeling, Spahnie?" Haney asked. "OK. I was a little too careful with Berra there, I think," Spahn replied. Haney asked Spahn if he had all his pitches, and Spahn said he did.[257]

Spahn promptly gave up a single to center off the bat of Carey, scoring Howard and sending Berra to third. Haney marched right back to the mound while signaling to reliever Ernie Johnson, who later wound up as a longtime commentator on Braves games.

Spahn was removed after 5 1/3 innings, permitting seven hits and three runs. Johnson went two-thirds of an inning and then was replaced by rookie Don McMahon. Ford went the distance and gave up only five hits and one run. New York won 3–1 to take the lead in the Series.

Game Two was the next day, back at Yankee Stadium before 65,202 fans. The starters were Lew Burdette for the Braves and lefty Bobby Shantz for New York. Spahn gave Burdette some advice.

"The big thing out there today, Lew, is not to let the Yanks awe you," Spahn said. "Forget about the name on their uniform. I've just got a feeling that this is your day. You've got to do what I didn't do yesterday. Watch Mantle. He's got the fastest reflexes I've ever seen. Keep that ball low and away to Mickey. Keep the pitch around the ankles. Give him a couple of fast ones, then the slow ball."[258]

Spahn actually kissed the ball and handed it to Burdette.

Shantz had a listed weight of 139 pounds and stood just 5-foot-6, but was the 1952 American League MVP. He was a crafty pitcher, but the Braves solved him early, reaching him for six hits and four runs through three innings. This was a critical game for the Braves, who did not want to return to County Stadium trailing 2–0.

The Yankees received their first serious taste of Henry Aaron in the second inning when he led off with a triple to the spacious area in center field. A recovered Joe Adcock singled him home for a 1–0 Milwaukee lead. The Yankees nicked Burdette for a run, but Johnny Logan homered in the third. Shantz came out for the fourth but gave up consecutive singles to Adcock, Andy Pafko, and Wes Covington.

Shantz's next move was to the showers, and Stengel's next move was to insert Art Ditmar in relief. The Braves came out of the inning with two more runs, and Ditmar stuck around for four innings total. All the runs were charged to Shantz, and Ditmar allowed just one hit. Bob Grim threw two innings and also gave up only one hit. But it was too late. Burdette went all nine innings and the final score was Braves 4, Yankees 2. It was going to be a Series, after all.

Hank Bauer made the last out on an infield grounder and Logan ran the ball over to Burdette to keep. "Lew, you deserve this souvenir," Logan said.[259]

Both Spahn and Burdette held grudges against Yanks manager Casey Stengel, Spahn from pre-war days when Stengel sent him to the minors and Burdette from the early 1950s when he traded him away without offering him much chance to pitch.

"Maybe Casey knows my name today," Burdette said.[260]

At last the Series moved to Milwaukee for Game Three on October 5. Wouldn't you know it, but Milwaukee, which could have been practicing for the Tournament of Roses Parade, tossed another parade to welcome the Braves back to the Midwest. There were an estimated 10,000 fans at the airport to greet the team plane and another 200,000 people lining the parade route. It was cuckoo.

The sophisticated Yankees were even met by 2,000 polite fans, including one farmer who wanted a member of the team to step off the train and milk a cow. There were no good sports among the Yankees, who yukked it up at Milwaukee's expense. Even Casey Stengel, once popular managing in Milwaukee, drew the ire of fans for snubbing them. Stengel was grumpy and turned what started as cheers for his return into boos. These were people reveling in hosting their first World Series, their ascension to the big-time, and the Yankees did their best to make them feel small.

Buhl, an 18-game regular season winner, drew the assignment on the mound for the Braves and alas for him and those enthusiastic Milwaukee fans, the Yankee bats did make them and their heroes feel small in Game Three. New York clobbered Buhl and were no kinder to Juan Pizarro, Gene Conley, or Bob Trowbridge. Ernie Johnson, in the middle, threw two fine innings and Don McMahon at the end also fared better with two clean innings. In between, New York ran up 12 runs and allowed just three, Bob Turley starting out a bit wild, but Don Larsen settling into 7 1/3 innings of two-run ball.

Schoendienst had three hits and Logan and Aaron two apiece, but they didn't amount to much. The Braves were in the same spot as they had been after the opener in New York. They were down 2–1 in games and couldn't afford to fall behind 3–1.

Spahn wanted the ball again. He wanted to atone for the first game loss. He was like a warrior on the mound for Game Four. He wanted to beat the Yankees so badly in front of the home fans. This was a big opportunity, a second chance in the Series, a critical one to draw his team even. This was going to be no easy chore, but Spahn might have thrown a sinker at Haney if he tried to take him out this time.

The Yankees scored one run in the top of the first. The Braves rebounded with four in the fourth to ease anxiety for the 45,804 at County Stadium. Tom Sturdivant started for New York and seemed in command of his pitches with just one single allowed until the bottom of the fourth inning. Logan led off with a walk. Eddie Mathews doubled, and immediately Sturdivant was in trouble with men at second and third. Things got worse. Aaron cleared the bases with a three-run homer to left. One out later Frank Torre homered to right field.

The 4–1 lead looked impregnable the way Spahn was pitching—until the top of the ninth when he gave up a three-run, tying homer to Elston Howard that shocked the Milwaukee fans. They got edgier when New York scored a fifth run for the lead in the top of the 10th inning, the key being a Hank Bauer triple that knocked in Tony Kubek. Kukek was a Milwaukee native, so he was given a few cheers even though he wore an enemy uniform.

It was desperation time for the Braves, trailing 5–4. Nippy Jones, pretty much a third-string first baseman who got into 30 games for the Braves that year, pinch-hit for Spahn. Yank hurler Tommy Byrne hit him with a pitched ball, putting the tying run on before being lifted for Bob Grim. Initially, plate umpire Augie Donatelli called the pitch that stuck Jones a ball, and he was told to stay in the batter's box. However, Jones protested. Braves players produced a ball with a mark on it and said it was shoe polish from Jones' spikes. He was able to take his base. This was the best-known play in Jones' eight-year career.

Milwaukee players moved around the bases like chess pieces, but finally, Felix Mantilla, who came in as a pinch-runner, was driven home by a Logan double, tying the game 5–5. Mathews stepped in and ended the game with a two-run blast to right field. The Braves won, 7–5. Spahn won, too.

Somehow, the Braves were simultaneously living large and living on the edge. Ford started again for New York in Game Five, Burdette for Milwaukee. Both pitchers were 1–0 in the Series.

After Burdette won his first game of the Series, he had pretty much dismissed the Yankees as nothing special.

"The Yankees are no better than some clubs in our league," Burdette said with insouciance when sportswriters present seemed to call for him to bow at the Yankee shrine. They quizzed him about his pitches, and he said he got New York players out with "Stuff I always use. Screwballs, sinkers. . . ."[261] The writers wanted him to admit to throwing that darned spitball, but he just smiled at them.

This was round two for Burdette and he was even better than before. He flummoxed the Yankees on seven hits, and shut them out, 1–0. Ford went seven innings and gave up the run, and he gave way to Turley for the last inning. Adcock drove in Mathews in the sixth inning. Lew Burdette was the man of the hour again.

The Series adjourned to New York. The Braves were back in town, not to attend a Broadway show, but to put on their own show at Yankee Stadium. Some show it was over the final two Series games. Suddenly, it was New York on the verge of Series extinction.

Righty Bob Turley, who was 13–6 during the regular season, kept New York alive in Game Six with a 3–2 victory. Once again Buhl was hit fairly hard, though Johnson took the loss when he surrendered just one run in 4 1/3 innings.

So there they were, on the cusp of the ultimate sports suspense, the seventh game of the World Series. The Braves so badly wanted to win their first Series in Milwaukee; the Yankees wanted to brush aside this assault on their superiority.

Game Seven was scheduled for October 10, three days after Burdette's shutout. Spahn had been ill with a virus and a temperature of 103 degrees, and when Haney came to him and asked if he was ready to throw for all the marbles, he had to truthfully but regretfully decline. He was too weak. So going with the hot hand, Haney chose Burdette to hurl the seventh game. He was the one Milwaukee pitcher the Yankees had not solved. Right choice.

If anything, Burdette was better than he had been in winning Game Five, overcoming the jitters that often come with a Game Seven start. It is the game where memories and reputations are made. The world is watching the World Series and usually even a larger segment of the world is watching Game Seven.

Don Larsen started for the Yankees, as if Stengel was trying to rekindle the perfect-game magic of 1956 at the perfect time for New York. It did not work. One by one Stengel trotted out reinforcements to the mound, Larsen followed by Shantz, Ditmar, Sturdivant, and Byrne, a parade of pitchers.

The Braves scored four runs in the third inning. Bob Hazle, the summer phenom who had two hits in this game, started the rally with a single. Logan reached base on an error and Mathews doubled them both home. Aaron, who batted .393 in the Series, singled Mathews home. Wes Covington singled and a Torre groundout scored the fourth run. The Braves added a single run in the eighth on a Del Crandall home run.

The Yankees managed three hits in the ninth inning off Burdette without scoring after compiling just four others in the game. Bill Skowron grounded out on a force play at third and that was it. Milwaukee triumphed, 5–0, to win the World Series crown. Burdette captured three of the Braves' four wins, making him the Series MVP.

Burdette's three victories in a World Series remains a rare feat since the event began in 1903. The first pitcher to win three was Bill Dineen of the Boston Red Sox that year. The last was Randy Johnson with the Arizona Diamondbacks in 2001. At the time of Burdette's trifecta, the St. Louis Cardinals' Harry Brecheen in 1946 was the most recent pitcher to perform the feat, although Brecheen and Johnson did not win all three of their games as starters. Before Burdette's trio of masterpieces, it had been thirty-seven years since a pitcher had started and won three games in one Series, that being Stan Coveleski for Cleveland in 1920. Burdette was the first pitcher to toss two shutouts among his three wins since Christy Mathewson in 1905.

"In the Series, Burdette was the big difference, mostly because of his amazing control," Mantle said. "Lew Burdette surprised us Yankees."[262]

Burdette, who never sugarcoated comments to spare feelings, had his own take on how he beat New York three times.

"Everybody said I fooled the Yankees," Burdette said. "Well, they fooled me. I thought they were better hitters."[263]

Touché. Yes, Burdette and the Braves were allowed to gloat a bit.

Even though Spahn was not the pitcher for the seventh game, the result was the peak of his career to that point. Playing on the big stage, his team winning the big game, was something he cherished. In the late innings Spahn warmed up in the bullpen—capable of giving a few innings in an emergency—but Burdette eliminated the need for Haney to wave in Spahn.

"I don't care if you play in 100 World Series," Spahn said, "You can't escape the feeling you are part of something big and important."[264]

Thinking back to April when he made brash predictions in a national magazine about the Braves winning the National League pennant and the World Series and beating the Yankees, to boot, Spahn could take satisfaction in being right about it all.

There was a huge party in Milwaukee when the Braves won, with seemingly everybody in the city and the vicinity flooding the community in celebration. Nobody really knew exactly how many people toasted the Braves with their favorite beer—maybe 750,000, maybe a million—but the city once called "bush league" finally had its championship.

21

ANOTHER PENNANT

THE BRAVES' 1957 championship would forever overshadow their 1958 season. A first World Series championship for a community has a way of eclipsing everything else. But the Braves were not done. They felt they had paid dues for several years with their close calls, so they wanted the glory ride to continue. They still believed they were the best team in the National League and were determined to re-prove it.

While the Braves continued to look great on paper, even if some of their top players were aging, no two teams are alike. There is never an instant-replay season. Some players do not live up to their reputations. Some players play better than ever. Players hurt one year are healthy another. Players healthy the first time around get injured the next year.

Champs have targets on their backs, receiving every team's best game, all anxious to knock them off their pedestal. Other teams beef up lineups or pitching staffs. It is easy for a title team to stand pat. If you are already anointed as the best, urgency to improve may be lacking.

Owner Lou Perini, general manager John Quinn, and manager Fred Haney did not want to stop at one pennant. They had built meticulously, but they seemed to realize if some changes were not made they might get caught short, perhaps the next August when someone was injured. So although they embraced the 1957 offseason as a special time for the franchise and a time worthy of celebration, they did not get lazy.

In hindsight, reviewing his career record year-by-year, one has to wonder what the fuss was all about when the Braves obtained right-handed pitcher Bob Rush from the Chicago Cubs at the winter meetings in December of 1957. The main players the Braves gave up in the multi-player deal were Taylor Phillips and Sammy Taylor, who were not significant players on their roster.

The rest of the National League was shocked Rush was obtain-able for such an inexpensive price. Philadelphia Phillies general manager Roy Hamey spoke as if the Braves had just robbed a bank in Dodge City.

"What did they use on those poor Cubs, a shotgun?" Hamey said. "Why, that's awful. I couldn't believe it when they told me about it."[265]

This is what the Braves were getting: a thirty-one-year-old thrower coming off a 6–16 season with a 4.38 earned run average, a pitcher who only once in a thirteen-year major-league career won more than 13 games, and one whose 20 losses in 1950 led the NL. Why such excitement? Mostly it was because the Cubs of that era were woeful and any pitcher who survived looking half-decent might transform into a star for a first-class winning team. Indeed, in 1950, when Rush finished 13–20 he was selected for the All-Star team. He was chosen a second time in 1952 with a 17–13 mark and a 2.70 ERA. Rush was better than most of his surroundings, except for Wrigley Field, and everyone seemed to know it. The

Giants were trying to swing a deal for Rush at the same time and admitted offering what they believed was a more valuable package of five players.

Dodgers vice president Buzzie Bavasi said of the Braves post-trade, "Let's face it, it makes it that much tougher for us next year."[266]

Many baseball people wondered if Spahn, thirty-seven years old at the start of the season, would go gray, go arthritic, or suddenly look as if his salary was supplemented by Social Security. Spahn, keenly aware that age withers every athlete's prowess, always safeguarded his livelihood by exploring new ways to counteract his aging body and his slowing fastball. He had added the sinker and that proved wise.

After the World Series victory, Spahn contemplated the 1958 campaign and what he could do to prepare for another 20-win season. The Braves hired a new pitching coach, Whitlow Wyatt, a 106-game winner as a big leaguer and a four-time All-Star, even though a chunk of his career pre-dated the creation of the All-Star Game in the 1930s.

This appointment met with Spahn's approval. Wyatt had as much respect as a pitching coach as he did as a pitcher and Spahn's fresh idea was to add a slider to his pitching lineup. When attending a winter baseball banquet in Wisconsin in January of 1958, Spahn made his pleasure and thinking known. "Boy, I can't wait until I talk to Wyatt," Spahn said. "I know he'll be able to help me with my slider."[267]

The Braves' everyday lineup looked much the same as in 1957, though players who were injured, like Joe Adcock and Billy Bruton, were back at full strength. The Braves needed Bruton. Wes Covington, the emerging outfield star, hit .330 in

1958 with 24 home runs but only appeared in 90 games due to a knee injury suffered in spring training.

Frank Torre played a bit more first base than Adcock, but he was on the field for 100 games. Andy Pafko still provided some steadiness off the bench for 95 games. Catcher Del Rice and Felix Mantilla could always be counted on. But after his miraculous 1957 season, Bob Hazle began his big fade.

Eddie Mathews smacked 31 homers and Henry Aaron just kept getting better, at twenty-four totaling 30 homers and 95 RBIs while batting .326. He played in 153 games.

Of course, coming off his spectacular World Series, everyone expected Lew Burdette to continue doing what he did in October. Burdette came through, winning 20 games with a 2.91 earned run average. Bob Buhl was an 18-game winner the year before, so adding Rush to this mix seemed to create an impressive four-man group of starters.

However, this is when the unexpected intervened. Buhl got off to a swift start in 1958 with a 5–2 record. Only the ache in his arm that flared up periodically in 1957 which he shrugged off became worse and worse. He was bewildered, and doctors at first seemed baffled, too.

"It wasn't fun throwing the ball," Buhl said. "I couldn't even lift my arm to put on a jacket."[268]

For the moment, it appeared the Braves were in for a repeat of 1948 when the Spahn and Sain and pray for rain business took hold. Only it would be Spahn and Burdette and praying for rain.

Buhl also couldn't lift his arm to get the ball over the plate and his fastball was lagging. Haney stopped using him, and the team sent Buhl to the Mayo Clinic for inspection. It wasn't until a dentist spotted nerve damage in two teeth and pulled them that

Buhl felt all better. By August he wanted to return, but Haney refused to activate him.

While it may seem difficult to swallow, such tooth problems can cause widespread effects on other places on the body, although it was hard for Buhl to prove the two issues were related. All he knew was that when one place was fixed, the other got better.

In the interim, to the surprise of Haney, the team, and the rest of baseball, a group of young pitchers emerged from the shadows and began having success. It was a tag-team effort behind Spahn and Burdette (and yes, Rush, who won 10 games). In 1958, Carl Willey, Juan Pizarro, and Joey Jay made important contributions. Willey went 9–7 with a 2.70 ERA. Pizarro, who was just twenty-one despite being part of the 1957 team, went 6–4 with the same ERA. Jay, whose future lay ahead of him mostly with the Cincinnati Reds, went 7–5 with a 2.14 ERA.

Even more inexplicable than Buhl's fall was the 1958 collapse of Gene Conley, who finished 0–6 in 26 games.

So not everything was the same as it was in 1957, but still the Braves and Haney made do by mixing the pieces.

By mid-May Spahn was 6–0 with a 1.86 earned run average. If anyone suggested Spahn was too old to keep pitching in the majors they said it in a whisper. This was a man who kept re-inventing himself, a man at this stage of his career without a fastball that would dent a window. He was not going to blow the heat past Willie Mays or Roberto Clemente. By now it seemed as if the word "crafty" had been invented for Spahn. He was still being paid to get hitters out, but he was more than ever being paid to fool them, to apply deception to his pitch choice. He was the master of control, of placing the ball right where he wanted it to land in catcher Del Crandall's mitt.

"People always ask me what makes Spahn so great," Whitlow Wyatt said. "I tell them, 'Two and oh. Three and one. Three and two.' The tough spots. The worst thing you can do—with good hitters, I mean—is to come in with your fastball. Understand, I'm not talking about .220 hitters. You can sometimes blow it by them. But I'm talking about (Willie) Mays, and (Duke) Snider, and (Ernie) Banks. In that spot you need the slow curve, maybe, or the change, or the slider. A fellow is not a pitcher until he can control those pitches under pressure. Spahn is a great pitcher, maybe the greatest, because he gets them with that clutch pitch."[269]

The Braves adjusted to their problems throughout the season and 1958 happened to be a year of change and weakness in the National League. Milwaukee won 92 games, compared to 95 the year before. But this time the Braves rather comfortably outdistanced the pack.

Of all teams, the Pittsburgh Pirates, who only a few years earlier were the hands-down worst team in baseball, finished second with 84 wins. The Braves were still eight games better in the standings, but Pittsburgh was on the move, about to culminate a long rebuilding process. The Dodgers had gone off to Los Angeles and played miserably. The Giants had moved to San Francisco and the kindest description of their season was so-so at 80–74. What of Cincinnati and its power hitters? The Reds finished 16 games behind the Braves with a losing record. And St. Louis, those hard-to-kill Cardinals of 1957? They were four games worse than Cincinnati and 20 games in arrears of the Braves.

The Braves moved into first place for good on July 30, taking up residence there for so long they could have found a new place to vote. The Braves had been heavy favorites to repeat, although few prognosticators considered the Pirates would be runners-up and the previous contenders would be flops.

"This time we did what people expected of us, despite our injuries," Haney said.[270]

"Old Folks" Spahn threw 290 innings and won 22 games, equalling the second-most victories for him in a single season and his ninth time winning at least 20 in one year. He won his 20th with a complete game on September 13, beating the Cardinals, 4–2.

Especially since the advent of the designated hitter, few baseball people talk about the prowess of pitchers who can hit unless it pops up while they are at the plate during a televised game and a commentator thinks of it.

Although Spahn's lifetime average was just .194, he could defend the plate better than most hurlers and on many occasions surprised the opposing pitcher. He belted 35 home runs during his career. Wes Ferrell, who won 193 games pitching between 1927 and 1941, hit 37, the record for a pitcher. Spahn is tied for second on the all-time list with fellow Hall of Famer Bob Lemon.

One of the most amazing aspects of Spahn's 1958 season was that he batted .333, gathering 36 hits to help himself. On June 4, 1958, the Braves were on the road against the Giants.

Bob Rush started for Milwaukee and was hit hard. Bob Trowbridge followed him and was also hit pretty hard. Joey Jay, Humberto Robinson, and Don McMahon took turns on the mound and halted the Giants' offense. Ernie Johnson, who got the win, also had a blown save and Gene Conley received the save. Throughout most of the three-hour, thirty-five-minute game Spahn was a spectator.

After the Giants slugged their way into an early lead, the Braves chipped away at the margin after starter Mike McCormick pretty much held them in check. They scored off Al

Worthington and Pete Burnside, and Stu Miller came in to slam the door. Henry Aaron had three hits, Pafko and Adcock two apiece, and Covington had three runs batted in. At the end of nine innings, the score was 7–7. In the 10th inning the hopeful Braves scored two runs. But in the bottom of the 10th, the Giants tied it again at 9–9.

Haney used twenty-three players, sending up Mel Roach, Frank Torre, Harry Hanebrink, and Del Rice as pinch-hitters and sending in Lew Burdette and Bruton as pinch-runners. Bruton made it into the game in the top of the 11th after Covington walked. Johnny Logan sacrificed Bruton to second. Pafko flied out to right field for the second out.

Johnson was due up. He was a .180 lifetime hitter and hit one homer in his career. Of all people, Haney, who was almost out of players, turned to Spahn to pinch-hit. Spahn stepped in to face Miller and slashed a single to center that sent Bruton around with the run. The Braves had one more out to spend and then Conley retired the side in the bottom of the 11th for the 10–9 win.

When sportswriters interrogated Spahn about what type of pitch he struck for the game-winning hit, he said, "The same kind of pitch I missed by nine million miles the first time I swung."[271]

Burdette was not the hitter Spahn was. He hit just 12 home runs during his career. However, on July 10 of that season, Burdette made like, well, Henry Aaron. The Braves were facing the Dodgers in California, in their temporary home of the Los Angeles Memorial Coliseum. In the fourth inning, when it was Burdette's turn to hit, Crandall, Logan, and Pafko each had a foot on a base. Sure enough, Burdette blasted a grand slam, the key blow in his 8–4 win, although LA pitcher Johnny Podres was likely so shaken by the unlikely sight of Burdette circling the bases he lost his concentration and allowed the Felix Mantilla homer that followed.

It was of no surprise to anyone that while the Braves were repeating as National League pennant winners, the Yankees were doing likewise in the American League. New York also won 92 games, but the Yankees were 10 games better than the second-place Chicago White Sox. If the Braves were nervous about the rematch it didn't really show. If the Yankees were overconfident this time, that didn't show either.

Burdette was the star of the previous Series, so the *New York World-Telegram and Sun* sought him out as a guest columnist to offer the Braves' point of view. Burdette began cranking out his opinion on September 30, before the Series began, but after the opponents were decided.

"I don't really know too much about the Yankees," Burdette said. "But I didn't know much about them last year either [when he went 3–0 in the Series] and I haven't given 'em much thought lately. I do think they're nice fellows, even though they don't have a hankering for me. About the Series, we'll win it. I don't know how many games it'll go this time."[272]

Spahn was Haney's choice to pitch the opener on October 1, this time in County Stadium, not Yankee Stadium. Although Bob Turley was the American League Cy Young Award winner with 21 victories, Casey Stengel picked Whitey Ford to start because of his postseason experience.

This time Spahn was not staggering around with a 103-degree fever and performed like his usual self, relying on control, never tiring, going the distance and pitching Milwaukee to a 4–3 Game One win in 10 innings. Bill Skowron and Hank Bauer did reach Spahn for solo homers.

"I don't lose easily," Spahn said.[273]

The headline on Burdette's column read, "We Win Close Ones." He wrote a game analysis, and of Spahn he said, "One thing about Spahnie that sets him above most other pitchers is that he seldom has two bad innings in a row. That's his history. That, plus the fact he gets stronger as he goes on."[274]

In a humorous aside, Burdette wrote of the Braves receiving a telegram of encouragement from actress Gwen Verdon who starred on Broadway in the play *Damn Yankees*. She said, "Now please go out and beat those damn Yankees."[275]

Burdette started Game Two against Turley and the Braves crushed those damned Yankees, 13–5. Milwaukee scored seven runs in the first inning and Bruton and Covington each ripped three of the Braves' 16 hits. Three other guys clouted two hits each. Burdette even hit a home run, although Bauer hit his second of the Series and Mickey Mantle bashed two.

Burdette had a string of 24 straight scoreless innings going in the Series, and Babe Ruth held the record with 29 2/3 such innings. In his column, Burdette made fun of his hitting. "Besides," he said, "maybe now I can start chasing Ruth's home-run records."[276]

The Braves were up 2–0 in the Series and definitely looking like sure things to win again. The Yankees were still the Yankees, though, and they weren't going down easily. In Game Three, Don Larsen topped Bob Rush, 4–0, at Yankee Stadium, the home field agreeing with the Yanks.

Game Four was Spahn versus Ford for the second time. The two Hall of Famers dueled scorelessly into the sixth inning, but Ford yielded first. The Braves scored one run in each of the sixth, seventh, and eighth innings, Spahn allowed just two hits, and Milwaukee won 3–0 for a 3–1, seemingly safe lead in the World Series. Spahn, Mr. Hitter all of a sudden, even had a run-scoring single.

"He has taken charge of us and made us respect him the way Lew Burdette did last year," Mickey Mantle said in his own New York newspaper column. "You simply don't figure any pitcher, especially an older fellow like Spahn, to close down on you like that in the late innings."[277]

Catcher Del Crandall was even more effusive about Spahn. Spahn fanned seven Yankees. Overall, the home plate umpire signaled 28 called strikes in the game, all pitches that fooled New York batters. "His control was really uncanny," Crandall said. "He was hitting the corners, inside, outside. Mostly a fastball. It was so good we didn't need many screwballs."[278] That was a news flash Spahn could still summon the fastball when he needed it.

They definitely were revving up for another parade in Milwaukee, more beer toasts, and a party that might never end as the Braves seemed poised to clinch a second World Series in a row. After Spahn's dominating win he and Burdette entertained sportswriters with their cheerful banter.

"The stage is now set for my roomie to wrap it up," Spahn said of Game Five. "You will, won't you?"[279]

Only he didn't. As overpowering as Burdette was in 1957, he was that beatable in this Series outing, losing to Turley, 7–0. Six of the runs scored in the bottom of the sixth. So the Yanks reduced Milwaukee's lead to 3–2.

Going for the kill, Haney started Spahn again on October 8 in Game Six, three days after his masterpiece and back at County Stadium. Whitey Ford started for New York. While Spahn gave up another homer to Bauer, Ford lasted just 1 1/3 innings, yanked after giving up five hits and two runs. The Yankees tied it 2–2 in the sixth and the score stayed that way past the ninth inning.

Once again Spahn played the stalwart, mowing down batters, walking purposefully to the mound inning after inning. The Yankees got to him in the 10th, starting with a leadoff homer from Gil McDougald. There were two outs and two men on, both with singles, when Haney lifted Spahn for Don McMahon. Haney made the hard walk to the mound and put his arm around Spahn. When Spahn made the harder walk to the dugout, the 46,367 fans gave him a standing ovation.

A single scored one more run charged to Spahn before McMahon got out of the inning and the Braves got their last at-bats to try and erase the two-run lead. The Braves came close, Aaron scoring Logan on a single off reliever Ryne Duren. Turley came on, but Frank Torre's line drive ended the game. The Braves and Spahn fell 4–3. Spahn could not replicate Burdette's three wins of 1957. The Braves could not clinch the Series.

"I wanted to stay in," Spahn said. "The ball game hinged on so little."[280]

Larsen started Game Seven for New York but was removed early. Burdette started for the Braves. It was 2–2 after seven innings, but the Yankees broke things open in the eighth, scoring four runs. The lead held up, and New York won at County Stadium, 6–2. Turley was the winner. During the Series Spahn and Burdette had both started games on just two full days rest. Turley, too, was on short rest—desperate measures for both sides. This was the first time in twenty-five years a team had bounced back from a 3–1 deficit to become the champions.

"They never quit and I say more power to them," Burdette wrote afterward. "They take advantage of every opportunity and every break."[281]

This was one of those wait-till-next-year losses. There was no reason to think the Braves' run was over. Surely they would be pennant favorites in the National League again in 1959.

22

TRYING FOR A THIRD PENNANT

THERE WAS SLIPPAGE at the gate. Even Milwaukee could not sustain its frenzied outlook on the Braves. The first six years the Braves were located in Milwaukee they led the National League in attendance, four times topping two million. In 1958, as the Braves won a second NL pennant in a row, attendance dipped to 1,971,101. In 1959, after capturing a World Series crown and two straight pennants, attendance dropped to 1,749,112.

After the Braves won the Series, the parade was surreal, with those hundreds of thousands of citizens lining the streets. When the Braves returned from New York after losing the seventh game of the World Series in 1958, they were met by some fans once again, numbering only in the hundreds.

Was this the herald? Was this the first crack in the relationship? How could such deep love and devotion dissipate so quickly when the team was a big winner? The Braves never could quite understand why Milwaukee fans loved them so intensely before they accomplished anything. Now it was difficult to fathom why Milwaukee fans' passion was fading. To a man, after the 1958 season, the Braves felt they were good enough to win a third straight pennant.

General manager John Quinn was gone. He moved to the lowly Philadelphia Phillies with hopes of rebuilding them and was replaced in Milwaukee by John McHale. Quinn had been with the Braves in Milwaukee from the beginning and he saw the job through there with two pennants.

Player faith may have been shaken going for a third one when for the second year in a row Milwaukee made huge news in the offseason. Unlike the acquisition of pitcher Bob Rush, this was not good news, however. Future Hall of Fame second baseman, Red Schoendienst, who brought so much energy and experience to his position, was revealed to have contracted tuberculosis. At one time in the United States that was a death sentence. That was not the case in the late 1950s, although it was a debilitating illness requiring a long recovery time and there was no guarantee a thirty-six-year-old athlete could return to competitive form.

The diagnosis shocked Schoendienst, the Braves, and all of baseball. During the 1958 World Series there were days he did not feel well. He played on, but when he was home between games he rested in bed all day. He was nauseous at times. His wife Mary said his face would sometimes be chalky white. After the Series, Schoendienst, who said he had been feeling off almost all season, went to a doctor for his annual checkup and some medical tests.

"You have tuberculosis, Red," Mary said her husband told her as he replayed the doctor's comments. "The findings are unmistakable. I want to take you—right now—to a sanitarium. You've got a tough road ahead. You'll have to lie on your back, hardly moving an inch, for perhaps as long as six months."[282]

Mary Schoendienst said she was never prouder of Red than the way he fought to conquer the disease.

A sportswriter who visited Schoendienst in the Mt. Rose Sanitarium found him talkative and upbeat. Thousands of get-well notes filled cartons in his room.

"TB don't hurt," he said. "You don't feel it at all. If anybody'd seen me on TV, they wouldn't even think I was sick."[283] He rested and rested some more.

Schoendienst disappeared from view all through spring training but was available for another hospital-bed interview shortly before being released as April dawned. By then he had had a lung operation.

"I think I'm one of the luckiest guys alive," Schoendienst said. "Sure, it's going to be tough. But I'm confident I can still play baseball, if not this year, then next. If I never play again, I'll have no regrets. I've had 16 wonderful, happy years in baseball."[284]

So the Braves were missing an important piece before the season began, although Schoendienst did get well enough to play four more seasons, and even got into five games for the Braves in 1959.

Felix Mantilla was the natural replacement, but he batted just .215 that year in 105 games. Bobby Avila, who won an American League batting title earlier in the 1950s, was thirty-five and at the end of his career. He began the year with the Baltimore Orioles, was placed on waivers, picked up by the Boston Red Sox, and put on waivers again. The Braves grabbed him on July 21 and started him. Avila played in 51 games but hit just. 238. He was no Red Schoendienst at the time.

The other usual suspects were in the everyday lineup. Joe Adcock was a 25-homer man at first base in 115 games. Billy Bruton was healthy again and hit .289. Johnny Logan hit .291 and Wes Covington .279. Eddie Mathews and Henry Aaron were both stupendous. That duo gave every opposing pitcher the shakes.

Mathews, twenty-seven that season, led the league with 46 homers, drove in 114 runs, and batted .306.

"Losing Red really hurt us," Mathews said. "It would be hard to overstate how important he was in our winning the pennant in 1957. Leadership is hard to define. It involves clutch hitting, turning the key double play, a whole list of things. Red did them all. If Red had stayed healthy, I really believe we would have run away from the pack. He made that much of a difference."[285]

Aaron, playing every game, hit 39 home runs, drove in 123 runs, and batted .355.

"I was never a better hitter," Aaron said of 1959 and especially in the early season when he was hitting .508 at the end of April and fans were talking about him batting .400. "I've never been in a groove quite like I was at the beginning of 1959."[286]

Having punch in the lineup like Mathews and Aaron could cover up a lot of deficiencies. Scoring was not a problem since the Braves scored 100 runs more than they allowed.

When it came to pitching it always returned to Warren Spahn, Lew Burdette, and the backup singers. At least Bob Buhl was reeled back in from the garbage dump. But the rest of the staff did not live up to either the achievements or the promise of the year before. Spahn won 21 games again at thirty-eight with a 2.96 earned run average. Burdette matched him with the 21 victories, but his ERA skyrocketed to 4.07. Buhl bounced back with 15 wins.

It was a serious problem when Bob Rush went 5–6, Joey Jay 6–11, and Carl Willey 5–9. Young Juan Pizarro finished 6–2, being very useful when given a chance. Don McMahon was 5–3 with a 2.57 earned run average and 15 saves, so at least when manager Fred Haney wanted to pull a starter he had some insurance.

But the best insurance policy any manager could have was Spahn, despite his age. He was still a workhorse, throwing 292 innings as he appeared in 40 games. The typical laws of aging did not seem to apply to him or his left arm. Right from the start, pitching Opening Day on April 10 in Pittsburgh, Spahn handcuffed the Pirates with a seven-hit shutout as Milwaukee won 8–0. Spahn moved to 2–0 on April 21 as the Braves beat the Reds, 7–4. In the first game, he was superb; in the second win he got the job done the hard way. Those two contests encapsulated Spahn's long-term performance. If he had his good stuff, nobody could hit him. If he was a tad off he could fight through and probably still beat you.

In the late 1950s, when the Braves were truly in the national limelight, there was considerable talk that their best players were somehow overlooked in recognition because they played in small-town Milwaukee. But the excellence demonstrated by Mathews, Aaron, Burdette, and Spahn cut across regional boundaries. Spahn was especially well-known because he had pre-dated them all and been winning for so long his statistics kept mounting up.

The exquisite baseball writer Roger Kahn wrote a lengthy "Sport Special," as the longer, in-depth pieces were labeled in *Sport* magazine.

"Judged by any reasonable standard, Warren Spahn of the Milwaukee Braves has been the best pitcher of the last 10 years," Kahn said. "[H]is earned run average stands close to a record low for any decade." Kahn stated Spahn "has become a complete master of his craft. He knows the tricks, the angles, the percentages."[287]

While she still marveled at her husband's computer-like mind in retaining baseball knowledge, LoRene Spahn had become a very serious baseball fan.

"Years after a game, he can tell you what somebody hit," she said. "Then I send him to the grocery for three items and he has to call me up because he's forgotten what two of them were."[288]

Someone taking the man's side here might chime in that clearly Spahn knew what was important.

From Opening Day on in 1959 the Braves did what they were supposed to do—win. Except for one day through the end of the month, they were in first place. They kept up the solid play, and at the end of play on July 5 they were still in first, their record 44–33. One win along the way was particularly notable.

On May 26, 1959, southpaw Harvey Haddix pitched the perfect game that wasn't against the Braves at County Stadium. On a rainy night, 19,194 fans chose not to stay home. They witnessed a unique bit of baseball history. Overall, Haddix was a successful pitcher during his 14 seasons in the majors, winning 136 games and being chosen for three All-Star teams. A good fielder, Haddix also won three Gold Gloves. He did not break into the big leagues until 1952 when he was twenty-six years old, and his finest season was 1953 when he won 20 games.

Slightly built at 5-foot-9 and 170 pounds, Haddix woke up on the morning of his scheduled start not feeling well and almost cancelled out. Instead, he threw the best game of his life and didn't even win it. Throwing a perfect game is an extraordinary baseball rarity. As of 1959 there had been six of them, including Lee Richmond and John Montgomery Ward's duo of perfectos in 1880 when the rules were somewhat different. Cy Young did it in 1904 for the Boston Americans, aka the Red Sox, and Addie Joss pulled off the achievement in 1908 for Cleveland. Charlie Robertson, one of the least heralded of those who managed the feat, threw a perfect game for the Chicago White Sox in 1922, and Don Larsen had achieved perfection in the 1956 World Series.

For inning after inning Haddix and Lew Burdette matched zeroes on the scoreboard. However, Burdette did so in decidedly different fashion, seemingly pitching out of jams constantly. He permitted 12 hits, and Pittsburgh had a stampede of baserunners. Meanwhile, Haddix was allowing no hits, walking nobody, and avoiding errors and hit batsmen. The men struggled that way through nine innings. Neither team had a run, and Haddix still had a no-hitter and perfect game underway.

The Pirates had men on base in the second, third, fourth, fifth, ninth, 10th, 11th, 12th, and 13th innings. It was a miracle Pittsburgh did not score, but Burdette was pitching a Spahn-style game, toughing it out. For the Braves batters, nada, no hits, no threats. Pittsburgh's batting order featured Bill Mazeroski, Bill Virdon, Dick Stuart, Bob Skinner, Smoky Burgess, and Don Hoak, although Roberto Clemente did not play that day. When it came to rounding third base it seemed as if each of them wore a ball and chain.

The fans were in ecstasy. On a lousy weather night they were rewarded with a remarkable spectacle as Haddix winged his pitches past Aaron, Mathews, Adcock, and Covington time after time. The end came suddenly and awkwardly in the bottom of the 13th, rather than cleanly.

Mantilla led off and hit a grounder to Pirates third baseman Don Hoak. He fielded the ball and made an error on the throw to first. That ended the perfect game and gave Milwaukee its first baserunner. Mathews bunted, sacrificing Mantilla to second base. If ever there was an occasion to play for one run this was it. Now that the perfect game was gone (though the no-hitter was intact), but with the game still at stake, Pittsburgh manager Danny Murtaugh ordered Aaron be intentionally walked.

Adcock was the next hitter, and he clubbed a double into confusion. He smashed the ball to deep right-center for a home run, sending Mantilla across the plate with a run. Aaron knew the ball was not caught, but didn't realize it went over the fence and thought the game had ended when Mantilla scored so he did not continue in the basepaths. Adcock, unaware Aaron stopped running, passed him and was declared out and his hit was reduced to a double.

Aaron felt badly later about his mistake.

"I had cost him [Adcock] a home run, but thank goodness my dumb mistake was lost in the attention given to the incredible and heartbreaking game that Haddix had pitched," Aaron said. "I am sure Adcock wanted to strangle me, but he never said much about it."[289]

There was no doubt the game was no longer perfect, nor a no-hitter, and the Braves were the winners. The umpire declared Milwaukee a winner 2–0. However, the next day, league president Warren Giles ruled that only Mantilla's run scored and the final was 1–0.

"One of the strangest things that happened that year was the finish of Harvey Haddix's 12-inning perfect game against us," Mathews said.[290]

Harvey Haddix was perfect for 12 innings, an unprecedented mark. He was credited with a perfect game despite the loss. In 1991, however, the majors reviewed all no-hitters thrown to that date and established a new definition. A no-hitter didn't count unless a pitcher threw for at least nine innings and the no-hitter remained intact until the completion of the game. Under that definition, Haddix's "perfect game" was retroactively taken away from him, yanked out of the record books.

The 1959 pennant race left room for anyone who truly got hot to walk away with the flag. There were not many great teams. The Pirates were on the way up but still finished 78–76. The San Francisco Giants were pretty decent but finished 83–71. The Braves were erratic. They were out of first place for almost all of July and August and did not rally to claim the top spot until September 21 after bouncing between second and third for a few months. Milwaukee won 15 of its last 20 regular season games.

The Braves were seasoned, had two league championships on their resume, and were to be feared by the other teams. In that September 21 game Spahn was on the mound and the opponent was the Pirates. His performance was no masterpiece a la Haddix but more a show of perseverance. Over eight innings he gave up 12 hits and six earned runs but won his 20th game of the year as the Braves beat up on four Pirates pitchers to win 8–6. That put Milwaukee into a tie for first. As the hours and days trickled down on the season, the Braves hung tough, battling with the revived Dodgers, who were a completely different ballclub than they had been in 1958.

Spahn won his 21st game 3–2 over the Phillies on September 26, and the Braves were tied for first at bedtime. The next day Bob Buhl won 5–2 over Philadelphia, and the pennant race ended in a tie between Milwaukee and Los Angeles, each with 86–68 records. This set up only the third tie-breaker playoff in National League history.

In 1959, the Chicago White Sox were the American League champs and sitting around waiting for something to do after going 94–60. The Sox finished five games ahead of the Indians and 15 games ahead of the out-of-sorts Yankees.

The Dodgers won a coin flip for home-field advantage versus the Braves, and Game One was September 28 at County

Stadium. Stunningly, with the pennant at stake, only 18,297 fans showed up. Without a layoff before the playoff, the Braves had to start Carl Willey instead of the too-tired Buhl or Spahn. Willey was neither untouchable nor an easy mark. He went six innings and gave up three runs with McMahon finishing. However, those three runs, one at a time in the first, third, and sixth innings, were trumped by LA pitching that allowed the Braves only two runs in the second.

The playoff resumed 2,000 miles away at the Coliseum on September 29 with no rest day. Burdette started and was not that effective. Spahn appeared in relief but also was not on. The Dodgers eliminated Milwaukee, 6–5.

The Braves came close to snatching a third straight pennant, but overall it was an uneven season. "We looked like world beaters one day and we were horrible the next," Spahn said.[291]

Within days of the playoff defeat, manager Fred Haney resigned. He said coming up short at the end of the pennant race was not his reason for going. "I am quitting for myself and my family."[292]

Three weeks later, Johnny Logan ripped Haney. He blamed the manager for the loss of the pennant and said neither he nor other players would miss him in the dugout.

"We should have won by 10 games without any question," Logan said, although that may have been an optimistic outlook.[293]

The popular Braves, who put Milwaukee on the baseball map, seemed to be fraying in the front office and losing favor with the fan base, although there seemed to be no good reason for that as well as the club had played annually since relocating from Boston.

The drop in attendance by almost 500,000 since 1957's World Series–winning year was as alarming as it was inexplicable for a place that prided itself on being a baseball town. One tactical error, it seemed to Mathews, was no longer permitting fans to bring their own beer into the ballpark. He and the other players were surprised at the low turnout for the playoff game, even though there was no advance notice of the game and all tickets went on sale game day.

"Maybe," Mathews said, "the novelty had worn off."[294]

The novelty of pitching had not worn off for Warren Spahn. In 1959 he won 20 or more games for the tenth time and despite his age had no intention of retiring or of failing to reach that milestone several more times.

23

AGELESS WONDER

THE MILWAUKEE BRAVES were still new, residents of the community for less than a decade. Yet somehow they seemed tarnished to the fans. There was no good reason really, but attendance continued to plummet, in 1960 to 1,497,799. That was more than 700,000 fewer people than came out to County Stadium in 1957.

That year the Braves won the World Series. In 1958, the Braves reached the World Series. In 1959, the Braves tied for first place and lost a playoff. In 1960, the Braves finished second in the National League with a record of 88–66. In the big picture, that was a heck of a stretch. Only the Yankees had been better in that time span. My, how a Chicago Cubs fan would have embraced such a streak. The Braves fan had it good, but apparently didn't really know it.

This was a team in 1960 that still had Del Crandall (19 homers, 77 RBIs, .294) at catcher, Joe Adcock (25 homers, 91 RBIs, .298) at first, Eddie Mathews (39 homers, 124 RBIs, .277) at third, Bill Bruton (12 homers, 54 RBIs, .286) in center, and Henry Aaron (40 homers, 126 RBIs, and .292) in right. A visitor to the ballpark could count on seeing the home team score runs. Although Chuck

Cottier spent more time at second than anyone else, Red Scho-endienst did return from illness for 68 games.

The departure of Fred Haney led to the hiring of Chuck Dressen as manager. Dressen, a flamboyant figure with the Brooklyn Dodgers, was already a senior citizen when he got to Milwaukee. He was a hardliner who believed in disciplining the troops.

The core of the pitching staff Dressen inherited was the same as it had been during the Braves' successful run. This was both good and bad news. Lew Burdette won 19 games, and Bob Buhl won 16. The inexperienced pitchers of two years earlier were now seasoned. However, they were not much better. Carl Willey and Juan Pizarro each finished 6–7. Joey Jay went 9–8. Don McMahon was battered out of the bullpen, going 3–6 with a horrendous 5.94 earned run average.

Burdette was grumpy because he wanted a better contract for the 1960 season and the Braves were not as sympathetic as he expected.

"I'm holding out," Burdette said, as if announcing he was supporting an altruistic cause more than looking for a raise, "because I don't think it's fair to all the pitchers in baseball if I were to sign for the same money after winning 21 games."[295]

It was easy to make the case the Braves were not being fair to Lew by not giving him a salary increase, though the net result was that Burdette was late to spring training. Burdette said he was so insulted by the first contract sent calling for a pay cut, he threw it in the trash. Then he turned his nose up at $36,000, the figure from 1959. The Braves front office argued Burdette lost more games and gave up more hits and home runs than in any of his other Milwaukee seasons, even if he won more than ever and led the National League in wins. And fans wonder why players got agents. It was not publicized how much Burdette played for in 1960.

Above all, when it came to pitching, although he was threatening to challenge Methuselah as the oldest player in the game, the Braves still had Warren Spahn. Spahn turned thirty-nine at the beginning of the season, yet there he was, the ace of the staff taking his turn like a metronome, appearing in 40 games and still winning. This season it was 21 victories with a 3.50 earned run average. He threw 267 1/3 innings, rather high by Old Man standards but not by Warren Spahn standards.

Two years before he became Spahn's boss, Dressen praised what the pitcher brought to a team. "Spahn is what I call a go-to-sleep pitcher. The manager says Spahn is going to pitch tomorrow and then gets a good night's sleep. He doesn't have to stay up thinking. Spahn will be thinking for himself."[296]

This was the season of Spahn's September no-hitter, the first of his long career. He was still a team leader, still the pitching staff leader. He also had a good rapport with Crandall, who was the lefty's main catcher throughout almost all of the 1950s and into the 1960s.

"I never shook them off," Spahn said of catchers. "But I did stare them off. And location was more important to me than the pitch. I wanted the catcher to give me the location. So it didn't matter what pitch he'd call for, but it was important about the location of it. And also, one pitch sets up another one. You throw a fastball by a hitter and boy he's going to be reared up to hit that next one. And if you change up on him, he screws himself into the ground. I think this is the attitude I had when I was pitching . . . that I could nullify any hitter that came up there. And it wasn't with throwing a ball by him but changing speeds."[297]

While Burdette played it coy with sportswriters and other players about whether or not he threw a spitball as a weapon, many years into retirement Spahn admitted throwing one in a game in either the late 1950s or early 1960s when Walt Moryn was playing outfield for the Chicago Cubs. Moryn, who hit 101 homers during his eight seasons in the majors, had a knack for batting well against Spahn, no matter what the southpaw tried. Standing on the mound, Spahn thought about that and thought about Burdette and decided this once he was going to throw an illegal spitball.

"And he hit it for a home run," Spahn said. "When he went around third base I said, 'Hey, Walt, you hit my spitter.' He said, 'It didn't spit.' So that's the last time I ever tried to throw it."[298]

Over the later years of his career and in retirement, Spahn was constantly asked how he did it, how an older pitcher could keep up the same kind of work as he did in his twenties, how he could defeat time. Spahn was engaging on the subject, enjoying explaining how he outsmarted hitters.

The last year of Ted Williams's memorable career was 1960. The great Boston Red Sox hitter, who broke into the majors in 1939, loved to banter about hitting and pitching with Spahn. Neither of them shied away from instigating arguments for argument's sake. They had fun teasing each other about the baseball world from opposite sides.

One time when they were both visiting Cooperstown for a Hall of Fame dinner, Williams took his turn speaking and cracked that all pitchers were stupid.

"And about twelve or thirteen of those people were pitchers," Spahn said. "I was about the third person that spoke after Ted and I said, 'Well, Ted, if all these pitchers are stupid, how come you only hit .406? Fifty percent is .500 and you didn't hit that.'

"I used to get him to deliberately talk about hitting just to hear him. And the older that Ted got, the greater a hitter he was when he was playing. Ted is one of my favorite people and a student of the game."[299]

That was Spahn comparing Williams's talk to a fish story, about how the farther away the angler got from the lake the larger the fish got. However, for a time it was true that the older Spahn got the better his pitching became. Certainly that was counterintuitive, but he was a smart man who took care of his body, added new tricks, and wanted to stay in the game and at the top of his game.

Pitching coach Whitlow Wyatt, who stayed with the Braves after Haney left and Dressen came, understood Spahn's methodology. Spahn was right to think the two were going to be on the same wavelength about pitching.

"He just knows how to pitch," Wyatt said. "He pitches to weaknesses. He has different kinds of curves and different motions and different speeds and he's a competitor. I don't say he's the best thrower, just the best pitcher."[300]

In 1960, Spahn's 20th win of the season was his no-hitter that topped the Phillies, 4–0. He was so overpowering that day he collected 15 strikeouts. After that victory Milwaukee was within 5 1/2 games of first place and in second. Nine days later, after a stretch that included a five-game winning streak, the Braves were no closer to first.

On September 21, Spahn won his 21st game, beating Cincinnati 3–1. By then the Braves were in third, 7 1/2 games out, and definitely not gaining. The final two games of the regular season had Milwaukee at Pittsburgh in Forbes Field, but the Pirates had already clinched the pennant. The Braves lost both games and finished seven games behind Pittsburgh, which would go on to win one of the most suspenseful World Series of all. This was a runner-up finish that wasn't as dramatic as a couple of the Braves' other second places. This was the eleventh time Spahn won at least 20 games in a season. And as the season concluded it seemed likely that in 1961 he would be able to join elite company by winning 300 games in his career. He was at 288 wins and, yes, counting.

As of the start of the 1961 major-league season, a dozen pitchers had won 300 games in their careers, led by Cy Young with a record 511 victories and Walter Johnson with 417. No one has approached the totals of either titan.

Grover Cleveland Alexander and Christy Mathewson were next on the list (and still are), with 373 wins apiece. Pud Galvin, Kid Nichols, Tim Keefe, John Clarkson, Eddie Plank, Charles Radbourn, Mickey Welch, and Lefty Grove followed. Grove retired with 300 wins after reaching that total in 1941, then the most recent member to join the club.

During the course of regular business, following the patterns of his seasons, Spahn should have been approaching the milestone sometime over the summer of 1961.

However, he took a little detour on the way, throwing a different type of milestone game. Spahn pitched a second no-hitter. After missing out on the satisfaction of doing so for so many years up until 1960, he tossed a second one the next season. Just about any no-hitter can be classified as a thing of beauty the way any Miss America nominee can be. They are all special in their own way.

The scene was County Stadium on the night of April 28, 1961, five days after Spahn's fortieth birthday, and the shame of it was attendance was just 8,518. It was not nice weather, quite cold, and the *Milwaukee Journal* game story called those present "hardy souls" while referring to the setting as "the refrigerator that was County Stadium."[301] But in the old days not even a blizzard would have held Braves fans back with the club at home. Spahn beat the San Francisco Giants 1–0 while facing the nine-inning minimum of 27 batters. He issued two walks and erased those runners on double plays.

Sam Jones was the opposing pitcher, and he was almost as good, scattering five hits while striking out 10. Milwaukee's run was unearned, scoring in the first inning. Second baseman Frank Bolling singled and went to second on a passed ball while Eddie Mathews was at the plate. There were two outs when Henry Aaron singled Bolling home. Bolling was the only player in the game that day to get two hits. It was hardly a milquetoast Giants lineup Spahn faced. Hall of Famers Willie Mays, Willie McCovey, and Orlando Cepeda were the heart of the order, which also included the 1959 American League batting champ Harvey Kuenn, future NL batting champ Matty Alou, and his slugging brother Felipe Alou.

Spahn was unfazed by the artillery. Kuenn and Cepeda hit into double plays after Chuck Hiller and McCovey walked. Both plays started with the batters grounding to Spahn on the mound. Both times he spun and threw to second with shortstop Roy McMillan covering. McMillan twice relayed the ball to Joe Adcock at first. Spahn also fielded a bunt dropped down by Matty Alou and barely nailed him after flipping the ball backhand to Adcock.

"It's a crazy, wonderful world," Spahn proclaimed in the locker room. "It takes me 15 years to pitch a no-hitter. That should be enough for anyone. Then I get another in a hurry. This one was easy. I made a lot of mistakes, but I was lucky and they didn't hurt me."[302]

Milwaukee's catcher that day was Charlie Lau, not Del Crandall. Lau laughed at Spahn's characterization of making mistakes. Lau thought Spahn only made one mistake, throwing a high screwball to Mays. Mays got a piece of it but not all of it and tapped the ball back to the mound.

"When he talks about mistakes he means the ball didn't always go quite where he wanted it," Lau said, "like it might be inside, but a little higher or lower than he meant it to be. Spahn calls those mistakes, but nobody else would."[303]

If Spahn's so-called errors were noticeable, not even Mays noticed.

"You ask me, I would say he was not fast," Mays said, "not even what you'd call sneaky fast. But he was all pitcher, with amazing control. He kept the hitters off-balance with his changing speeds and he never put the ball where you could get much bat on it."[304]

At the time, Spahn was the second oldest pitcher in major-league history to throw a no-hitter. Cy Young was the only one who accomplished the feat at an older age. That changed when Nolan Ryan pitched his seventh and last no-hitter at the age of forty-four in 1991, thirty years after Spahn's.

One aspect of Spahn's no-hitter at forty that struck him and sportswriters funny was his sudden decision to embrace the old adage "Life begins at forty."

"I used to be a little bit concerned about reaching 40," Spahn said. "But now I think it's a helluva age."[305] Spahn had already celebrated the actual day of his birthday on April 23 by beating the Pirates, 3–1.

Former teammate Earl Torgeson was in his last year in the majors, indeed his last few weeks, in 1961 after being picked up by the Yankees. He sent Spahn a telegram that read, "Congratulations on your no-hitter. Mayo Clinic wants your body for medical science."[306]

Although Spahn was as good as ever, the Braves weren't. They were on their way to their worst finish since moving to Milwaukee. Their 83–71 record was only good enough for fourth place. Dressen didn't even make it to the end of the season, with Birdie Tebbetts taking over with 25 games left.

After playing two games for the team in 1960, Joe Torre became the mostly regular catcher in 1961 and was runner-up as Rookie of the Year. Brother Frank was gone by then, though. Adcock had one of his finest years with 35 homers and 108 runs batted in. Newcomer Frank Thomas (not to be confused with the later White Sox's Frank Thomas, who is now in the Hall of Fame), hit 25 homers at age thirty-two and added even more pop. Eddie Mathews hit 32 homers and batted .306. Aaron remained in a class of his own (or at least in a class with few others) by bashing 34 home runs with 120 RBIs while batting .327.

Spahn said he knew right away Aaron was going to be great after watching him make a stupendous outfield catch while falling down.

"And I thought, 'God gave this guy the kind of ability that he's going to do great things in baseball,'" Spahn said. "And he proved that right. I think Hank could have been a 20-game winner if he wanted to pitch. That's how good he was. And, you know, his endurance, his physique, he was a perfect ball player. If, you know, if you had to clone ball players, he might be the one to clone."[307]

One of Spahn's greatest moments on the diamond occurred August 11. There were 40,775 people at County Stadium for a contest with the Chicago Cubs. The Braves won, 2–1, over Jack Curtis. Spahn went the distance, allowing just six hits to players like Ernie Banks, Billy Williams, Ron Santo, George Altman, and Don Zimmer. Milwaukee scored one run in the fifth and one run in the eighth and Spahn made them stand up.

This was the occasion of Warren Spahn's 300th victory.

"It was fantastic, the most exciting game I ever pitched," Spahn said. "This was even more exciting than the World Series or the two no-hitters." He said he didn't worry about reaching 300 in prior days because he figured he would definitely win another game. But on game day, in the hours leading to his appearance, Spahn felt differently. "The pressure began to build up. About six o'clock I was wishing we could start the game right then and there. I wanted to get it over with."[308]

Son Greg, twelve, who was born right around the 1948 World Series, was as energized as Spahn. He issued his own game report.

"Was mom ever excited," the younger Spahn said. "I never heard her yell so loud."[309]

Greg Spahn's grandmother and Warren Spahn's mother Mabel was keeping tabs from Buffalo. "I can't explain exactly how I feel, it's wonderful," she said afterward when she sent a telegram to her son.[310]

As he told the sportswriters, Dad was pretty darned excited, too. Spahn knew his stuff, but he seemed to play poker with his comments in the days after his no-hitter, talking in a self-deprecating manner about his assets, possibly to psyche out future young hitters.

"Hell, look at me now," Spahn said. "I'm not a big guy and I'm 40 years old. I stand up there looking at a big, strong 25-year-old and I know I can't overpower him. I have to outthink him. I have to keep him off-balance. This is hard work for a 40-year-old."[311]

Poor Warren. Somehow he kept getting that next generation to make outs.

24

TWILIGHT

AFTER WINNING AT least 20 games in a season for six straight years, when Warren Spahn won only 18 in 1962 it was stop-the-presses news in Milwaukee. *Gasp.* Was he mortal, after all? Inevitably, since he was forty-one years old at the time, all manner of scrutiny was focused on Spahn's left arm to detect possible signs of deterioration.

It does not matter if you are the greatest left-handed pitcher of all time and one of the all-time greats in Major League Base-ball, if you are forty-one and look the part (Spahn was very much balding and craggy-faced by now) people are going to be skeptical about whether or not you still have it. Of course if some previously unknown twenty-one-year-old came along and won 18 games in a season baseball people would be gushing about his future.

Only four years had passed, but much of the Milwaukee starting lineup was different than it was for the 1958 pennant-winners. The Braves were on their third manager since and there was much other turnover as next Birdie Tebbetts, who disappeared between the 1962 and 1963 seasons, and then Bobby Bragan sought to bring another pennant to Milwaukee.

The Braves still had plenty of power, with Henry Aaron blasting 45 home runs and Eddie Mathews and Joe Adcock adding 29 each. One intriguing new player was a rookie named Tommie Aaron, Henry's younger brother. There were great expectations for the twenty-two-year-old, but while good enough to make the majors, the younger Aaron did not have the talent to leave a major mark.

As always the pitching staff was structured around Spahn, Lew Burdette, and question marks. Burdette finished 10–9 with a bad earned run average of 4.89, and Spahn had his minor dropoff with a few less wins. A nice acquisition was Bob Shaw, a key hurler for the Chicago White Sox's 1959 American League pennant-winners. Shaw won 15 games for the 1962 Braves.

There were also three young starters management believed in: Bob Hendley (who made his debut in 1961 and won 11 games for this team), Denny Lemaster (3–4), and Tony Cloninger (8–3).

In 1963, a headline appeared in the *Milwaukee Journal* reading, "Braves Beat Bongos Over Hendley As 'New Spahn.'"[312] Didn't happen. In 1964, the same newspaper referred to the Milwaukee attitude toward Lemaster with this headline: "Braves Preen Head Feathers Over 'Second Spahn' Lemaster." The story included this sentence: "For some time now, the Braves have looked upon Lemaster as a second Spahn and this could be the year he becomes one."[313] In 1965, another nominee arose as this headline read, "Braves Feel Blazer Ready To Blossom As 'New Spahn.'"[314] The third candidate in three years to be thus anointed was Wade Blasingame.

Apparently after that there was no more mention of Warren Spahn clones, replacements, or second comings. There were no additional Warren Spahns to be had, not fifty-plus years ago and not since. Lifetime, Hendley ended up 48–52 and Lemaster 90–105. Blasingame's career won-lost total was 46–51, although in 1965 he won 16 games, if never more than nine before or after. At 113–97, Cloninger, whom no one made the mistake of calling another Warren Spahn, out-did all of them.

In 1962 and 1963, despite advancing age, Spahn was still busy being Spahn, if also doing double duty as a twice-their-age pitcher ahead of Hendley, Lemaster, and Cloninger in the rotation.

The Braves finished the 1962 season with an 86–76 record, but that did not keep them in the pennant race. In a season when the San Francisco Giants won 103 games, the Dodgers 102, the Reds 98, and the Pirates 93, that made them also-rans.

In 1962, the Braves exiled long-reliable reliever Don McMahon to the Houston Astros, shocking and dismaying the pitcher, who recorded a 1.53 ERA with the Astros and in June of that season was the winner in a 3–2 victory over the Braves. McMahon and Birdie Tebbetts had not seen eye to eye on strategy.

McMahon said Tebbetts ordered him not to use his fastball, which he was doing to great effect in Houston, and ignored him for a month before McMahon was dispatched to Houston. McMahon trashed Tebbetts in the newspapers before the June series began, and when McMahon came in late to pitch, Tebbetts shouted, "You still look the same to me." McMahon seethed and retorted, "Drink another beer, you fat so-and-so."[315] McMahon was pleased to get the victory. Soon enough Tebbetts was glad to go home and be replaced by Bobby Bragan.

The Braves remained steady winners, if not always threatening for first place, but on most days there were plenty of good seats still available at County Stadium. It was a case of love lost by the Milwaukee baseball fan, despite the presence of three of the best players on the planet, three Hall of Famers, in Spahn, Aaron, and

Mathews on view in the lineup for a decade. It was not only the Hall of Famers, either. Milwaukee still featured Del Crandall (an eleven-time All-Star), Bill Bruton, Johnny Logan, and slugger Joe Adcock and mixed in other solid players like Frank Bolling, Joe Torre, and Roy McMillan. The team had no dissension.

"It still bothers me that we were only able to win two pennants and one World Series with the team we had," Aaron said years later. "We should have won at least four pennants in a row. I wish I knew what kept us from winning more because there is no question we had the talent. Besides that, half our guys would fight their mothers to win a ball game. Damn it, we were better than that."[316]

Attendance dipped to a shocking 766,921. Instead of drinking their beer at the ballpark, the suds-loving Milwaukee fan was drinking at home or in the neighborhood tavern.

Rarely has the ardor of a town cooled so quickly on baseball as this remarkable reversal. Bud Selig, the eighty-three-year-old retired commissioner of baseball who is now in the Hall of Fame, had an enormous influence on Milwaukee Major League Baseball before leaving town for higher office.

Selig was three years old when he began attending Milwaukee Brewers minor-league games with family members and in the early 1950s was the largest public stockholder in the Braves. Few people have been as passionate about Milwaukee baseball for as long. Later, after the Braves abandoned the city for Atlanta, Selig played a major role in luring the Seattle Pilots to town to reincarnate the Brewers as a major-league substitute for the Braves. Selig was appalled when the Braves fled.

Years later Selig still called it tragic the Braves left town because the team had done so much good for the community and the community had done so much good for the team.

"It's hard to say exactly why it stopped working," Selig said, "but I can say that the Braves were not aggressive marketers. And by saying that, I'm being kind. Very, very kind."[317]

Warren Spahn could do many things, but he could not make the people of Milwaukee care deeply again, not even in 1963 when he stunned the baseball world by winning 23 games for the second time in his career, with an ERA of 2.60 at age forty-two. Not even by pitching a game for the ages, one still talked about in baseball circles for the jaw-dropping nature of its length and conclusion, could Spahn single-handedly woo back the vanishing fan.

Spahn was the king of the clubhouse, partially due to his longevity and partially because of his prankster sense of humor. He and Lew Burdette often teamed up on jokes. It came naturally to them, unlike the quieter Henry Aaron or Eddie Mathews. Spahn and Burdette were close friends and roommates. They often went out on the town and drank together on the road. They could be dangerous together, playing pranks more introspective and laid-back players never thought of doing.

It's not clear how much the sportswriters knew about these shenanigans, but many years later Aaron wrote about a few of them in an autobiography. He said most of the time Spahn and Burdette got back what they dished out. Wes Covington, Aaron noted, repeatedly made fun of them because they were not stylish dressers. However, the brunt of many jokes, although he was beloved within the team, was Donald Davidson.

Davidson, who as a youth was a Braves bat boy in Boston, joined the team in 1948 and served in more than one front office capacity, although primarily in public relations. He loved baseball, but when he was five Davidson caught a sleeping sickness disease that stunted his growth. In adulthood, Davidson stood 4 feet tall and weighed 85 pounds. He was known for his own snappy wit and he engaged in banter with the players. However, sometimes Spahn and Burdette took advantage of Davidson's size disadvantage by scheming against him with stunts that would certainly be considered politically incorrect today.

"It seemed like they were always at war with Donald," Aaron wrote, "irritating him with little tricks, like messing with the special car Donald had, lowering the brake pedals so he couldn't reach them. They also warned Donald that if he ever came on the field, they'd take off his pants." Once, the duo caught Davidson off-guard and did so, stranding him in the outfield before fans came in. Manager Fred Haney finally brought Davidson a pair of trousers. Another time the pitchers locked Davidson in the whirlpool during a game. Davidson retaliated once by nailing shoes belonging to Spahn and Burdette to the floor in the locker room and throwing their clothes into a running shower, so they had nothing to wear home.[318]

Spahn was on his way to a 23–7 record in 1963 and the Braves were on their way to an 84–78 mark, another winning year not substantially different than the season before. Attendance was 773,018, very similar to the year before.

Spahn won his 20th game of the year, 3–2, over the Philadelphia Phillies with a complete game on September 8 with the Braves piling up 11 hits. Don Hoak, the old Pirate, collected three of the nine hits off Spahn. The losing pitcher was Dallas Green, who in 1980 won a World Series managing the Phillies.

Spahn won that 23rd game, equaling his career high, on the last day of the regular season by shutting out the Chicago Cubs, 2–0, on four hits. The losing pitcher that day was his old Braves pal Bob Buhl, who was sent to Chicago in 1962. This was to be Spahn's last great season, his last of 13 seasons winning 20 games, the last time he was chosen as an All-Star. There was no hint of that at the time, however.

The astonishing game Spahn was part of in 1963 took place on the chilly night of July 2 in Candlestick Park against the Giants with 15,921 the paid attendance. Those fans would get the equivalent of two games for their money, though some would describe the experience of watching Spahn and the Giants' future Hall of Famer Juan Marichal as priceless. Spahn was 11–3 on the season coming in. Marichal was 12–3.

Marichal was twenty-five, sometimes called "The Dominican Dandy," for his place of origin. He was a right-hander, but intriguingly, his own signature motion involved high kicking as much as Spahn's did. The two of them resembled people in rocking chairs tilting back so far they were in danger of going over backwards. When the Giants unveiled a statue to honor Marichal much later, he was posed throwing a pitch and his left foot was pointed skyward, higher than his shoulder. That season Marichal won 25 games, the second-most in his career to 1968 when he won 26. In all, Marichal won 243 games in 16 major-league seasons and is a treasured national hero in the Dominican Republic.

The funny thing was that growing up in the Dominican Marichal might have heard of Spahn but did not know what his pitching delivery was like. Later, after being in the big leagues, he said, "Nobody kicks his leg higher than me. I learned to pitch like that in the Dominican Republic. Then I see Warren Spahn pitch. He does just like me."[319]

On this day nothing but zeroes went up on the scoreboard. An epic by any standard, the Braves versus Giants pitching duel lasted 16 innings. Clubs did not keep track of pitch counts with the same avid curiosity as they do now, and not much was made of the total number of pitches each man threw at the time. They were calculated later, and in these days of yanking pitchers almost automatically when they reach 100 or 110 pitches regardless of how well they are throwing, the numbers would give front office mavens and managers heart attacks.

Marichal threw 227 pitches. Spahn threw 201 pitches. Neither complained of sore arms, felt they had to immediately retreat to the disabled list, or rest for a month. Their view was they were just doing their jobs. They came to the park, took the ball as starting pitchers, and tried to beat the other guy, going as long as it took. They just couldn't guess that as long as it took might seem like forever.

The game took 16 innings and four hours, ten minutes to finish. Three Braves—Crandall, Bolling, and Denis Menke—accumulated two hits each out of Milwaukee's total of eight. Orlando Cepeda and the much lesser-known Ernie Bowman were the only ones in the Giants' lineup with two hits each. Bowman, the San Francisco shortstop, was in his last of three big-league seasons and hit .184 that year.

In the top of the fourth inning, Norm Larker, playing first for the Braves that day, was thrown out at home plate after walking. That was the closest Milwaukee came to scoring. Despite the double shutout going it was not as if Braves manager Bobby Bragan and Giants manager Alvin Dark, who broke in as a player with the Braves more than a decade before, were unaware of the possible fatigue factor for the pitchers.

In the ninth inning, Willie McCovey, one of several Hall of Famers involved in the game, ripped a pitch deep and very high to right field. The umpire ruled it foul, although McCovey never gave up believing it was really a fair ball and a home run.

"He didn't make the call right away," McCovey said. "I hit it so high and so far he waited until it landed . . . which was in Oakland. He was the only person in the ball park who thought it was foul."[320]

Spahn knocked the most powerful hit off of Marichal, a double in the seventh inning that hit the wall, but didn't clear it. Greg Spahn, the pitcher's son, was an eyewitness.

"It was about a foot too low to go out," the younger Spahn said. "He would have won his own game. That would have been perfect."[321]

In the ninth inning, Dark trekked to the mound intending to relieve Marichal, not because he was doing anything wrong, but because he had been pitching for such a long time. Marichal refused to leave the game.

"I am not going to come out of that game as long as that old man is still pitching," Marchial said.[322] Dark tried to coax Marichal to the bench a couple of more times as innings passed, but Marichal retained the same outlook. Across the diamond Spahn was pretty much doing the same thing, saying if this young whippersnapper could still throw, so could he. It was a matter of pride for both pitchers. Marichal said he laughed when he later heard the same dialogue was going on between the opposing pitcher and manager. A day after the contest the pitchers huddled out of sight as Spahn provided advice based on his experience for how the younger pitcher should treat his arm over the next few days.

"The day Warren Spahn and I pitched 16 innings, nobody expected that," Marichal said. "We didn't expect it and we didn't even really expect it while it was going on."[323]

It was not a perfect game but a perfect baseball night—a game to be remembered forever. When the end came, it was sudden. In the bottom of the 16th inning, Spahn retired Harvey Kuenn on a fly ball. In stepped the redoubtable Willie Mays, and he did his friend Juan Marichal a favor by hitting the first pitch out of the park, the ball landing in the left-field stands. Final score, 1–0, Giants. This was one of the 52 shutouts Marichal threw during his career, including 10 in one season in 1965.

After both men were retired and members of the Hall of Fame they spent time together annually during induction week events.

"I liked Warren as a pitcher and a human being," Marichal said. "We got so close from visits in Cooperstown. Warren Spahn was such a great pitcher. Now that he has passed away, I miss him."[324]

There was another very special occasion for Spahn during the 1963 season. Taking note of his incredible accomplishments, overall fabulous career, and his longevity with the team dating back to Boston days, the Braves honored him with "Warren Spahn Night," sometimes called "Spahnie Day."

In connection with the festivities, two-inch-wide red, white, and blue Spahnie pins with the September 17, 1963, date and a picture of the pitcher were manufactured and sold for 25 cents each. The money raised was earmarked for a scholarship fund aimed at sending qualified Wisconsin students to college. By the time of the game enough pins had been sold and donations collected to announce a $30,000 start-up. Spahn himself gave $500 to the fund. Spahn and his wife LoRene and son Greg were presented with gifts. Greg, fourteen going on fifteen, received a western saddle, no doubt the connection being made that the Spahns lived on a ranch in Oklahoma much of the year.

Spahn received hundreds of congratulatory messages from friends and former players, including one from President John F. Kennedy, who would be killed by an assassin's bullet about two months later. The JFK letter read in part, "Dear Warren, You are one of the few men in the history of baseball who has the distinction of establishing new records in each game in which you play. Few athletes in our time have won the universal admiration which you have in your many years as a player." Although Kennedy was likely not worried about the competition, fans held up a sign at County Stadium reading, "Wisconsin Nominates Warren Spahn For President."[325]

Comedian Bob Hope sent his regrets, saying he had obligations in British Columbia that would keep him away from Wisconsin. Present for the celebration (which also included a daytime luncheon at five dollars a plate in Spahn's honor) were two renowned left-handed pitchers of the past, Carl Hubbell and Lefty Gomez, Spahn's old friend and teammate Johnny Sain, then pitching coach of the Yankees, and Gabby Hartnett, the former Cub catcher in the Hall of Fame. Messages from each National League team were also presented to Spahn, some displaying a sense of humor based on his longtime success against them.

"In recognition of his greatness from the team he has beaten the most," read the note from the St. Louis Cardinals. "You have our vote for the Hall of Fame—if you retire now," was the note from the Los Angeles Dodgers.[326]

As the 400 guests departed the luncheon, an orchestra played "On Wisconsin," the University of Wisconsin fight song.

Spahn took the field in uniform before game's start to address the fans and expressed his gratitude for this attention.

"I'm the luckiest guy in baseball," Spahn said into a microphone. "My sincere thanks, from the bottom of my heart, for making this occasion and this foundation possible. God bless you. It looks like World Series time out here. Let's keep it that way."[327]

Spahn said he was "choked up" by the adulation he received on the field prior to the game. "It's a heck of a lot easier pitching a game," he said.[328]

The Braves faced the Giants that night at County Stadium, with 33,676 fans in attendance and Spahn starting against Bobby Bolin. It was one of Spahn's worst games that season. The Giants hit him hard (five hits and four runs), and he lasted just three innings in an 11–3 defeat.

"I was all right," Spahn said. "My arm felt fine. I just couldn't do the job I wanted to do so badly. Don't make excuses for me. It's results that count and I just wasn't able to contribute anything."[329]

He already had 20 wins in the bank for the season and won his next three, giving him 350 for his career. Warren Spahn Night was one of the greatest nights of Warren Spahn's baseball career, but what neither he nor the fans could know was that it was also just about the last great night of his career.

Later, Spahn was presented with a massive scrapbook—in height, weight, and content—containing photographs from the celebrations, telegrams received, newspaper stories from all around the country, and copies of schedules for the luncheon and special night at the park. Three of the Spahnie buttons were clipped to the front.

It may have been something Spahn's wife LoRene said in the days leading up to the festivities that sparked the scrapbook idea. "It used to be easy to remember all the records," she said. "Now there are so many we have to keep a scrapbook handy."[330]

Also tucked into the scrapbook, although it did not pertain to the special night, was a handwritten, congratulatory note from Hall of Fame pitcher Waite Hoyt, himself a 237-game winner, on the 1961 occasion of Spahn's 300th victory. Hoyt, who enjoyed a long broadcasting career after retiring as a player, penned the note on the stationery of the Warwick Hotel in Philadelphia on August 10. Hoyt's Reds had just completed a series against the Phillies and were on their way to San Francisco to play the Giants.

"My day may be long past," wrote Hoyt, who retired in 1938, "but I can still admire and respect a fine pitcher—a fine competitor. It has been a pleasure watching you."[331]

Those many millions in Milwaukee, and those who crammed into County Stadium for Warren Spahn Night, would agree it had long been a pleasure watching Warren Spahn pitch.

25

IT'S OVER

THE 1964 SEASON was the one so many feared sneaking up on a pitcher well into his forties. Warren Spahn more resembled Bob Hendley at his worst than Warren Spahn at his best. He went from the 23–7 marvel of 1963 to the 6–13 disaster of 1964, accompanied by a grim earned run average of 5.29.

Concurrent with Spahn's dismal year was the continuing lukewarm interest of the fans. County Stadium drew just 910,911 for the year as the Braves bore up well enough without counting on Spahn, finishing 88–74. The lineup was rebuilt with such players as Rico Carty, who hit .330, and Lee Maye, who hit .307, alongside Henry Aaron, who hit .328, and Joe Torre, who hit .321. Eddie Mathews slumped but still clouted 23 home runs. Tony Cloninger won 19 games and Denny Lemaster 17.

One intriguing career overlap occurred in 1964 as Spahn's tenure with the Braves was running out. A rookie pitcher in spring training, trying to cling to the roster (he appeared in 10 games that season) was Phil Niekro. Niekro was about to embark on a 24-season career marked by 318 victories just as Spahn was headed out the door.

Niekro was in Bradenton spring camp with Spahn, but was a timid rookie who was almost too frightened to engage superstars like Spahn, Henry Aaron, and Eddie Mathews in conversation. "I thought they were all gods," Niekro said. "I was so young. I was a greenhorn. I didn't want to ask any questions. I was glad to be there."

However, Niekro did watch how Spahn worked out and even how he dressed, because he was the symbol of being the best. "Spahn was the biggest player in the game as far as a pitcher went," Niekro said. "I wanted to be a right-handed Warren Spahn. Of course, I didn't have that leg kick. He was great. He was exceptionally great."[332]

Of course, Niekro's bread and butter turned out to be the knuckleball, so true pitching role models were rare for him.

Besides briefly being teammates, Niekro had a few other things in common with Spahn, one of them being his own longevity, staying in the big leagues until he was forty-eight. Also, he too was able to stick around late into games. Four times, Niekro led the National League in complete games.

"You win a lot of games in those seventh, eighth, and ninth innings," he said of Spahn.[333]

Spahn endured the worst pitching season of his life and manager Bobby Bragan essentially declared him through. After that 1964 season, the unthinkable occurred. Warren Spahn and the Braves parted company and it was not through retirement. On November 23, 1964, the Braves sold Spahn to the New York Mets. Bragan predicted Spahn would not win six games the next season.

Bragan said only Spahn's "name" had kept him in the majors during the 1964 season and accused him of caring only about himself.

"Spahn could have helped us as a reliever late in the season if he hadn't been thinking about that $80,000 salary of his," Bragan said. "He's not thinking of the team. He's thinking about Warren Spahn—the great Spahnie! He's a future Hall of Famer and an immortal and all that stuff. But let me tell you that if any other pitcher had been shelled the way he was last season, he would have been shipped to Denver. But this was Warren Spahn and he had to be handled with great care, even if he couldn't get anybody out. He got old all of a sudden. He was dead on his feet. His legs were gone."[334]

That insult-laden commentary was a strange way to treat a local icon, who was as shocked as the manager about losing his stuff so abruptly. The fact was you don't send a Warren Spahn to Denver because of who he is and what he has meant to baseball and to the franchise.

Spahn had a few choice comments for Bragan.

"He hasn't said anything about me that he hasn't said about other players who left the club," said Spahn, who suggested Bragan didn't really want to win because he played untried, non-achieving talent. "Lew Burdette, Del Crandall, you name them. Talk to the other players about him. You'll find out how much he was disliked. But I prefer not to get into a running argument with him. All I'm interested is having a good year with the Mets and proving that Bragan is wrong."[335]

When Spahn referred to Bragan not wanting to win, he meant Bragan wanted to avoid a resurgence in the team's popularity that might derail a rumored move to Atlanta. As it was, Warren Spahn of the Boston and Milwaukee Braves did not continue his franchise relationship when the Braves did leave for Atlanta in 1966. Spahn left town a year before the team, some might argue a year too late since the knowledge the team was abandoning the city drove attendance down to 555,584 in 1965.

Although forty-three going on forty-four, Spahn refused to believe he was done. After all, just a year previously he had compiled the best pitching season of his life. It did not seem possible he could lose his touch completely overnight or over the winter. From his late thirties on, sportswriters repeatedly quizzed Spahn about when he was going to retire. Since he was still winning 20 games a season that was not a question he pondered much. He used to tell them that it had only been five months since the end of the season to spring training, so how much could have changed? Well, this time something changed.

When the New York Mets announced Spahn's acquisition they called his new job pitcher-coach. When Spahn met the press he said, "Pitching is first, then coaching. Being a starting pitcher is the best job in baseball. For the second half of last season I wasn't getting that opportunity. I have to work a lot to do my best. I don't think that anybody goes from middle age to old age in one year. There were any number of factors that brought that sharp drop. I lost my timing and not working steadily I could never get it back."[336]

In February of 1965, in a lead-up to the new season, *Sport* magazine gave Spahn a forum to speak his mind about his career. The headline read, "I Still Can Win."[337] That was very much on his mind. Spahn said the first time he heard, "You know, Spahnie, you're not getting any younger . . ." was when he was thirty-four and had a 17–14 season.

"But my best years were still ahead of me," Spahn wrote. "I won 20 or more games in each of the next six seasons and threw two no-hitters." He said he knew as soon as he had an off-year the issue would arise again. "They're wrong. I'm not through. I think I have at least one more 20-game season in me. In a pitcher, age isn't a factor, as Satchel Paige proved. Nobody knew how old he was when he helped pitch the 1948 Indians to a pennant, but he was almost certainly older than I am now."[338]

Actually, it was believed Paige was a forty-two-year-old major-league rookie that season, but he pitched parts of four additional seasons in the majors and made a single appearance when he was fifty-three.

"That is all that counts in a pitcher, physical condition and the condition of his arm," Spahn said. "I'm a young 43 (44 in two months) and I can still do most of the things I always could do. My reflexes are a little slower, but they were unusually sharp when I was younger and they're still good."[339]

Spahn explained what he thought went wrong during the 1964 season, not in terms of any injury, but that he had lost touch with his longtime form and it took a while to figure out the flaw and solve it. "Until last spring I never had to worry about each little step leading up to the release of the ball. I had repeated them so often they were all second nature to me. But when my pitches stopped doing what I wanted them to do I realized I would have to go through each motion step by step to find the trouble. It took just a split second to say I was finishing on the heel of my foot, but a long time to pinpoint that as the trouble. I had to throw and throw and throw while saying over and over to myself, 'What am I doing wrong? Where am I making the mistake?' When I finally found the answer, then I had to pitch often and regularly to regain my control and timing. A control pitcher like me feeds on confidence because he must be precisely accurate."[340]

Spahn said his confidence—even after all of those years of success—was done in by the lack of faith shown him and being pulled early from games instead of being allowed to complete them as he so often had while wiggling out of difficulty before. "In the past I had always been allowed to try and clean up my own messes, and often succeeded."[341]

It did seem as if Spahn was bringing fresh confidence to New York and the Mets, a team desperately needing any kind of boost after beginning life in the early 1960s as the worst team in history. Alas, even in 1965, neither the Mets nor Spahn were much better. New York finished last for the fourth year in a row with a 50–112 record. Ironically, New York's manager was Casey Stengel, Spahn's first manager with the Boston Braves before World War II. In-between, of course, Spahn had become a 300-game winner and Stengel had delivered 10 pennants in 12 seasons for the New York Yankees.

This made for an odd later-in-life pairing.

"Yes, I said, 'No guts' to a kid who wound up being a war hero," Stengel said of the player he insulted and sent to the minors in 1942, "and one of the best pitchers anybody ever saw. You can't say I don't miss 'em when I miss 'em."[342]

Stengel did not even finish out the season, ending his long and illustrious baseball career after 95 games in 1965, going 31–64. This reunion led to a memorable utterance from Spahn about Stengel's career. "I'm the only guy to play for Casey Stengel before and after he was a genius."[343]

But Spahn did not last through the season for the Mets either. His optimism about regaining his form was misplaced. Bragan's comments about him being done seemed accurate. Spahn's record for the Mets was 4–12 in 20 starts with a 4.36 earned run average. Spahn learned that it was hard to win games with the Mets.

The Mets let Spahn go on July 17. Stengel was still in charge and wanted to shift Spahn to the bullpen. Spahn refused. *New York*

Times columnist Arthur Daley said Spahn was like many athletes who refuse to recognize time is up, in his case partially because he had proven himself again and again with terrific performances in his forties. "So brazenly successful had he been in his defiance of time that this stubbornly proud man was deluded into dreaming that he could continue indefinitely," Daley wrote.[344]

Yet only a day passed before Spahn cut a fresh deal with the San Francisco Giants to pitch for them through the rest of the season. The Giants wanted to believe.

"I feel I can help them win the pennant," Spahn said, thinking of being a spot starter and reliever. "I'll do whatever manager Herman Franks wants."[345]

Out on the West Coast, Spahn started 11 games, appeared in 16, and went 3–4, but with a very respectable earned run average of 3.39. Not bad, supporting Spahn's argument that perhaps he could still do more. But he never got that chance in the majors again. The Giants released him in the offseason and no team made him an offer. He kept hoping the phone would ring over the winter at his Oklahoma ranch, but it did not. No one asked Spahn to show up for spring training. He was forty-five years old and it seemed he was the only one in the country who thought he could still pitch major-league ball.

"Maybe I'm just an old man trying to play a young man's game," Spahn said in May of 1966 with the season a month gone. "But I still like to pitch. I think I could get ready to pitch in the majors in a week or two. The question is whether it would take longer than that to get my control back."[346]

He said Chuck Tanner, his old Braves teammate, was managing in Double-A El Paso and asked him if he wanted to throw some for his team. Spahn thought it over but did not go. Instead, he briefly joined up with the Mexico City Tigers in the

Mexican League as pitcher and coach but spent only a matter of weeks there.

"I didn't retire," Spahn said in July of 1966. "Baseball retired me. Retirement isn't as bad as you might think, but I still feel that I could win for some major-league club." Of his time in Mexico, he said, "It was sort of a paid vacation."[347]

Across the country from Spahn's ranch, the Braves were now situated in Atlanta, drawing a million more fans than in their last year in Milwaukee and Bragan was getting fired for his losing record after 111 games. In Milwaukee, diehards were fighting in court to regain the Braves and prevent them from doing business in Atlanta. That battle was going on as Spahn was battling to return to the majors. No one out there was listening to either argument.

"I admire the people of Milwaukee and Wisconsin who have fought for a ball club," he said. "I hope it comes out all right. I think Milwaukee deserves a major-league club. But whether baseball can boycott Milwaukee, or whether it gives Milwaukee another chance to get another big-league club, this is something for the lawyers to decide."[348]

"Baseball was good to me, especially Milwaukee, and I have no regrets. I'll never forget Milwaukee and the fans."[349]

Although he wanted to keep going, keep winning a few more games, Spahn never got the chance. He concluded his major-league pitching career with 363 victories, sixth most on the all-time list, the most by any left-hander. Cy Young, 511, Walter Johnson, 417, Christy Mathewson and Grover Cleveland Alexander, 373, and Pud Galvin, 365, are the only ones who won more. Right behind Spahn is Kid Nichols with 361 wins, Greg Maddux with 355, and Roger Clemens with 354. The last two are the only pitchers of recent vintage who had a shot to surpass Spahn.

As Spahn was nearing the end of his career, *Sport* magazine carried an article that raised the issue of "Is Warren Spahn The Best Ever?" In it, Branch Rickey, the Hall of Fame baseball executive, said when comparing Spahn to the others, "Spahn is just as good, if not better. He had wonderful physical qualities to start with. He had exceptional speed. The general public underrates him in that respect. He has what I call mysterious speed." Of Spahn's commitment to staying in shape and retaining his mental focus, Rickey said, "In this category he is unexcelled by past greats. In my opinion there has never been a better pitcher in the history of baseball than Warren Spahn."[350]

Ford Frick, a former commissioner of baseball, echoed Rickey, concluding Spahn's credentials put him in the mix for best-ever consideration.

"Spahn is one of the top pitchers of all time," Frick said. "It is hard to compare a 1904 and a 1906 pitcher because the game has changed. But Spahn must rank with the greatest of all time such as Young, Ed Walsh, Matty, Alexander, and Johnson. I think I'm safe in saying that measured by any system Warren Spahn is on par with the greatest who ever lived—any of them."[351]

That was a flattering portrayal, though on the whole Spahn would rather have still been pitching. Instead, he did the next best thing, accepting other jobs in baseball.

26

STILL LOVING THE GAME

WARREN SPAHN WANTED to keep pitching in the majors, but no one wanted him, making him a reluctant retiree. So he adapted. An he was able to remain in baseball for many years in different capacities.

Spahn's wife LoRene was a native of Oklahoma, and after they married he made Oklahoma his year-round residence. They lived on what started out as a fifty-acre spread in 1948 and grew into a 2,800-acre ranch in Hartshorne called the Diamond Star, 105 miles from Tulsa. Spahn raised Hereford cattle, although he was not a hands-on rancher while tied up being a hands-on pitcher. Oh, they also struck oil on his property and he received decades of royalties from that. For a guy whose peak earning year in baseball was $87,500, Spahn later had many options, including making speeches and signing autographs at card shows.

In 1963, when he was still active, Spahn was invited to make an appearance in a popular television series of the time called *Combat*. Of all things, the American war hero played a German army sergeant, leading a group of five men. He had a very small speaking part. His baseball teammates teased him constantly leading up to the filming, urging Spahn onward with such helpful hints as, "Don't forget to pull the pin out of the grenade before you heave it, dumpkopf."[352]

Spahn was on the set in Culver City, California for only a short time and then joined the Braves at Chavez Ravine for a game against the Dodgers. He pitched and won his 16th game of the season that same night. The *Combat* episode aired on November 5, 1963, but did not lead to a film career for Spahn.

Several years before Spahn ceased pitching, one winter on his ranch he speculated about a second, non-playing career in baseball. "I'd like to manage, if I could try out my own theories on the ideas I've picked up. I'd want to work with young players, maybe as sort of a trouble-shooter and instructor in some major league's minor league system. If I could not improve their technique, maybe I could teach them desire."[353]

Spahn so wanted to keep pitching, but not a single team offered a phone-call invitation to try out or come to spring training.

"There's a feeling of emptiness at first," Spahn said of his forced retirement, "as though you don't exist anymore. You think no one gives a damn about you. I was never divorced, but it must be like that. You just have to go out and build a new life for yourself. Some athletes can never handle it and that leaves them bitter. Well, I decided I was going to be productive until I die. I know I'd be lost if I retired and was out of the mainstream."[354]

After his 1966 intermission, when he was hoping for a team to give him a last chance, Spahn dove back into baseball. By 1967 Spahn had his first managing job as boss of the Tulsa Oilers, the Triple-A team in the St. Louis Cardinals' minor-league chain. He was forty-six.

"This job isn't easy," he said. "In fact, it's tougher than I expected. But that doesn't mean I don't like it. This offer to manage the Tulsa club came suddenly, early this spring." Spahn said the fact that it was the high minors for a top-flight organization and it was in Oklahoma made it easy to take the job. "And I'm near home. I have an apartment in Tulsa, so as to be available at all times and I don't get out to the ranch very often, but my wife and son can get to Tulsa any time they want to. So it's a good deal all around."[355]

When Spahn took over the Oilers in 1967 they were in the Pacific Coast League, even though the closest coast in either direction was more than 1,000 miles away. Tulsa was not very good his first season, but the team won 95 games and the league championship in 1968. After two years, Tulsa moved to the American Association. Spahn remained manager for two-plus more years, into the 1971 season before the Cardinals fired him. Before that, however, St. Louis offered Spahn the job of the big club's pitching coach. He preferred to stay in Tulsa.

In 1970, in the middle of his tenure with Tulsa, Spahn underwent surgery to spruce up both of his knees. For a time afterward he was in a wheelchair and then switched to a walker, but he was ready for the 1971 season, his last with the Oilers. He chose to double his operations, he said, because "I felt if I didn't have the work done simultaneously, I'd chicken out on the other knee."[356]

Cards general manager Bing Devine flew to Tulsa in late August to inform Spahn he wasn't going to be invited back the next season. Although Spahn said he respected Devine for taking the trouble to travel to Tulsa to tell him, he chose to leave the team right then.

The next season Spahn was hired as pitching coach of the Cleveland Indians under manager Al Lopez and general manager Hank Greenberg. "I think it's a real challenge and an opportunity for me to get back in the big leagues," Spahn said.[357]

Spahn spent two years as the Indians' pitching coach. On the sidelines, instead of the mound, Spahn covered some territory, starting with those five seasons in Tulsa, working with the Indians, helping the Mexico City Tigers, the Hiroshima Toyo Carp in the Japan League, and the California Angels. Spahn found working with Japanese players interesting but was not so keen on the style of the game he encountered there in the 1970s.

"It's a whole different ballgame over there," he said. "They don't have the brushback pitch over there. That is such an important part of pitching. When you don't throw the brushback you give the batter the liberty to lean over and crowd the plate. You are taking away one of the pitcher's most valuable weapons. The game is oriented toward the offense because that's the way the fans want it."[358]

There was never any doubt of his enshrinement in the Baseball Hall of Fame with those 363 victories looming, but in 1973 it became official when Spahn was inducted, voted in on the first ballot of eligibility. Spahn was visiting his father Ed in Buffalo when he received the telephone call notifying him of the results. Talk about Dad being proven right about his son's pitching prospects years before.

"I'll never forget the look on his face when I told my dad," Spahn said. "I think for me the biggest kick was seeing that look on his face."[359]

Warren Spahn was fifty-two years old and if they had let him he probably would have tried pitching a complete game at Doubleday Field in Cooperstown.

Calling his election the "greatest victory of my life," Spahn was thrilled at being chosen. "Cooperstown, it's great to be there," he said. "My head on a plaque behind Babe Ruth, Ty

Cobb, Walter Johnson and all the others. What more can a man ask?"[360]

When he notified son Greg of his selection, he also threw in a dad-like comment. "You're going to have to start calling me 'Sir' again," Spahn said.[361]

The ceremony itself in August of 1973 did not go as smoothly as hoped. Spahn was the only living inductee. Roberto Clemente, the Pittsburgh Pirates star who died on a mission of mercy in a plane crash, had the waiting period for eligibility waived. Old-timers, pitcher Mickey Welch, another 300-game winner, and Billy Evans, an umpire and administrator, were also inducted.

When Spahn began to speak his brother-in-law Leo Curran collapsed in the crowd and his crying children followed him out. Spahn was shaken but recovered to complete his remarks. Spahn stressed it was exciting his father, then eighty, and son, then twenty-five, could be in Cooperstown with him. He also spoke about the integrity of baseball.

"As much as it hurts to lose," he said, "I was never prouder than to have been part of a game of such high standards."[362]

Spahn very much enjoyed returning to Cooperstown each year to schmooze with the other Hall of Famers at each induction ceremony. They tossed back a few beers, told jokes, and reminisced about their times in the game.

Phil Niekro the rookie couldn't say he really knew Spahn during their short time together with the Milwaukee Braves, but he did get to know the lefty better after he too was inducted into the Hall of Fame in 1997.

Each summer, when a new class is inducted, the selectees are feted at a dinner in Cooperstown and are presented with their Hall of Fame rings. Older Hall of Famers come back and revel in sharing their baseball experiences.

Typically, the players gather on the back porch of the Otesaga Resort Hotel, drinking beer or wine, as a matter of taste. Spahn was a beer drinker with Braves teammates and Niekro believes his drink of choice at these get-togethers was Heineken. "They're telling war stories," Niekro said.[363]

Other honors began piling up for Spahn, as well. He was very rooted in Oklahoma and even maintained his ranch for a number of years after his wife passed away. Eventually, Spahn gave up the ranch that had been a huge part of his life and moved into the nearby community of Broken Arrow. A little later on an Oklahoma company produced a beer named after Spahn called "Spahnie 363." He remained very popular in the Sooner State.

In 1991, Spahn's granddaughter Kara brought him to school for a variation on show-and-tell. It was "Grand Person's Day." Actually, Spahn had to leave town, so he showed up a day early to introduce himself to her fifth-grade class. The kids asked questions, including what was his grandest moment in the game.

Spahn replied, when he "went up to the big leagues and had that major-league uniform on. It didn't fit, but I had it on."[364]

Adopted as one of the state's own, Spahn was inducted into the Oklahoma Sports Hall of Fame in 1999 and the Oklahoma Sports Museum created the Warren Spahn Award, each year bestowed on the best left-handed pitcher in Major League Baseball. Among those who have been honored are Randy Johnson, a four-time winner who joined Spahn in the Baseball Hall of Fame with 303 victories, and CC Sabathia. More recently Clayton Kershaw of the Los Angeles Dodgers has been a repeat winner.

That year, the Sports Museum threw an autograph party featuring Spahn and calling it "Warren Spahn Day." Another Hall of Fame pitcher, Ferguson Jenkins, was part of the festivities, as was former Harlem Globetrotter and Harlem Magicians basketball player Marques Haynes.

In August of 2003, a statue of Spahn throwing a pitch was unveiled at Turner Field in Atlanta, at the time the home of the Atlanta Braves, Spahn's old franchise. Spahn worked closely with sculptor Shan Gray on the design. Spahn was eighty-two years old when the monument was dedicated. There were a number of other statues honoring Braves players at Turner, such as Henry Aaron and 300-game winner Phil Niekro, as well as Hall of Fame manager Bobby Cox. Also included in the display was superstar Ty Cobb, known as "The Georgia Peach" for his nearby roots. The Braves moved into a new park, SunTrust Park, for the 2017 season and brought the statues with them.

Also in August of that year, an Atlanta sportswriter had a lengthy visit with Spahn talking about his baseball career. Spahn was not as spry as he had been, described as needing a caregiver and the help of son Greg to rise after chatting, then leaning on two canes to start walking. It was obvious at eighty-two Spahn was not the athlete he once was, and when a photographer asked him to pose with a baseball, he said, "Damn thing's heavy." This Spahn had suffered with several physical problems over the preceding year, needed surgery, punctured a lung, broke ribs and a leg. "I'm glad I don't have to make a living with this [the ball] now."[365]

The story appeared a few days before the unveiling of the nine-foot-tall, 1,000-pound statue paid for by a $95,000 private fundraising campaign. On the same day, Del Crandall was inducted into the team Hall of Fame, a place where Spahn already had a spot. Spahn never pitched for the Braves in Atlanta, but the Braves were still his team, whatever city they represented.

"I'm delighted," Spahn said. "I'm sorry I didn't get to play in Atlanta. But I'm honored and thrilled that the statue will be there for posterity."[366]

Spahn was in fading health, and he died in Broken Arrow on November 24, 2003, officially of natural causes. Five days later a service was conducted at the Boston Avenue Church United Methodist in Tulsa that was called "In Celebration for the Life of Warren Spahn." Words of remembrance were delivered by Gary Caruso, the former sports editor of the *Atlanta Journal-Constitution*, but someone who grew up as a fan of Spahn's during the heyday of his pitching career. A picture of Spahn in his Braves uniform was on display at the church, as well as flower arrangements in the shape of a baseball and one of his No. 21 jerseys. Spahn's casket, as is offered for all veterans, was draped with an American flag as a salute to his World War II military days.

"Warren Spahn was the Wyatt Earp of the National League," Caruso said. "No one maintained law and order against the larger-than-life hitters of baseball's grandest era better or longer than the man we are here today to remember."[367]

Those writing obituaries that week, and baseball writers who so appreciated what the winningest left-handed pitcher in baseball history brought to the sport, filed thousands of words in praise of the high-kicking, balding, hook-nosed southpaw who dazzled batters for two decades and astoundingly won at least 20 games in a season 13 times and retired with a 363–245 record.

"He became Milwaukee's first superstar 50 years ago," one Milwaukee commentary began. Despite those brief late-career stops in New York and San Francisco, Commissioner Bud Selig said of Spahn, "he was a Brave and he loved Milwaukee. He was something. The likes of Warren Spahn will not come down this road any time soon."[368]

The *New York Times'* lengthy obituary read in part, "Confounding batters with a fluid, high-kicking motion and an assortment of pitches that nicked the corners of the plate or darted just outside the strike zone, Spahn was a craftsman on the mound." Just how much of one was noted by one-time Dodger lefty Johnny Podres who said his teammate Sandy Koufax was the best over a few-year period in the 1960s, but Spahn was the best of them over time, "for the long haul, for year-after-year performance, Warren Spahn was the best I ever saw. He was just a master of his trade. I couldn't take my eyes off him."[369]

They made it personal in the *Buffalo News*, representing the city where Spahn grew up and lived in until he went into the Army. The story there noted he "rose from the sandlots of South Buffalo to the Baseball Hall of Fame." The story reminded local readers Spahn had pitched in an Old-Timers' Game in Buffalo as recently as 1990. Spahn became the first inductee of the Greater Buffalo Sports Hall of Fame.

"It means very much to me to be honored by my hometown," he said on the occasion. "I've bounced all over the country and Buffalo has never forgotten that I was a local product."[370]

At various times different baseball people suggested that if Spahn had gotten an earlier start in the majors and had not missed more than three years of playing during World War II, he might have won 400 games, finishing behind only Cy Young and Walter Johnson. Spahn may have believed that, but he never really said so, indicating he gained so much maturity during his Army days that he was a different guy when he came out.

When Spahn died, however, Bob Feller made the case for Spahn winning many more games under different circumstances. The same was said for Feller, as well, who won 266 major-league games while also missing several years in the service. "He was a war hero,"

Feller said. "Who knows how many games he would have won if it hadn't been for World War II?"[371]

There has been considerable talk about whether any more pitchers will ever win 300 games in a career. One thing Phil Niekro is sure of is that no one will come along and win 20 games in a season 13 times, as Spahn did.

"Oh, no, no," Niekro said. "You won't see that [a 13-time, 20-game winner] again."[372]

Henry Aaron, Spahn's longtime teammate in Milwaukee, attended the funeral and said when he was a young player in the early 1950s and the Braves journeyed to away games by train the players sat around and talked baseball and he listened to the master talk about pitching.

"He never bragged about anything," Aaron said. "But he always tried to be better than everybody else. Everything he talked about as a pitcher I listened to, and I learned a lot." Aaron said Spahn seemed to take it personally when he gave up a mere run or two and that spark gave other players motivation. "If he gave up one run, you'd think he had lost the World Series."[373]

For the 2004 season, the Atlanta Braves honored Spahn passing by attaching No. 21 patches to players' uniforms on their left sleeves.

The Oklahoma legislature passed a resolution of tribute to the Hall of Famer. In part it said the older Spahn's residence in the state for more than fifty years made "him a genuine Okie" and it was resolved that in 2005 his April 23 birthday be proclaimed "Warren Spahn Day."

Decades earlier, Spahn had fallen in love with Anna Maria Island in Florida and built several cottages in his vacation getaway area (and spring training home) with baseball-themed names. Sometimes Braves teammates joined him there. Son

Greg tells the story of listening on the radio with Braves stars in 1964 as Muhammad Ali and Sonny Liston fought for the heavyweight championship. Most of the properties were sold late in Warren Spahn's life, many for significant sums. One house, called "Infield," remained in the family until Greg Spahn donated it to the Anna Maria Island Historical Society in 2012. Society officials talked of turning it into a baseball museum.

Warren Spahn's Hartshorne Ranch (and then his home in Broken Arrow) was a baseball museum itself. He was a saver who kept his baseball memorabilia and displayed it. One sportswriter visitor said it was essentially a mini-Cooperstown.

In 2013, Greg Spahn, by then nearly sixty-five, decided to put his father's memorabilia up for sale, including such items as his 1957 Cy Young Award trophy, baseballs from the last out of about 120 of his 363 victories, his Baseball Hall of Fame induction ring, and his 1958 National League championship ring. Those were big-ticket offerings, but there were hundreds of other things also available through an auction house.

The Cy Young Award sold for $126,500 at auction, and the Hall of Fame ring sold for $55,000. In all, the Spahn memorabilia brought $900,000 at auction. "My father's items deserve to be among the fans who cherish the pieces and properly enjoy them," Greg Spahn said.[374] There were about 400 items for sale.

"He saved everything," said Greg Spahn, who held onto items of personal significance. "If he had known during his playing days that old pairs of spikes and sanitary socks were going to be worth something, he'd have saved those, too. But he kept all the important stuff. There is just so much stuff . . . a lot of it wasn't properly stored. Deterioration would have happened sooner or later. I would rather sell it now than have it stay in the attic above my ranch house for another 20 or 30 years and leave my kids with the burden of sorting everything out."[375]

Warren Spahn died in the 2000s, not very long ago, but time moves so quickly, generations of athletes pass through their teams so swiftly, that young fans will mostly hear about him by reading history, unless they attend Atlanta Braves games and pause at the statue that illustrates his famous pitching motion.

It would have been something if a pitcher born in 1921, just after the Deadball Era ended, won 400 games, 37 more than his lifetime total of 363. Spahn's protestations aside, he probably would have without such lengthy World War II service. Given the heart, determination, and belief the man had in his own talents, perhaps he would have been able to pick off another 11 wins if a major-league team summoned him for the 1965 season. He needed just two more to pass Pud Galvin and 10 to tie Grover Cleveland Alexander and Christy Mathewson.

Baseball is a sport of statistics more than any other. Spahn's place in history is secure, and the way the game is played now no one else will ever catch him. Greg Maddux with his 355 wins stopped trying in 2004. Roger Clemens, with his 354 wins, stopped trying in 2003. Spahn is sixth on the all-time wins list and the only ones in shouting distance of 250 are Bartolo Colon with 240 and CC Sabathia with 237. Both are closer to retirement than that interim milestone. As of the 2017 season, Colon was forty-four and likely to be through. Sabathia was thirty-seven and with all of his injuries was pitching on borrowed time.

At one point after retirement, Spahn, with those 363 wins in a safe deposit box, considered the greatest left-hander of all, a key contributor to three pennant-winners and one World Series championship, a 13-time, 20-game winner, made light of the poetic commentary of 1948 applied to him and his friend Johnny Sain.

"First we'll use Spahn, then we'll use Sain; then an off day, followed by rain. Back will come Spahn, followed by Sain, and followed, we hope, by two days of rain."

And all that most baseball fans remember is "Spahn and Sain and Pray for Rain," words which author Gerald Hern did not pen.

"Life's funny, huh? I used to think that rhyme was silly," Spahn said. "But I guess it's how I will be remembered."

ABOUT THE AUTHOR

Lew Freedman is an award-winning journalist who is the author of about 100 books, many on baseball history.

Presently a writer for the *Cody Enterprise* in Wyoming, Freedman has previously worked on the staffs of the *Chicago Tribune*, *Philadelphia Inquirer*, and *Anchorage Daily News* in Alaska. He has won nearly 300 journalism awards.

A graduate of Boston University and the owner of a master's degree from Alaska Pacific University, Freedman and his wife Debra live in Wyoming and Indiana.

ENDNOTES

CHAPTER 1: A NO-HITTER AT LAST

1   John P. Carmichael, *My Greatest Day in Baseball* (New York: Tempo Books, 1968).

2   Roger Kahn, "Mind Over Batter: Nobody Had a Better Head for Pitching Than Warren Spahn," *Sports Illustrated*, December 8, 2003.

3   Al Silverman, *Warren Spahn: Immortal Southpaw* (New York: Bartholomew House/Sport Magazine Library, 1961), 144.

4   Ibid., 143.

5   Ibid., 144.

6   Ibid.

7   Ibid.

CHAPTER 2: BUFFALO AND BEYOND

8   A sportswriter asked Spahn what goals he had left to achieve and he immediatley responded that he wanted to win 300 games. He was in a hurry to do so too and was disappointed he couldn't accomplish that record before season's end.

9   Jim Kaplan, *Spahn, Sain, and Teddy Ballgame: Boston's Almost Perfect Baseball Summer of 1948* (Burlington, MA: Rounder Books, 2008), 146.

10 Ibid.

11 National Baseball Hall of Fame Library interview with Warren Spahn, transcription, October 11, 2004.

12 Ibid.

13 Kaplan, 146.

14 Al Silverman, *Warren Spahn: Immortal Southpaw* (New York: Bartholomew House/Sport Magazine Library, 1961), 32.

15 National Baseball Hall of Fame Library interview with Warren Spahn, transcription, October 11, 2004.

16 Ibid.

17 Milton J. Shapiro, *The Warren Spahn Story* (New York: Julian Messner, Inc., 1958), 20.

18 National Baseball Hall of Fame Library interview with Warren Spahn, transcription, October 11, 2004.

19 Roger Kahn, "Mind Over Batter: No One Had a Better Head for Pitching Than Warren Spahn," *Sports Illustrated*, December 8, 2003.

20 Ibid.

CHAPTER 3: HIGH SCHOOL AND AMERICAN LEGION

21 Milton J. Shapiro, *The Warren Spahn Story* (New York: Julian Messner, Inc., 1958), 22.

22 Al Silverman, *Warren Spahn: Immortal Southpaw* (New York: Bartholomew House/Sport Magazine Library, 1961), 34.

23 National Baseball Hall of Fame Library interview with Warren Spahn, transcription, October 11, 2004.

24 Staff American League preview, Detroit Tigers, *Sports Illustrated*, April 18, 1966.

25 National Baseball Hall of Fame Library interview with Warren Spahn, transcription, October 11, 2004.

26 Ibid.

27 Ibid.

28 Ibid.

29 Ibid.

30 Ibid.

31 Ibid.

CHAPTER 4: LEARNING THE TRADE IN THE MINORS

32 Milton J. Shapiro, *The Warren Spahn Story* (New York: Julian Messner, Inc., 1958), 13.

33 Ibid.

34 Ibid, 33.

35 Jim Kaplan, *Spahn, Sain, and Teddy Ballgame: Boston's Almost Perfect Baseball Summer of 1948* (Burlington, MA: Rounder Books, 2008), 147.

36 Ibid.

37 Al Silverman, *Warren Spahn: Immortal Southpaw* (New York, Bartholomew House/Sport Magazine Library, 1961), 42.

38 Ibid, 43.

39 Ibid, 45.

40 National Baseball Hall of Fame Library interview with Warren Spahn, transcription, October 11, 2004.

41 Marty Appel, *Casey Stengel: Baseball's Greatest Character* (New York, Doubleday, 2017), 126.

CHAPTER 5: WAR AND RETURN

42 Milton J. Shapiro, *The Warren Spahn Story* (New York: Julian Messner, Inc., 1958), 58.

43 National Baseball Hall of Fame Library interview with Warren Spahn, transcription, October 11, 2004.

44 Ibid.

45 Ibid.

46 Jim Kaplan, *Spahn, Sain, and Teddy Ballgame: Boston's Almost Perfect Baseball Summer of 1948* (Burlington, MA: Rounder Books, 2008), 148.

47 National Baseball Hall of Fame Library interview with Warren Spahn, transcription, October 11, 2004.

48 Ibid.

49 Alan Schwarz, "Feller Proud to Service in 'Time Of Need,'" (2006 interview), reprinted *New York Times,* December 16, 2010.

50 Ibid.

51 Kaplan, 148.

52 National Baseball Hall of Fame Library interview with Warren Spahn, transcription, October 11, 2004.

53 Ibid.

54 Ibid.

55 Ibid.

56 Dwight Jon Zimmerman, "Warren Spahn, Hall of Fame Pitcher, Was Seasoned by World War II," DefenseMediaNetwork, October 25, 2014.

57 National Baseball Hall of Fame Library interview with Warren Spahn, transcription, October 11, 2004.

58 Ibid.

59 Ibid.

60 Ibid.

CHAPTER 6: ROOKIE WARREN SPAHN

61 Harold Kaese, *The Boston Braves, 1871–1953* (Boston: Northeastern University Press, 1954), 261.

62 Jim Kaplan, *Spahn, Sain, and Teddy Ballgame: Boston's Almost Perfect Baseball Summer of 1948* (Burlington, MA: Rounder Books, 2008), 148.

63 National Baseball Hall of Fame Library interview with Warren Spahn, transcription, October 11, 2004.

64 Ibid.

65 Ibid

66 Milton J. Shapiro, *The Warren Spahn Story* (New York: Julian Messner, Inc., 1958), 58.

67 Al Silverman, *Warren Spahn: Immortal Southpaw* (New York: Bartholomew House/Sport Magazine Library, 1961), 61.

CHAPTER 7: A STAR IS BORN

68 Harold Kaese, *The Boston Braves, 1871–1953* (Boston: Northeastern University Press, 1954), 261.

69 Ibid., 262.

70 Richard Goldstein, "Johnny Sain, Who Inspired Baseball Rhyme, Dies At 89," *New York Times*, November 9, 2006.

71 Ibid.

72 National Baseball Hall of Fame Library interview with Warren Spahn, transcription, October 11, 2004.

73 Ibid.

74 Ibid.

CHAPTER 8: A PENNANT FOR BOSTON

75 Gerald V. Hern, "Spahn & Sain," *Boston Post*, September 14, 1948.

76 National Baseball Hall of Fame Library interview with Warren Spahn, transcription, October 11, 2004.

77 Grantland Rice, "Setting The Pace: Look Out For Billy Southworth," syndicated column, March 1948.

78 Ibid.

79 Bill Corum, "Sports: A Harvard Man Wins In The Hub; Why Not?," *New York Journal-American*, September 28, 1948.

80 Brent Kelley, "Bill Voiselle Was Key Member Of '48 Braves," *Sports Collectors Digest*, July 19, 1991.

81 "Star For Braves, Dies At 39," *Sporting News*, May 18, 1960.

82 Ibid.

83 Ben Epstein, "Knuckleball Bob," *New York Mirror* (date missing, National Baseball Hall of Fame Library Archives).

84 Ibid.

85 Bob Cooke, "Barrett's Clowning Earns Him Role of Braves Morale Builder," *New York Herald-Tribune*, March 6, 1947.

86 Jack McCarthy, "Antonelli: He Took Braves' Bonus, But Returned Dividends To Giants," *Boston Herald-American*, May 14, 1978.

87 Johnny Antonelli and Scott Pitoniak, *Johnny Antonelli: A Baseball Memoir* (Rochester, NY: RIT Press, 2012), 20–21.

88 Ibid., 21.

89 Harold Kaese, *The Boston Braves, 1871–1953* (Boston: Northeastern University Press, 1954), 272.

90 Arthur Daley, "Sports of the Times: The Comeback Kid," *New York Times*, July 6, 1953.

91 John Gillooly, "Earl Of Snohomish II," *Sporfolio*, September 1947.

92 John Shea, "Alvin Dark, Giants, A's World Series Manager, Dies At 92," *San Francisco Chronicle*, November 14, 2014.

93 Tom Mortenson, "SCD Remembers Sibby Sisti," *Sports Collectors Digest*, November 16, 1990.

94 National Baseball Hall of Fame Library interview with Warren Spahn, transcription, October 11, 2004.

CHAPTER 9: THE BRAVES' WORLD SERIES

95 National Baseball Hall of Fame Library interview with Warren Spahn, transcription, October 11, 2004.

96 Ibid.

97 Gene Schoor, *The History of the World Series* (New York: William Morrow and Company, Inc., 1990, Baseball Hall of Fame Library Archives photocopies).

98 Milton J. Shapiro, *The Warren Spahn Story* (New York: Julian Messner, Inc., 1958), 98.

99 National Baseball Hall of Fame Library interview with Warren Spahn, transcription, October 11, 2004.

100 Shapiro, 102.

101 Shapiro, 104–5.

102 Brent Kelley, "Conatser Recalls Playing Days With Boston Braves," *Sports Collectors Digest*, April 5, 1991.

103 National Baseball Hall of Fame Library interview with Warren Spahn, transcription, October 11, 2004.

CHAPTER 10: PENNANT HANGOVER

104 Harold Kaese, *The Boston Braves, 1871–1953* (Boston: Northeastern University Press, 1954), 278.

105 Arthur Sampson, "Billy Southworth, The Pennant Man," *Look*, May 24, 1949.

106 Ray Birch, Society for American Baseball Research, "Johnny Cooney," "Letter from Johnny Cooney," *Christian Science Monitor*, December 1, 1944.

107 Milton J. Shapiro, *The Warren Spahn Story* (New York: Julian Messner, Inc., 1958), 112–13.

108 Ibid., 114.

109 Ibid., 114.

110 Ibid., 117.

111 Fay Vincent, *The Only Game in Town: Baseball Stars of the 1930s and 1940s Talk About the Game They Loved* (New York: Simon & Schuster, 2007), 143.

112 Arthur Sampson, "Billy Southworth, The Pennant Man," *Look*, May 24, 1949.

113 Ibid.

114 Rich Marazzi, "Goodnight Sibby Sisti, Wherever You Are," *Sports Collectors Digest*, July 28, 1995.

115 Ibid.

116 Brent Kelley, "Conatser Recalls Playing Days with Boston Braves," *Sports Collectors Digest*, April 5, 1991.

CHAPTER 11: THE COLLAPSE

117 Milton J. Shapiro, *The Warren Spahn Story* (New York, Julian Messner, Inc., 1958), 117–18.

118 Al Silverman, *Warren Spahn: Immortal Southpaw* (New York: Bartholomew House/Sport Magazine Library, 1961).

119 Ibid., 75.

120 Michael Madden, "He Ran Into a Fenway Wall," *Boston Globe* (National Baseball Hall of Fame Library Archives, date missing), 1993.

121 Dan Daniel, "Jethroe Clears Race Obstacle in St. Pete," *Sporting News*, March 29, 1950.

122 Rich Marazzi, "Batting the Breeze: Sam Jethroe," *Sports Collectors Digest*, November 11, 1994.

123 Jim Auchmutey, "Sam Jethroe, The First Black Braves Player at 79 Fights Barriers to Baseball Pension," *Atlanta Journal*, June 22, 1997.

124 Ibid.

125 Silverman, 76.

126 Jack McCarthy, "Max Surkont: Ex-Brave Now Serves Highballs," *Boston Herald,* December 25, 1977.

127 Harold Kaese, *The Boston Braves, 1871–1953* (Boston: Northeastern University Press, 1954), 281.

CHAPTER 12: LAST DAYS IN BOSTON

128 Ralph Wimbish, "He Was Original 'Big Daddy,'" *New York Post,* October 5, 1997.

129 Al Silverman, *Warren Spahn: Immortal Southpaw* (New York: Bartholomew House/Sport Magazine Library, 1961), 87.

130 Ibid., 88.

131 Ibid.

132 Ibid.

CHAPTER 13: THE BRAVES MOVE TO MILWAUKEE

133 John Klima, *Bushville Wins!* (New York: Thomas Dunne Books, 2012), 5.

134 Clif Keane, "Frick Opposes Braves Shift Now, But Lacks Power to Block It," *Boston Globe,* March 15, 1953.

135 Ibid.

136 Arthur Daley, "Sports of the Times: The Moving of Plymouth Rock," *New York Times,* March 19, 1953.

137 Ibid.

138 John P. Carmichael, "Milwaukee Gets Boston Braves; League Grants Shift This Year," *Chicago Daily News,* March 18, 1953.

139 John Gillooly, "Braves Take It in Stride," *Boston Herald,* March 15, 1953.

140 Ibid.

141 Ibid.

142 Klima, 7.

143 Clif Keane, "Frick Opposes Braves Shift Now, But Lacks Power to Block It," *Boston Globe*, March 15, 1953.

144 John Gillooly, "Hub Fans Wish Lou Nothing But Worst," *Boston Herald*, March 25, 1953.

145 Klima, 15.

CHAPTER 14: THE LOVE AFFAIR BEGINS

146 Milton J. Shapiro, *The Warren Spahn Story* (New York: Julian Messner, Inc., 1958), 126.

147 Al Silverman, *Warren Spahn: Immortal Southpaw* (New York: Bartholomew House/Sport Magazine Library, 1961), 89.

148 John Klima, *Bushville Wins!* (New York: Thomas Dunne Books, 2012), 26.

149 Silverman, 91.

150 Shapiro, 128.

151 Paula Parrish, "Ballplayer Bill Bruton Dead at 69," *Wilmington News-Journal*, December 6, 1995.

152 Norman Macht, "Billy Bruton Recalls How the Game Was Played in 1950s," *Baseball Digest*, August 1990.

153 Ibid.

154 Ibid.

155 Pat Harmon, "Didn't Know He Was Fast Till He Was Told," *Cincinnati Post*, April 17, 1953.

156 Earl Lawson, "Adcock Won Statewide Acclaim When He Played Basketball with University of Louisiana Five," *Cincinnati Times-Star*, May 12, 1952.

157 "Sausages, Sauerbraten and Sympathy," *LIFE*, July 6, 1953.

CHAPTER 15: A SURPRISE PENNANT RACE

158 Eddie Mathews and Bob Buege, *Eddie Mathews and the National Pastime* (Milwaukee: Douglas American Sports Publications, 1994), 70.

159 Ibid., 84.

160 Milton J. Shapiro, *The Warren Spahn Story* (New York: Julian Messner, Inc., 1958), 137.

161 Bob Buege, *The Milwaukee Braves: A Baseball Eulogy* (Milwaukee: Douglas American Sports Publications, 1988), 41.

162 Ibid., 43.

163 Andy Pafko and Dave Condon, "I'm Lucky to Be a Brave," *Sport*, June 1954.

164 Ibid.

165 Ibid.

166 Ibid.

167 Ibid.

168 Gregory H. Wolf, "Bob Buhl," Society For American Baseball Research, no date.

169 Arthur Daley, "Sports of the Times: Tough As a Paratrooper," *New York Times*, March 29, 1960.

170 Ibid.

171 Bob Wolf, "Riot Almost Breaks Out As Dodgers Renew Year-Old Feud with Braves' Lew Burdette," *Milwaukee Journal*, August 4, 1953.

172 Ibid.

173 Associated Press, "Burdette Says Winning 'No Fun' When His Pal, Spahn, Is Victim," *Dayton Daily News*, July 26, 1963.

174 Gene Schoor, *Lew Burdette of the Braves* (New York: G.P. Putnam's Sons, 1960), 90.

175 Ibid.

CHAPTER 16: HENRY AARON

176 Howard Bryant, *The Last Hero: A Life of Henry Aaron* (New York: Pantheon Books, 2010), 52.

177 Ibid. 51–52.

178 Ibid., 52–53.

179 Hank Aaron and Lonnie Wheeler, *I Had A Hammer: The Hank Aaron Story* (New York: HarperPaperbacks, 1991), 118.

180 Bryant, 95.

181 John Klima, *Bushville Wins!* (New York: Thomas Dunne Books, 2012), 56.

182 Aaron and Wheeler, 122.

183 Bryant, 99.

184 Aaron and Wheeler, 122.

185 Ibid., 127.

186 Ibid., 128.

187 Al Hirshberg, "Big Brave from Milwaukee," *Saturday Evening Post*, May 28, 1955.

188 Ibid.

189 Ibid.

190 Gregory H. Wolf, "Joe Adcock," Society of American Baseball Research, *Sporting News*, August 11, 1954.

191 Gregory H. Wolf, "Joe Adcock," Society of American Baseball Research, *Sporting News*, January 23, 1957.

192 Milton J. Shapiro, *The Warren Spahn Story* (New York: Julian Messner, Inc., 1958), 141.

CHAPTER 17: BRAVES TRYING TO TAKE OVER

193 Milton J. Shapiro, *The Warren Spahn Story* (New York: Julian Messner, Inc., 1958), 145.

194 Bill Nowlin, "Chet Nichols," Society For American Baseball Research, no date.

195 Ibid.

196 Hank Aaron and Lonnie Wheeler, *I Had A Hammer: The Hank Aaron Story* (New York: HarperPaperbacks, 1991), 132.

197 Howard Bryant, *The Last Hero: A Life of Henry Aaron* (New York: Pantheon Books, 2010), 114.

198 Aaron and Wheeler, 131.

199 Norman Macht, "Billy Bruton Recalls How the Game Was Played in 1950s," *Baseball Digest*, August 1990.

200 Lou Chapman, "Looks Like Real Hill Package to Braves," *Milwaukee Sentinel*, March 20, 1955.

201 Al Silverman, *Warren Spahn: Immortal Southpaw* (New York: Bartholomew House/Sport Magazine Library, 1961), 97.

202 Ibid.

CHAPTER 18: ON THE CUSP

203 John Gillooly, "Braves Value Conley's Arm at $100,000," *Boston Record*, February 6, 1952.

204 Ibid.

205 Ibid.

206 Donald Honig, *Baseball Between the Lines* (New York: Coward, McCann & Geoghegan, 1976), 194.

207 Edward Prell, "'Moscow Agents' Kidnapped Conley in 1948 Idaho Raid," *Chicago Tribune*, May 8, 1955.

208 Joe Williams, "Conley Keys Braves' Hopes, New Boss Says," *New York World-Telegram and Sun*, June 23, 1956.

209 "Versatile Fred Haney Is Dead at 79," *Sporting News,* November 26, 1977.

210 Ibid.

211 Ibid.

212 John Klima, *Bushville Wins!* (New York: Thomas Dunne Books, 2012), 69–70.

213 Bob Wolf, "Failure to Run Out Bounder Costs Danny O'Connell $25," *Milwaukee Journal,* July 17, 1956.

214 Larry Powell, "Bob Buhl: Former N.L. Moundsman Was All Pitcher," *Sports Collectors Digest,* May 28, 1993.

215 Milton J. Shapiro, *The Warren Spahn Story* (New York: Julian Messner, Inc., 1958), 152.

216 Ibid., 153.

217 Ibid., 154–55.

218 Klima, 101.

219 Klima, 101.

220 Klima, 76.

221 Klima, 76.

CHAPTER 19: A PENNANT FOR MILWAUKEE

222 Warren Spahn and Furman Bisher, "I Say Milwaukee Will Win the Pennant," *Saturday Evening Post,* April 20, 1957.

223 Ibid.

224 Ibid.

225 Ibid.

226 John Klima, *Bushville Wins!* (New York: Thomas Dunne Books, 2012), 96.

227 Ibid.

228 Bob Wolf, "Young Tex Covington Could Solve Braves' Problems in Outfield," *Milwaukee Journal,* January 9, 1956.

229 Bob Wolf, "Covington Started As Football Player; Found He Could Hit," *Milwaukee Journal,* March 5, 1956.

230 Wolf, "Covington."

231 Rich Marazzi, "Batting the Breeze: Frank Torre Celebrates the Anniversary of His First Full Year with a New Heart," *Sports Collectors Digest*, September 26, 1997.

232 Ibid.

233 Ibid.

234 Klima, 129.

235 Klima, 130.

236 Gregory H. Wolf, ed., *That's Joy In Braveland!* (Phoenix, AZ: Society For American Baseball Research, 2014), 119.

237 Cleon Walfoort, "Pennant Rides on 'Felix the Cat,' Now the Club's Only Shortstop," *Milwaukee Journal*, August 21, 1957.

238 Ibid.

239 Wolf, *That's Joy In Braveland!*, 125.

240 Klima, 134.

241 Klima, 136.

242 Hank Aaron and Lonnie Wheeler, *I Had a Hammer: The Hank Aaron Story* (New York: HarperPaperbacks, 1991), 164.

243 Ibid., 168.

244 Thad Mumau, *An Indian Summer: The 1957 Milwaukee Braves, Champions of Baseball* (Jefferson, NC: McFarland & Company, Inc., 2007), 97.

245 Clifford Evans, "Warren Spahn Interview," tapes for Baseball Hall of Fame Library Archives, no date.

246 Bob Wolf, "Too Much Time Off Hurt Pitching, McMahon Says," *Milwaukee Journal*, November 16, 1958.

247 Ibid., 140.

248 Howard Tuckner, "Rookie Is Hitting .507," *New York Times*, August 30, 1957.

249 J. R. Hillman, "Bob Hazle: The Hurricane Left His Mark," *Sports Collectors Digest*, May 9, 1997.

250 Tuckner, "Rookie Is Hitting .507."

251   Klima, 177.

252   Klima, 164.

CHAPTER 20: WORLD SERIES

253   John Klima, *Bushville Wins!* (New York: Thomas Dunne Books, 2012), 186.

254   Klima, 190.

255   Steve Contursi, Yankee History, "A Birthday Party Nightclub Brawl (1957)," www.yanksgoyard.com, January 15, 2017.

256   Klima, 185.

257   Milton J. Shapiro, *The Warren Spahn Story* (New York: Julian Messner, Inc. 1958), 171.

258   Gene Schoor, *Lew Burdette of the Braves* (New York: G.P. Putnam's Sons, 1960), 114–15.

259   Ibid., 119.

260   Ibid.

261   Jack Mann, "Yanks Just Another Team to Hear Burdette Tell It," *Newsday*, October 4, 1957.

262   Gene Schoor, *The History of the World Series: The Complete Chronology of America's Greatest Sports Tradition* (New York: William Morrow & Co., 1990), 256.

263   Lew Burdette and Joe Reichler, "The Yankees Know Me Now!" *Saturday Evening Post*, February 15, 1958.

264   Al Silverman, *Warren Spahn: Immortal Southpaw* (New York: Bartholomew House/Sport Magazine Library, 1961), 115.

CHAPTER 21: ANOTHER PENNANT

265   Bob Wolf, "Braves' Rush Deal Stuns Rival Teams," *Milwaukee Journal*, December 11, 1957.

266   Ibid.

267 Al Silverman, *Warren Spahn: Immortal Southpaw* (New York: Bartholomew House/Sport Magazine Library, 1961), 117.

268 Gregory H. Wolf, ed., *That's Joy in Braveland!* (Phoenix, AZ: Society For American Baseball Research, 2014), 36.

269 Silverman, 118.

270 Bob Buege, *The Milwaukee Braves: A Baseball Eulogy* (Milwaukee: Douglas American Sports Publications, 1988), 184.

271 Ibid., 203.

272 Lew Burdette, "Braves' Hurler Calls Opponents Nice Fellows Who'll Finish Second," *New York World-Telegram and Sun*, September 30, 1958.

273 Silverman, 122.

274 Lew Burdette, "We Win Close Ones," *New York World-Telegram and Sun*, October 2, 1958.

275 Ibid.

276 Lew Burdette, "How to Beat Yanks: Keep the Ball Low," *New York World-Telegram and Sun*, October 3, 1958.

277 Mickey Mantle, "Gives Spahn the Credit," *New York World-Telegram and Sun*, October 6, 1958.

278 Associated Press, "His Control Was Uncanny," *Syracuse Post-Standard*, October 6, 1958.

279 Dick Young, "Spahn, Burdette in Comedy Act," *New York Daily News*, October 6, 1958.

280 Silverman, 131.

281 Lew Burdette, "A Game of Inches," *New York World-Telegram and Sun*, October 10, 1958.

CHAPTER 22: TRYING FOR A THIRD PENNANT

282 Mary Schoendienst, "My Proudest Moment: No Crowds Cheered Red," *St. Louis Parade*, September 13, 1959.

283 Bill Furlong, "Red Tells of Lonely Fight with TB," *Cincinnati Enquirer*, February 20, 1959.

284 Herb Kamm, "Champions in Courage: Stricken Schoendienst Sure He'll Play Again," *New York World-Telegram and Sun*, April 1, 1959.

285 Eddie Mathews and Bob Buege, *Eddie Mathews and the National Pastime* (Milwaukee, WI: Douglas American Sports Publications, 1994), 183.

286 Hank Aaron and Lonnie Wheeler, *I Had A Hammer: The Hank Aaron Story* (New York: HarperPaperbacks, 1991), 191.

287 Roger Kahn, "The Art of Warren Spahn," *Sport*, June 1958.

288 Ibid.

289 Aaron and Wheeler, 192–93.

290 Mathews and Buege, 183.

291 Al Silverman, *Warren Spahn: Immortal Southpaw* (New York: Bartholomew House/Sport Magazine Library, 1961), 138.

292 Cleon Walfoort, "Haney Resigns—'To Spend More Time With Family,'" *Milwaukee Journal*, October 5, 1959.

293 Milton Gross, "Fred Haney Blamed By Johnny Logan for Pennant Loss," *Pittsburgh Press*, October 23, 1959.

294 Mathews and Buege, 191.

CHAPTER 23: AGELESS WONDER

295 Dick Young, "Burdette Can't Savvy Braves' Salary Logic," *New York Daily News*, March 13, 1960.

296 Roger Kahn, "The Art Of Warren Spahn," *Sport*, June 1958.

297 National Baseball Hall of Fame Library interview with Warren Spahn, transcription, October 11, 2004.

298 Ibid.

299 Ibid.

300 Kahn, "The Art Of Warren Spahn."

301 Bob Wolf, "Spahn Beats Giants On Second No-Hitter," *Milwaukee Journal,* April 29, 1961.

302 Cleon Walfoort, "'Crazy, Wonderful,'" *Milwaukee Journal,* April 29, 1961.

303 Ibid.

304 Ibid.

305 Bob Wolf, "'Just Plain Lucky,' Chirps No-Hit Ace Spahn," *Sporting News,* May 10, 1961.

306 Bob Wolf, "Ex-Teammate Torgy Wires Spahn After His No-Hitter," *Sporting News,* May 10, 1961.

307 National Baseball Hall of Fame Library interview with Warren Spahn, transcription, October 11, 2004.

308 Bob Wolf, "'Most Exciting Game I've Ever Pitched,'" *Sporting News,* August 23, 1961.

309 Ibid.

310 "Everyone in Act," *Milwaukee Journal,* August 12, 1961.

311 Tex Maule, "'Everything Seemed Easy,'" *Sports Illustrated,* May 8, 1991.

CHAPTER 24: TWILIGHT

312 Bob Wolf, "Braves Beat Bongos Over Hendley As 'New Spahn,'" *Milwaukee Journal,* April 27, 1963.

313 Bob Wolf, "Braves Preen Head Feathers Over 'Second Spahn' Lemaster," *Milwaukee Journal,* April 11, 1964.

314 Bob Wolf, "Braves Feel Blazer Ready To Blossom As 'New Spahn,'" *Milwaukee Journal,* June 5, 1965.

315 Bob Wolf, "McMahon Tells Birdie to Get Another Beer, Gives Him Reason to Get Something Stronger," *Milwaukee Journal,* June 8, 1962.

316 Hank Aaron and Lonnie Wheeler, *I Had A Hammer: The Hank Aaron Story* (New York: HarperPaperbacks, 1991), 197.

317 Ibid., 244.

318 Ibid., 198–99.

319 Sandy Grady, "'Warren Spahn—He Does Just Like Me,'" *Philadelphia Bulletin*, July 12, 1963.

320 Daniel Brown, "Marichal-Epic Duel Was 50 Years Ago," Bay Area News Group, July 1, 2013.

321 Ibid.

322 Juan Marichal and Lew Freedman, *My Journey from the Dominican Republic to Cooperstown* (Minneapolis: MVP Books, 2011), 97.

323 Ibid., 101.

324 Ibid., 102.

325 Bob Lemke, "'63 Spahnie Buttons Funded Scholarships," Bob Lemke Baseball Blog, June 8, 2015.

326 Cleon Walfoort, "Cheers of 33,676 Fans, Message from Kennedy, Highlight Spahn Night," *Milwaukee Journal*, September 18, 1963.

327 Ibid.

328 United Press International, "Milwaukee Braves, Friends, Fete Pitcher Warren Spahn," *Greensburg* (PA) *Tribune-Review*, September 17, 1963.

329 Walfoort, Ibid.

330 Christine Czyrylo, Associated Press, "She's Right-Handed Woman to Baseball's Left-Hander," *Aberdeen* (SD) *American-News*, September 16, 1964.

331 Waite Hoyt personal note to Warren Spahn, August 10, 1961.

CHAPTER 25: IT'S OVER

332 Personal interview, November 5, 2017.

333 Ibid.

334 Bob Wolf, "Scathing Words Fuel Hot Feud As Bragan, Spahn Swap Insults," *Sporting News*, December 19, 1964.

335 Barney Kremenko, "'I'm Pitcher First, Then Coach' Says Spahn, Describing Met Job," *New York Journal-American*, December 5, 1964.

336 Warren Spahn and Al Hirshberg, "I Still Can Win," *Sport*, February 1965.

337 Ibid.

338 Ibid.

339 Ibid.

340 Ibid.

341 Marty Appel, *Casey Stengel: Baseball's Greatest Character* (New York: Doubleday, 2017), 127.

342 Ibid., 127.

343 Arthur Daley, "End of the Trail?" *New York Times*, July 16, 1965.

344 Associated Press, "Giants Sign Spahn," July 19, 1965.

345 Bob Wolf, "Spahn Feels He Can Pitch at 45—Mulls an Offer from El Paso," *Milwaukee Journal*, May 14, 1966.

346 Bob Wolf, "'Not My Idea,' Says the Retired Spahn," *Milwaukee Journal*, July 23, 1966.

347 Ibid.

348 Ibid.

349 Joe Reichler, "Is Warren Spahn the Best Ever?" *Sport*, May 1964.

350 Ibid.

351 Ibid.

CHAPTER 26: STILL LOVING THE GAME

352 Cleon Walfoort, "Spahn Turns Actor, a Villain Yet, As Braves' Advisory Staff Watches," *Milwaukee Journal*, August 24, 1963.

353 Cleon Walfoort, "Loyal Employees," *Milwaukee Journal*, December 9, 1958.

354 David Lamb, "Spahn Gives Word Brave New Value," *Los Angeles Times*, February 21, 1987.

355 Cleon Walfoort, "Manager Spahn Finds His Big Job," June 4, 1967.

356 John Ferguson, "Spahn Checks in Chair for 'Walk' Toward Camp," *Tulsa World*, February 15, 1970.

357 "No Pitch for Warren Spahn in Japanese Baseball," *Oneonta Daily Star*, August 7, 1978.

358 Jack Lang, "Shrine Doors Open at Spahn [headline cut]," *Sporting News*, February 10, 1973.

359 Associated Press, "Spahn Gets Life's Greatest Victory," *Tulsa World*, January 25, 1973.

360 "Greg Spahn Told: 'Call Me Sir Again,'" *Tulsa World*, January 25, 1973.

361 Bob Broeg, "Hall-Of-Famer Spahn Shows Old Poise Again," *St. Louis Post-Dispatch*, August 7, 1973.

362 Jack Wilkinson, "Warren Spahn Set Standard for All Left-Handers to Come," *Atlanta Journal-Constitution*, August 8, 2003.

363 Personal interview, November 5, 2017.

364 Wilkinson, "Warren Spahn Set Standard."

365 Barry Lewis, "Baseball Bids Farewell to Great Spahn," *Tulsa World*, November 30, 2003.

366 Michael Hunt, "Spahn: Game's Greatest Lefty a Complete Ballplayer," *Milwaukee Journal-Sentinel*, November 25, 2003.

367 Richard Goldstein, "Warren Spahn, 82, Dies: Left-Handed Craftsman of the Baseball Mound for 21 Seasons," *New York Times*, November 25, 2003.

368 Robert J. Summers, "Hall Of Fame Pitcher Warren Spahn Dies," *Buffalo News*, November 25, 2003.

369 Dan McGrath, "Warren Spahn, 1921–2003, Winningest Left-Hander Left Rich Legacy," *Chicago Tribune*, November 25, 2003.

370 Lewis, "Baseball Bids Farewell to Great Spahn."

371 Rich Mueller, "Sport's Collecting Gene Pays Off for Family," *Sports Collectors Daily*, July 24, 2013.

372 Personal interview, November 5, 2017.

373 Gary D'Amato, "Spahn's Son Putting Memorabilia Up for Sale," *Milwaukee Journal-Sentinel*, June 21, 2013.

374 Gerald V. Hern, "Spahn & Sain," *Boston Post*, September 14, 1948.

375 Mark Feeney, "Warren Spahn; High-Kicked and Hurled Way into Baseball Record Books, Braves Lore," November 25, 2003.

INDEX